# The Silver Pen

### Starting a Profitable Writing Business
### From a Lifetime of Experience

## A Guide for Older People

*Also by Alan N. Canton*

ComputerMoney: Making Serious Dollars In High-Tech Consulting

# The Silver Pen

## Starting a Profitable Writing Business From a Lifetime of Experience

## A Guide for Older People

Alan N. Canton

αβ

*Adams-Blake Publishing*

# Disclaimer

This book is designed to provide information in regard to the subject matter covered. It is sold with the understanding that the publisher and author are not engaged in rendering legal, accounting or other professional services. If legal or other expert assistance is required, the services of a competent professional should be sought.

It is not the purpose of this book to reprint all the information that is otherwise available to the author and/or publisher, but to complement, amplify and supplement other texts. The reader is urged to obtain other available material, and learn as much about writing as possible.

Writing is not a get-rich scheme. Anyone who decides to go into the business must expect to invest time, effort and money.

Every effort has been made to make this book as complete and as accurate as possible. However, there may be mistakes both typographical and in content. Therefore, this text should be used only as a general guide and not as the ultimate source of consulting information. Furthermore, this book contains information on writing only up to the printing date.

The purpose of this book is to educate and entertain. The author and Adams-Blake Publishing shall have neither liability nor responsibility to any person or entity with respect to any loss or damage caused, or alleged to be caused, directly or indirectly by the information contained in this book.

If you do not wish to be bound by the above, you may return this book to Adams-Blake Publishing for a full refund.

Adams-Blake Publishing
8041 Sierra Street
Fair Oaks, CA  95628  U.S.A.

Copyright © 1996 by Alan N. Canton
First Printing 1996
Printed in the United States of America
ISBN 1-883422-11-6
Library of Congress Catalog Number: 95-79412

# Table of Contents

# Acknowledgements

This book is dedicated to Jane Schweitzer and Helen Sperling for their faith, love, advice, and guidance. Without them, this work would not have been possible.

Finally, I salute all of you who have the courage, ambition, and motivation to embark on the journey of starting a new endeavor.

# About the Author

Al Canton has been an independent consultant for fifteen years. Born in 1947, he grew up in Great Neck, New York. Mr. Canton holds a BA degree from the University of Virginia, and an MA from the College of William And Mary. He started out as a school teacher and taught the entire 8th grade in an 8 room school house in Webster Springs, West Virginia. After graduate school, where he was introduced to computer technology, Mr. Canton worked for EDS in San Francisco and Dallas. Tired of making Ross Perot richer, Mr. Canton, on a whim, started his own consulting company in 1978. Over the years he has taught courses at National University and has given seminars throughout the country. As an active writer on technology issues, he has been published in numerous magazines and journals. Mr. Canton is married with four cats.

# A Note on Style

The author has tried his best to make this book gender neutral as much as possible. When he uses only "his" or "her" it is out of stylistic consideration and should not be considered a "political" statement.

# 1

· · · · · · · · · · · · · · · · · ·

# THE CONCEPT

## Are You With the Program?

You're a skeptic. That's OK, I'm glad you are. You can skip to the italics at the bottom of the next page to see if you should keep this book.

Welcome back!

I can see you now. You're standing in the bookstore. Or you're sitting in your living room. Or you're reading in bed. And I can hear what you're thinking. "What's this *Silver Pen* concept all about? Is this another one of those get rich quick books?"

There are no riches here (quick or otherwise). However, this book will teach you how you can earn from $10,000 to $20,000 a year in a clean, dignified manner using what you know from your life.

I'm going to teach you three specialized subsets of the writing business.

What's that sound I hear? Two loud cries!

The first cry is "I can't write! I don't know a subject from a verb. My spelling is terrible. I can't even put together a laundry list!" This book will teach you step by step how to go about learning and mastering the writing craft. Notice I don't say "developing your talent." Talent is not necessary. If you can read, you can write. Writing is a craft, like needlepoint or woodworking. It's easily learned by most people.

"Business? I don't know anything about business!" is the second shout. "I can't run a business; I don't know a credit from a debit." In the first place anyone who has ever worked for a business knows how a business should be run. You might not think you know, but you do. In the second place, starting and running a small home-based, low-risk business is a "piece of cake." If you can run a household, you can run a writing business.

---

**COMMENT**: Do you read the comics? Dagwood's wife Blondie never worked a day in her life and now she has her own catering company!

---

We are not talking rocket science here. I will present basic ideas along with specific procedures people all over the country already use to earn extra money and to make better and more productive lives for themselves.

So you can determine right now (especially if you skipped here) if you want to buy (keep) this book, here is the program in a nutshell.

You're going to be in business for yourself. It's not hard; at least not nearly as hard as you think.

The objective of the program is to give you a dignified, low-risk, easy-entry, part-time, and low-stress way to earn $10,000-$20,000 a year based upon what you already know.

*You're going to disseminate information about your subject area.*

*And what is this subject area? It's the area in which you have the greatest knowledge.*

*You're going to make a nice little retirement income on something from your life experience. You're going to be paid for what you know.*

*You're going to start your own little info-business by working in three areas: freelance writing, ghostwriting, and commercial writing. You can do one, two, or all three.*

You're going to be a **knowledgepreneur**.

---

**COMMENT**: I hope I have coined a new word. I have not heard it before, so if you have, I would love to know where your first read or heard it. Write me c/o the publisher.

---

## Here is a Term of Endearment for You

Because so many people object to the words "senior citizen" and because so many of the other labels used to describe retired people have negative connotations, I have come up with a term that I think will be acceptable to all who are in the retirement stage of life: "post-employed," or PE for short.

Just about all of you are PEs. For the most part, your regular work life is over. You have ended a career or vocation that paid you a living and hopefully has contributed to your retirement income. My definition of a PE is someone whose income is derived from investments, pensions, or other passive means. In a nutshell, you're neither employed nor self-employed. That part of your life is in the past; thus post-employed.

---

*COMMENT*: I also use this term for those who may have never worked. PEs who ran a household and raised children were, in a way, employed. These were jobs without paychecks.

---

## The Fixed Income Blues

One doesn't have to be a brain surgeon to diagnose one senior-citizen problem. Many of you have fixed incomes and are in a situation where either low interest rates or inflation have eroded your income base. If you want to earn an extra income through employment, nobody will hire you because they think you're too old. For many of you, it's not a pretty picture, but it's reality.

Yes, you can get a job. But it probably won't be as good as your last position. Why? Lots of silly reasons, all of which fall under the topic of age discrimination.

---

*COMMENT*: Since getting employment is not the topic of this book, I won't go into detail. However, it is very difficult for most PEs to reenter the job market at the same level they left it.

---

I will present you with an alternative to flipping burgers or selling Amway. But I must first open your minds a little bit. When I speak to PEs, I get the same refrain over and over again. After I outline my concept, they tell me they can't do it, it wouldn't work for them, they have no talent, they'll wash out, etc., etc., etc. So, please listen for a few moments. The closed mind of the post-employed is hard to open, but I'm going to spend a few pages trying. If I don't convince you of your ability to succeed, please return the book because it will be of no use to you.

## A Simple, Basic Truth

I'm going to tell you something that, at first, you'll probably argue with. But if you stop and think about it, you'll see that it's true. *The whole world and every institution in it is there to tell you "no."* It's the paramount purpose of the media, the government, our educational system, and even friends and family, to tell you that no matter what endeavor you attempt, you're going to fail. The "world" wants you "doomed" to the life prescribed to you by the system. This is not some counter-cultural rhetoric. It's a fact of life in modern society.

People will tell you things that relate to *themselves*, not to *you*. This is especially true of the negatives you'll hear about starting a business in retirement. What I just said above must sink in. Most of the people in the world and all of the institutions are there to tell you "no." The professionals, the media, the pundits, the government all function to impede you. Creativity is suspect, and successful creativity is what all these entities envy most.

Your bankers, lawyers, accountants, friends, your relatives - everyone will tell you at great length about any and every way that you can and will fail. In the long run, no one really wants to see you succeed, except people who loan you money or have something to sell you. *They will equate, in their own minds, your success with their failure.* When you talk to others about the writing business concepts this book offers, you'll think you're living in a temple of doom. People who have no idea about what they are talking about will tell you how hard it is and how perilous is the journey. They will tell you not to venture out. Don't listen. Don't believe. Steve Jobs, the father of the Apple Macintosh computer, had it right when he told his software developers, who were working 18 hours a day, "The journey is the reward." People you talk to will see the mountains in your path but miss the rivers, streams, valleys, meadows, vistas, and excitement that you'll encounter in crossing these mountains.

> **COMMENT:** *This is not a book on philosophy. But I always get asked "Why is there so much negativity?" Simple. If we honestly and truly believed that we could reach our real potential, we would all be doing our own things. Those who "influence" us - our churches, our political leaders, our media - would lose their power. We wouldn't be the sheep they want us to be. But this is a subject for another book.*

In our culture, people who break from the norm and follow their own minds *and succeed* are called *exceptional.*

Sorry, but I don't buy into the concept that people who succeed are *exceptional.* I don't believe that it takes a special type of person to make it in our system. Where is it written that you can't do anything (within reason) that you set out to do?

You have to either take it on faith or at least fool yourselves into believing that you can run your own life. You have to believe that, no, you're not too old. You're not stupid. You have the energy. You can succeed. You won't fail.

## Trust in Yourself or No One Else Will

I want to say a few words that may not apply to you. In fact they only apply to a minority of PEs. However, that's still a large number of people. *If you're confident in your abilities, then please skip this section.*

Some PEs have two traits that are, I think, special to their generation. They trust in everything but themselves and are fearful of failure.

Some PEs I talk with give me the feeling that I'm dealing with people who are so co-opted by the system, they can't or won't think for themselves. They have lived through years of people telling them what to do, how to do it, what to think, how to act, when to laugh, what to like - I could go on - that it's no wonder they have low self-esteem. They will buy 100% into something a stranger on TV tells them. They will accept as true whatever an authority figure or so-called expert says. They will listen to and trust just about everyone - except themselves.

So when I ask many of them "What do you know?" they say they don't know anything. When I ask if they think they can do such and such, their automatic response is "no."

I don't know if "I can't" is a conditioned response or if these people sincerely believe it. Whatever the cause, if you're among this minority, you must abandon this notion of not being up to the task. You're not going to be successful with the program if you have a defeatist attitude. You have to adopt the belief that you can do anything you set your mind to do. Please don't accept outside advice or input that tells you otherwise. I'm not telling you to ignore all advice, just to separate the facts from the editorials. For example, one of your children might say, "Mom, you should get a Macintosh computer; it's great. But, Mom, I think the writing business concept you read about in that *Silver Pen* book is never going to work." My suggestion is to take the computer advice and ignore the negative editorial.

---
**COMMENT**: *Outside of computers, what does your kid really know anyway!*

---

## FDR Knew, Do You?

As I said above, a second factor prevalent among a minority of PEs is fear. *If you're used to doing new things and always open to new ideas, then skip this section.*

Roosevelt once said there was nothing to fear but fear itself, but I don't think these people were listening. I meet a significant number of PEs who really believe that they have the skill, ability, and knowledge to work the program, but they don't try because they're afraid they will fail, through no fault of their own.

Obviously, there are lots of ways to fail in business. Let's say you opened a small store. You could fail because you bought the wrong inventory (that is, you made a bad decision). You could fail because Wal-Mart opened up next door (not your fault). You know something? People who have failed in business always say that the perception (fear) of failure was much worse than the reality.

The fear of failure is out of proportion with what actually happens. Sure, people do lose life savings in misadventures. But it doesn't happen as often as people *fear* that it will.

Having spoken to hundreds of PEs, I believe those in this group are less concerned with losing money than with losing self-respect, should a business venture bite the dust. It's not that these PEs fear losing some of their savings in a business or an investment. It's having to face their friends and family should their efforts crash and burn. Fear of failing is paralyzing. It keeps people from trying to reach their ultimate potential. PEs (as well as non-PEs) have to conquer any such fear.

One of the great things about the writing business program I will present is that it would be difficult to lose more than a few thousand dollars. The biggest costs are in office equipment, which can be sold to recoup at least some of the investment. Also, you don't have to work for years in order to achieve a feeling of success. If you follow the steps I lay out, you should soon achieve a feeling of confidence.

But if you're one of those PEs afraid to take a risk, no matter what the consequences of failure might be (large or small), then I advise you not to engage in the program. It's not that the risk is large. It's simply that, in order to be successful, you must achieve a mindset or attitude that you will be successful. Mind over matter, courage over fear.

Maybe I can pump you up a bit.

Show me a generation in American history that has faced as much change and adversity as yours? You grew up during the depression, the biggest economic contraction in history. You were tempered by World War II, the greatest conflagration in history. You lived under the threat of nuclear annihilation during the 50s. You endured the stress of the cold war abroad, and a witch-hunt at home. In the 60s you bravely watched your country march off to war in a land you never heard of or cared about. You watched the country you loved and fought for be torn apart during the civil rights movement and anti-war demonstrations. You perse-vered when the President was accused of committing crimes against your democracy and was forced out of high office. You might have grown up on radio, but watched TV as one of your own generation walked on the moon. You may have danced at your prom to Smoke Gets In Your Eyes, but you accepted the new sound of the Beatles. You were never a lost generation. You worked. You paid your taxes. You raised your children. You in-vented things. You created a new world, one totally unlike the one into which you were born.

Probably no generation is more prepared to face the prospect of change than yours. Sure a few PEs are a fearful lot, slow to accept what is new and modern. And, true, a few PEs can be gullible - if the government (or any authority) says it, it must be true. But when push comes to shove, PEs know deep down that they can face up to any challenge.

PEs are a tough bunch. This next phase of life, being a PE in the 90s will be hard. But it won't be as hard as what you faced in a strike or bread line in 1936, or on the beach at Normandy, or in a hospital in Korea, or on a march in Selma, or when you got the telegram in 1969.

You have a knowledge of life and of what makes things hap-pen. You have created a standard of living that is the envy of the world. You know a lot of stuff and you have a lot you can share.

This knowledge will get you through. You'll be paid for what you know. Your experience will help support you.

This is not a difficult business. It can be frustrating but success will happen probably sooner than you think. If you follow the advice and examples in the book, I can virtually guarantee success to most PEs who make the endeavor. It's worked for others. Why shouldn't it work for you?

Please accept the fact that if you have good reading skills and you know how to clearly express yourself on paper, you have the ability.

> If you've ever written business reports, you have the ability.

> If you've ever been secretary for a volunteer organization, you have the ability.

> If you've ever worked in sales or marketing, you have the ability.

> If you've ever written letters to the editor, you have the ability.

> If you've ever created a business proposal, you have the ability.

> If you've ever written a poem, short story, or play, you have the ability.

> If you've ever written a Christmas letter, you have the ability.

> If you've ever written an article for your school paper, you have the ability.

If you've ever written product descriptions, you have the ability.

If you've ever written an advertisement or press release, you have the ability.

If you've ever written an article for a club news-letter, you have the ability.

If you've ever documented a process, product, or event, you have the ability.

Most important, even if you've never done any of the above, but you want to learn a new craft, *you have the ability.*

But having the ability is not a guarantee of success. You must also have the desire. You must have the discipline to plan your work and work your plan. You must want to succeed and be will-ing to work to make it happen.

## If They Were So Smart, They Would All Be Rich!

The second great truth that I want to share with you doesn't just apply to PEs. In your life you've heard a lot about so-called conventional wisdom. In fact, by this time in your life, you're expected to have some of it. Here is one of life's biggest secrets: Conventional wisdom is almost always wrong. I'll repeat it. *Con-ventional wisdom is almost always wrong.*

I'm not talking about immutable laws of nature such as "buy low, sell high," or "all things being equal, bet post position," or "the poor you will always have with you." Some things are just always so in the world.

But conventional wisdom also tells people they're too old to start a business, that they should only buy a franchise, that no one over sixty can learn to work a personal computer, that only Republicans raise taxes, that only Democrats start wars (I could go on and on). *Conventional wisdom is usually wrong.* If you listen and subscribe to what passes for conventional wisdom, *you're going to be wrong.* Listening to conventional wisdom will guarantee your failure, whether you're thinking about starting a writing business, taking up a new sport, or doing anything that "old people" think is reserved for "young people." Worse, conventional wisdom will keep you from trying.

Do you remember how much strife there was between the generations about 20-25 years ago? No, it wasn't only the Vietnam war, or long hair, or rock music. It was due in part to the younger generation willing to question authority and conventional wisdom. They had faith in themselves. They had no fear. Did they do better than the older generation? The jury is still out on that question. However, people 25 years younger than you, even with heavy family and financial obligations, are starting businesses more than ever before. They believe in themselves. While they probably have fear, they don't let it get in the way. They also know that the so-called conventional wisdom which says they will probably fail, is worth ignoring.

## So, What Do You Know, Joe?

The response to this question is always similar to the response I get when I suggest that someone buy a lottery ticket. "I never win anything!" When it comes to life's knowledge, many PEs are adamant that they don't know anything. I can't figure out why.

Here are people who have worked their entire lives. Unless they were born to independent wealth, they all did something for a living. And those who were homemakers, while they didn't bring a paycheck home, they too filled important positions requiring many skills.

Yet, when I ask the question, the reply is almost always the same - "I don't know anything!"

To be successful with the program, you must hone in on what you *know* or *do*. Or, you must determine what you *want* to know or do. The concept of the business is that you must be expert or at least extremely knowledgeable at something.

There is something that you know a lot about. There is some area of knowledge where you know far more than the next guy or gal. Whether the knowledge came from your work experience, from a hobby, or from being a volunteer, you *know* something. For those who disagree, I'll try to help you figure out what it is in a later chapter.

The majority of you have a good deal of experience in an area that you're still interested in. Maybe you were a mechanical engineer. Maybe you're an expert in rebuilding carburetors. Perhaps you know and love bookkeeping. Maybe it's event planning you learned from volunteer activities. If you have a hobby you love, then you're probably knowledgeable on the subject, be it collecting stamps, coins, butterflies, or beer bottles. When I ask "what do you really know about?" you're the folks who answer without blinking an eyelash.

---

**COMMENT**: *What you "know" may not always work with the program. However, there is a good chance you can use a derivative knowledgebase. Stay tuned!*

---

Of course, many PEs have extensive knowledge in an area, but absolutely hate anything having to do with it. For example, I talked with a thirty-year veteran of the auto sales wars. Unfortunately he hated selling cars, hated the manufacturers, and hated the dealers. But, he found that he had an interest in auto racing and hot-rods. What you know can be applied in several different areas, as you'll learn later in the book.

> **COMMENT**: *In several cases, people worked the program in areas they didn't like. For them, the need for income and the ease of entry was more important than love of their speciality.*

As you read about the writing business program, begin thinking about just what your knowledgebase is. Try to determine what you know from your lifetime of experience that you can market as useful information others will be interested in "buying."

## The Yellow Brick Road

Have you heard the old saying that if you don't know where you're going, any road will take you there? That's the problem with so many books, courses, seminars and the like, that are targeted to PEs. Most are forcefully clear in telling you that you can do this thing or that thing, but they pretty much leave you to your own devices on how to go about accomplishing whatever they think you should be doing! Lots of sizzle, no beef.

> **COMMENT**: *"If you don't know what road you're on, you'll probably end up somewhere else!"* Yogi Berra

My intention is not to lead you down a road to a business in which you'll eventually fail. The program that I outline in this book is based on common sense (not conventional wisdom) and has worked over and over again for PEs all across the country. While the concept is not exactly brain surgery, you'll find you should follow some special procedures.

I hear your question. Is the writing business really a good way to make a PE income? I believe it's a good way for most. However, unless you're convinced beyond a reasonable doubt, the program won't work for you. Remember when I talked about conventional wisdom? Conventional wisdom always talks about skill, knowledge, and prior experience as being the keystones to success. Partly true, but. . . .

I want to know what Orville and Wilbur knew about flying? What did Shakespeare know about renaissance Italy? What experience does anyone ever have that prepares them for a journey down a new road? It's not experience or even ability that's the deciding factor, my friends. Desire is at least as important, and maybe more so. You have to want it badly enough so that you'll spend the time to do it. The Wright brothers and the Bard were smart and capable men. But without the desire, ambition, and self-confidence, all would have failed. At least that's the way I see it. And it's the way that PEs who desire success need to look at things.

OK, you're fifty-nine years old. You worked every day of your life in the women's fashion retail business - as a clerk, manager, buyer, or whatever. And here I come along and say that you can work a program that will pay you for what you know about selling clothes to women. And you can. However, you need to be aware of one issue before you start.

The issue is *work*. I want you to read a few pages on *why* working can be good for you, *why* you should consider a part-time endeavor, *why* it's a good idea for you to start your own business.

# 2

## YOUR OWN BUSINESS:
## A GOOD IDEA

### Load Sixteen Tons and What Do You Get?

Men and women who are still working, facing the daily rat race, commuting long distances, dealing with pressure from bosses, customers, and co-workers, often dream about what it must be like to be you. They sit at their desks, their steering wheels, or their computers, or they lean on their shovels and wonder if there's such a thing as too much golf, if fishing ever gets old, or whether two-hour lunchs get boring after a while.

They go home to their families or pets or significant others and bemoan the fact that they never have time to pursue their hobbies, their sports, or to sit down and read a book.

A billion words have been written about how destructive job-stress can be to the mind and body. No matter what the oc-cupation, there are stresses related to it. No working person is exempt. As we all know, overwork can kill. Sooner or later, many working people who cannot find a balance between work-life and play-life will receive an early admission ticket to Medicare, the Betty Ford Clinic, or City of Peace.

Fortunately, the vast majority of working people are not really overworked: they are simply poor managers of their time - disorganized and unfocused. They start projects without proper preparation, they allow last minute interruptions to distract them, and they only take a short-term view of their work. They create their own stress, then fall victim to it.

If you have spent time in a locker room, a styling salon, or any place younger working men and women let down their guard to strangers, you'll hear complaints about the working life. "I only have time for one forty-minute tennis game a week." "I wish I could get my nails done more often, but I can't find the time." "My boss keeps me so busy, I never get a chance to bowl with you guys anymore." "I love playing bridge but it seems we're always having clients over." What they are really complaining about is not the lack of time, but the lack of balance in their lives.

Surveys show that job stress from poor time management is a frequent complaint among working people. We all know we must achieve greater balance between work and play in our lives, but never quite accomplish that. Just like the disposable income we had in the past, our discretionary time has also disappeared. With the cost of living being what it is, working people don't have work/play balance because they can't afford to.

If you read studies that come out of research foundations and university business schools, you find that most people actually enjoy what they do to earn a buck. For years, researchers concluded that mental illness among a large number of working people could be attributed to job dissatisfaction -- people hated their jobs and did not have the ability or opportunity to do what they wanted. It was accepted as fact that all except so-called creative people hated their jobs.

*COMMENT: Did you ever hear of a poet who didn't like writing poetry, or an artist who hated painting, or an actor who thought life on the set was a grind?*

What studies now show is that most people like their work; they just do too much of it. Working people just don't have the time to find balance in their lives. They are going here and there, doing this and that, picking up the kids, preparing meals, commuting or traveling, cramming for a meeting, trying to meet deadlines, working overtime shifts, going shopping, lining up at the bank, struggling with the new computer, and, in effect, loading sixteen tons of whatever they do onto their overstressed minds and bodies.

Then vacation time comes. For two or three weeks, working and business people have a prime opportunity to de-stress, slow down, and smell the roses. But that's not what happens. They book a ten-city European tour, attempt a 2,000 mile motor trip or board a cruise with twelve ports of call and nonstop on-board activities. Even the Club Med organization, which boasts itself as the "antidote for civilization," has so many possible activities that guests feel obligated to participate instead of acting like outdoor couch potatoes relaxing on a beach.

And so it goes for 40 years. Working people sit and dream of the day they get the gold watch, hang up the brief case, turn over the keys, punch out for good, reformat the hard disk, give up the pager, put away the uniform, close the books, and wave good-by while walking away. People still in the workforce dream of retirement; they dream of being you.

## Dream the Impossible Dream

Outside of some financial considerations, did you make concrete plans for your retirement years? Did you really think about what you would do? I believe most of you did, but not in detail. Careful planning wouldn't have been possible. You were caught up in a dream. We all invest a lot of our fantasy time in dreaming about what we are going to do after the gold watch is bestowed upon us. Be it golfing, fishing, camping, hunting, reading, gardening, playing bridge, traveling, going to school, or doing nothing, we spend a good deal of our working lives dreaming about the time we won't have to work.

It's not until about two or three years before the gold watch that most people go into an active planning mode. They think about restructuring their investments, about moving to a different locale based upon their perception of what they want to do with their time.

Finally the real search for balance arrives. The concept is that since you worked your butt off for the past twenty years, your reward is twenty years of golf. It makes perfect sense to you at the time. I'm sure that the first day out on the course, at the fishing hole, on the cruise ship, in pottery class, or whatever was your dream, is one of the top ten days of your life. You made it. You realized the dream. You can now live it.

For a time everything is OK, or at least seems to be. Everyone asks you how you're adjusting to retirement and you hold up the nine iron, the fishing pole, the tennis racket, and smile. For most of you, an endless array of "things" to do stretches before you. There might be financial limits, but there are no limits on your time, energy, or purpose. You can do what you want. After all, "It's a great time to be silver," as the makers of a well-known product continuously remind us.

Yet, as the first year of retirement draws to a close, many of you note that things are not going so well. You can't put your finger on it, but you know that playing golf every morning, lunching at the club, having drinks on the boat in the afternoon, and staying up to watch the late movie is fun, but not stimulating. You're not happy. You're out of sorts. Something is missing.

---

*COMMENT: In talking with PEs I found that most felt the first pangs of disenchantment about six months after the gold watch, yet did not fully realize it until twelve to eighteen months had passed.*

---

It seems that many PEs find their dream faulty. They really don't want to play golf every day. Boating is fun, but gets old. Even afternoon bridge can be a drag. The dream of retirement becomes the nightmare of boredom.

## How Many Reruns Can You Watch?

Boredom. You didn't expect that, did you? I mean, you dreamed all your life about a life of fun and leisure. A year or so into it and you're bored and glassy-eyed. If you never see another three iron for six months, it will be too soon! If you hear the words "gin" or "three no trumps" you'll scream! If you have one more midnight cruise ship eating binge, you'll start a food fight! If you see a fish even at the grocery store, you feel sick. If you have to climb behind the wheel of the RV one more time, you'll drive it off a cliff! And if your kid says, on her Saturday morning call, "So Mom, how did you enjoy retirement living this week?" you're going to visit the lawyer and redo the will!

You're bored because, once again your life lacks balance. While your working years had too little play, your retirement years have too little work.

Work, you say? Yes, work! Sociologists and psychologists have not been able to pinpoint why, but apparently humans (or most of us) cannot, as Goethe put it, endure a long string of good days! You need to be productive at something more important than sinking a thirty-foot putt, or making a clay pot.

You miss the chase. You miss the fight. You may not admit it, but a lot of you miss whatever you once did for a living. Even those who held jobs that were not considered creative miss going to them. Not everyone misses their *old job*, but many miss *working*.

The experts in the field of gerontology agree that PEs not only miss the actual job, but also the satisfaction of feeling productive. The word "feeling" is key. PEs who had big and important positions almost always felt productive; others who held more mundane jobs cite on surveys that they too believed they were productive. For example, take Fred, a lifelong produce manager at a supermarket. His store went to great lengths to assure Fred and people like him that what they did was vital to the success of the store. Then Fred retired and no longer felt that sense of accomplishment. Is it any wonder many PEs become depressed during retirement?

It stands to reason that if you suddenly give up a role in which you felt important and productive, and take on a more passive life role, you're going to have to adjust. More and more PEs can't make the adjustment.

The woman who had a job as a buyer in the high-pressure world of women's fashions and who was an important element in the success or failure of a fashion house, finds difficulty in believing that creating a beautiful three-color glazed vase is just a different form of productivity. Yet generations of senior activity directors have tried to sell this substitute concept of productivity. It's a tough sell because fewer and fewer PEs are buying it.

The man who sold insurance for thirty years spent a lifetime helping others plan for catastrophe. He helped his company reach higher and higher sales goals. He worked hard and long, including most nights and weekends. He has a large retirement income which he uses to pilot his sixty-foot yacht. Yet, he is not a "most happy fellow."

The woman who worked as a clerk in the county food stamp office knew that her work had an effect on the well-being of others. In her PE years, she uses her pension money to travel to the places she could only dream about while sitting at her desk. Yet she longs for some activity that will make her feel productive again.

The man who worked all his life for a large printing company and then quit ten years ago and bought a franchise quick-print shop has a problem. He built up the business, sold it and retired on the income from the sale. But, he misses the smell of the ink, the sound of the rollers hitting the paper. Working on his stamp collection every morning, taking a swim in the afternoon, and catching an early-bird dinner special is not the life he wants to continue leading.

Millions of women who were never on a payroll but managed important charity events, planned countless rummage sales, and organized hundreds of people in community campaigns, are not content to attend flower-arranging classes in the morning, French classes in the afternoon, and cocktail parties in the evening.

People always think the man or woman who had the high-powered job, who worked in a professional capacity, who had broad authority, or was a mover, shaker, or rainmaker, is the PE most apt to find retirement a bore. However, as I cited above, those who had regular jobs are often just as discontented in retirement. It's people just like you who yearn to feel productive again.

---

**Comment:** *The writing business that I outline is designed for PEs to once again be productive. Writing about what you know or like will give you back a sense of productivity, a feeling of success, assurance that you have value to our economic system. Most importantly, it will keep you from being bored!*

---

## "Once a Marine, Always a Marine"

I heard that quote in some old John Wayne movie. I spoke with some ex-Marines to find out if they agreed. Whatever Marines go through to become Marines stays with them for life. Always a member of the corps, Marines become part of a giant fraternity.

PEs generally feel this way about their former occupations or industries despite the stereotype that PEs hated their jobs, hated the industry, and couldn't wait to get out.

---

*COMMENT: As soon as the recession came along and jobs were hard to come by, all of a sudden people told interviewers that they "liked" their jobs!*

---

Talk with a fair number of PEs and you'll find that most enjoyed what they did for a living. I was amazed. I always thought of insurance as the most boring business in the world. But I've met dozens of guys who loved selling it and thought the insurance industry was the most noble and rewarding occupational group that one could choose to work in.

I found the same type of allegiance with clerks in DMV offices, sales assistants at department stores, hospital orderlies, landscapers, auto workers, as well as people who worked all their lives on an assembly line.

Even though PEs often landed haphazardly in occupations when jobs were scarce (depression and post-WW II) most picked occupations and industries that they liked (or learned to like).

---

*COMMENT: I had expected retired professionals and those in the helping occupations where the rewards, either monetary or spiritual, were high to miss their careers. I didn't expect to find former utility linemen mourning the passage of their working lives.*

---

Those of you who liked your work and took pride in the industry probably suffered separation problems when you retired. We want everyone to like and to work hard at their jobs. Then, one day after they get the gold watch, we expect them to put it all behind them. That just doesn't happen. I called the subscription offices of several industry-specific magazines that keep records on the demographics of their subscribers. I was amazed to learn that the subscriber base of so many trade publications is made up of people who are retired from the industry.

---

**COMMENT:** *The same is true for associations. You may no longer sell women's lingerie, but you still maintain your membership in the National Association of Professional Saleswomen. You may no longer teach school, but you still belong to the NEA.*

---

I spent many years in the computer industry. At first it amazed me how many data-processing PEs stayed up-to-date on what was being manufactured, programmed, sold, and talked about in the wild world of computers. After talking to other PEs in other industry groups and professions, I'm no longer amazed. It makes perfect sense.

Why should people who are no longer working in an occupation turn off their interest in it? Earlier, I would have thought "enough is enough." After working thirty years as an elementary school teacher, who wants to read about new trends in education? Well, the truth is, millions do. And, of course, this leads to lots of problems.

Most people can understand why professional athletes go into a depression soon after they retire. Does running a restaurant or selling insurance compare with 75,000 people cheering you during the World Series? Of course not. Yet, it's not just those used to fame and fortune who become depressed. Recent studies cite increasing numbers of depression cases suffered by people leaving *ordinary occupations*. These studies point to five basic factors.

The first is that having been part of a business or industry for years, people formulate solutions to current problems. Something happens when people stop working for a business and no longer have the responsibility they once had. Their minds open up to other possibilities and solutions to problems they had when they were working. Retired engineers tell me about solutions they came up with for engineering problems. Financial people tell me about new investment strategies they've come up with since becoming a PE. Teachers, nurses, librarians, middle managers have all expressed frustration that they have some good ideas, but don't know how to put them to use. Robert, an ex-software engineer told me "I was fooling around with a program I had been working on when I was with IBM. I came up with a neat way to accomplish the task. I called my old pals, but none of them ever returned my messages. I guess they think that having been away for two years, I couldn't possibly know what was going on. But I've kept up."

The second factor of separation-distress occurs because PEs miss the people. Many told me they don't necessarily want to go back to work, but they miss working with the personalities. One woman who had been a teacher and librarian said: "Working in education could be a pain. The hours were long and the pay was low. But the people! Every day was filled with the intellectual stimulation that flowed from well-read, well-educated co-workers. My bridge group just doesn't have that." Studies show that men who have been part of a long-term bonding process in their jobs or professions are often victims of this type of distress. An ex-military officer said that he has enjoyed doing lots of things since retiring from the Army, but he misses his old buddies while doing them.

The third factor is what I call the "expert syndrome." People often confuse this with power, but power is not the missing component. Toward the end of their careers, people become experts. They are the in-house gurus, the industry heavyweights, the guys or gals we go to for help, advice, or to get something fixed. This is particularly prevalent in the construction and shop trades. Paul was a master pressman. There wasn't anything he couldn't do with a large web printing press. When the impossible had to be done, everyone came to Paul. He misses that. He enjoyed the attention as well as the challenge. And since the technology of printing has not changed much since his retirement two years ago, he is still an expert. Yet, he has no outlet for his expertise.

The fourth depression factor is what many gerontologists call the "missing out" factor. People who worked in industries that were always undergoing constant change or who left before a project was complete, are depressed because they miss being part of the action. Linda was an astronomer for a NASA contractor and worked for years on the Hubble Telescope project. For a year before her retirement, she was a member on the project to "fix" the telescope. "What could be more interesting than engineering a 'service' call to space," she said. Of course, she retired before the big event and was despondent because she was not an active part of the actual "rescue." PEs often miss the "action" of their previous jobs or professions, though they don't necessarily miss long hours and constant politics. It's hard to sit on the bench when you're used to being a player.

Finally, PEs believe they have a lot to offer their previous fields. How many times have you thought, "If they would only give me a call, I could really help them out with this project, or help get a new guy up to speed, or show the new workers some shortcuts, or give some pointers on using this machine?"

Many studies have shown that when people are forced to retire (or are laid off) from a company, they are often bitter and vow not to answer calls from their old employers. But as time passes, six or eight months later, they long for a phone call. They want to be useful to the old shop. They know they have knowledge to share and want to share it. In short, they want to reach out and give something back.

---

**COMMENT**: It's one thing to be laid off AND angry at 40; it can inspire you to attain greater heights doing something else, somewhere else. But at 61, what does anger get you? How can you successfully channel the anger when no one will hire you? You can't. This is why many PEs start their own businesses.

---

## "Your Money or Your Life?"

Do you remember the famous Jack Benny routine where he is accosted and the thief gives him the above ultimatum? Benny's reply was "I'm thinking, I'm thinking!" For those of you who don't think you need any extra money, skip this section and move to the next.

Money is more than just a medium of exchange. It's more than an entry on a bank statement or some ink on a check. Money is how we keep score.

If you're a baseball player whose team is ahead, you'll still be unsatisfied if *you're* having a terrible game. For many, many PEs the same applies to working. Some people can be doing the most meaningful volunteer work in the world. However, since they're not paid, they don't get the same satisfaction as they would if they were earning a wage. Most don't want to admit it, but I think you'll agree it's true.

Earning money gives people a sense of self-worth. It's one way people measure their productivity. We tend to keep score of our self-esteem by the number of dollars we earn. It shouldn't be the most important number on the score board, but it's still important.

We've been programmed to believe that paid work is better than unpaid work. In a well-publicized study several years ago, a research team formed two large groups of people and gave each group *the same set* of short stories to read. The subjects were to give their opinion of each story by filling in a form which rated the stories on several items. There was a trick. The first group was told that all the stories were from an unpublished author whose work had been rejected by large publishing firms. The second group was told the opposite, that the stories had been accepted for a new book and possible TV show. The second group gave much higher ratings to the stories than the first group. The researchers then used another set of stories and switched groups, telling the first that the stories were published, and the second that they were unpublished. The results were virtually the same; when told the stories were "bought and paid for," people gave them higher ratings.

It's a fact of life that something (or someone) must be of value if someone else is willing to pay. This is why many PEs who embark on volunteer work right after retirement do not receive the satisfaction they expected. Since they are not being paid, the work does not contribute this vital aspect to their self-esteem.

> **COMMENT**: *What killed Willie Loman in "Death Of A Salesman"? He wasn't able to earn a living. The money he received was a gift from his boss. But that didn't cut it for Willie. Nobody was "buying" him, and after all, what is a salesman actually selling?*

## The Business of America Is Business

This quote is probably the only thing Calvin Coolidge is known for (besides the picture of him wearing an Indian headdress!) But the quote is true; business has given America a standard of living that's the envy of the world.

---

**COMMENT:** *Dorothy Parker, when told that Calvin Coolidge had died, asked "How could they tell?"*

---

Some of you worked in the private sector, some in government and some not at all. It doesn't matter. Whether you ran a department of a mega-company, were a clerk in an obscure bureaucracy, or had to run a household on a limited budget, the principles of business practice are part of your experience. Find a need and fill it, buy low and sell high, and try to have more money at the end of the year than you had at the beginning.

I want to concentrate on what having a small business can mean to you from a dollars and cents point of view. No matter what business you start, it can serve as the best (and last) tax shelter around.

From a tax standpoint, Congress has whittled away almost all the shelters and deductions. Consumer interest is no longer deductible. Mortgage interest is deductible only up to a limit. The amounts of health deductions as well as other miscellaneous itemizations are subject to a percentage of your adjusted gross income. For example, you're a nurse and have to take a course to maintain your credentials. Your two day class costs $250. Your adjusted gross income is $30,000. The law says that you can only deduct miscellaneous (educational) costs in excess of 2% of your adjusted gross. So, 2% of $30,000 is $600. If this is your only miscellaneous employment cost, you can't write off your $250 tuition. If the tuition had been $900 you could have deducted $300, the excesss over the 2% limit.

However, if you own a writing business and the community college is giving a three-day workshop on interview and reporting techniques for $180, this is not a miscellaneous deduction. This is a *cost of maintaining your business skills!* There is no 2% limitation. You write this off as a business expense on Schedule C.

I cannot emphasize the above too strongly. With proper tax and accounting advice, you'll be able to structure your life so that almost everything you do is business related. No, you're not going to write off that Hawaiian shirt you bought, but you may be able to write off a good percentage (maybe all) of the trip to Hawaii. You may not be able to write off dinner out with your husband or wife, but you might be able to deduct part of dinner with an interview subject. Or if you write about food topics and about children, you might be able to deduct dinner with your grandchildren!

As I said before, I'm not a tax expert. I don't give specific tax advice, only generic examples that may or may not apply to your situation. Ask a friend who is or was an accountant or book-keeper about the ins and outs of deductions for business expenses. If you're like most PEs, you'll be amazed at the tax opportunities a writing business can provide.

An accountant will say that you can possibly write off part of your house, part of your car, many of your travel expenses, part of your utility bills, all of your office supplies, furniture, and ma-chinery, some of your meals, and almost every book you buy or magazine you subscribe to.

I'm not talking about loopholes. I'm talking about Schedule C. If you have never seen one, take a look. It's where you enter all your business income and expenses. The difference between what you make and what you spend goes on line 12 of your 1040.

Although everyone wants to make money in his or her busi-ness, that's not as important as living well. Nothing is wrong with taking a loss just as nothing is wrong with making a gain. You win either way.

Let's assume you gross $15,000 in your writing business and have $3,000 in expenses. You have $12,000 more in your bank account and will pay taxes on it. That's OK. You still come out ahead, even with the deduction from your Social Security of $4,000. What if you decide you need a new computer, must do some research in England, have to spend several weekends in New York City, or must get a new camera? These are business expenses. You're likely to have spent more than your business made. That's bad, right? Wrong! You'll have less money in the bank, but look at all the stuff you got, virtually tax free! Because they're legitimate business expenses, you're allowed to deduct them (or part of them) from your taxes. You can have either $100 in cash or a $300 camera. Which do you want? Neither choice is wrong. If you didn't have your own business you would have no choice!

However, you shouldn't enter your own info-business only for the tax shelter benefits. You have to work hard. And if you take too many successive yearly losses, the government may call your business a hobby and disallow all your deductions. You must be serious about this business. The tax courts are littered with the remains of people who tried to pass off bogus businesses as legitimate enterprises in order to take Schedule C deductions. However, being a writer is a time-honored business that can and should make a profit (at least every once in a while!) I'm not talking about raising worms, doing piece work, or embarking on some multi-level marketing scheme. I'm talking about a real business where customers purchase information from you.

Don't only take my word on this. Check out the tax concepts with your own resources. Remember, I'm not talking about a scam. I'm talking about a legitimate enterprise where you invest time and money and expect to make a profit. A small business is the last tax shelter left in America. And who needs it more than you, a PE on a fixed income. Think about it.

## Hi Ho, Hi Ho (You Know the Rest!)

So where are we on the issue of your going back to work? My thesis is that retirement of all play and no work is as unbalanced as a lifestyle that's all work and no play. People were not engineered for a life of leisure. We need some activity, some goal, yes, even some stress to keep us strong, fit, and awake.

---

**COMMENT**: *Some people would add "to keep us young." But I'm not sure what "young" is anymore. I've seen 30-year-olds who have a fitness factor (mental and physical) of zero and 80-year-olds who are full of energy, knowledge, and ambition.*

---

By embarking on a path of semi-work, you're more likely to stay healthy. And in the final analysis, that's the bottom line. Living a life of boredom (or quiet desperation) is no good; neither is a life full of stress and frustration.

Starting on a program of creating your own info-business will give you the best of both worlds. You'll be able to immerse yourselves in a subject area that you know and enjoy. You'll have some direction to your daily life, certain things to do by a certain deadline. You won't be bored. You'll have an opportunity to keep up with a field you know. You'll make some money. You'll have access to the last good tax shelter.

I'm not talking about getting up at 5:30 AM and working until dark. I am talking about putting in two to four good hours a day. Productive hours. Not fiddling around hours. You have to *want* to do it. This is more than believing you *can* do it (although that's also important). You have to have the drive and ambition to make the program work. Whatever your self-confidence level, if you put in the time, if you "just do it," if you are energized by the process, you'll succeed.

Please understand that I'm talking about something more than just having a winning attitude. I'm talking about *liking* what you're doing. We all know people who are positive, upbeat, self-confident, and have a winning attitude, but they hate their work and do poorly as a result. Outside of work they are great to be around, folks you want to work on your committee, folks who are active in your community, folks you call when you want something done. But at work, they meander and stumble. Why? Because they hate the process. They don't like the daily ins and outs of what they do.

---

**COMMENT**: *Even professionals get tired of what they do. How many contracts can lawyers write before the process gets old. How many kids can teachers teach before they feel beaten by the system.*

---

I've tried to give you some confidence and attitude building ideas. I'm hopeful that at this point, you have a "can do" attitude. As I continue, I want you to think about what I call "the process," my euphemism for what you actually do, physically, day by day, hour by hour, to make the dollar. If you can't stand the process, you won't be happy and you won't succeed. There is a difference between "the image" and the reality.

When I tell people they can start a business and make money writing about what they know from their life experience, their heads fill with the picture of a writer sitting at a bar in Key West, drinking margaritas and scribbling notes on the back of cocktail napkins. That's the *image*.

The *process* is totally different. It's hour upon hour of sitting in front of a screen and keyboard, hours on the phone, hours at the library, and hours running from the post office to the quick printers, to the office supply store, to the airport, etc. The process is far different from the image.

If you can't see yourself spending hours alone in front of a computer screen, then don't attempt this business. The process is research and write, research and write. The program is not going to work for you if you don't like the process.

If you have some doubts ask yourself this: "Why shouldn't I like it?" We're talking about a quiet, dignified, peaceful work environment in which you're limited only by your own creative abilities. Sure, some of you really might like to go back to the shop floor. Some of you would really like to spend a day or two each week back on the line, or in the showroom, or behind the counter. But for many, a writing business is an ideal situation. You get to be all of these things without leaving home.

---

**COMMENT**: I like to call the craft of writing a "virtual workplace".

---

## A Business of Your Own

By starting your own info-business of writing you will be doing many of the things you did before you were a PE. You'll also become more knowledgeable and may achieve public recognition as an expert on whatever it was you did. In short, we can say that *what you did, is now what you do.* Just in a different form! Think about it. Open your mind. The program could be what you're looking for. It might solve some of the lifestyle difficulties of retirement, as well as remove some of the financial constraints.

It's not my intent to bulldog you into doing what this book is all about. If it's not for you, it's not for you. I said earlier that this program is a collection of simple concepts. People tend to view simple concepts with some disdain. All I ask is that you keep an open mind about your own abilities to succeed as well as on what the process really is.

While many of you are well off and don't need any extra income to offset a possible economic dislocation, I've tried, in this chapter, to cover some of the non-financial reasons why it's a good idea to start a business.

For those of you who *need* an outside income, understand one fact. There is no part time, simple, and easy way that you're going to make an extra $30,000 a year. But, if you want (or have) to make up some $10,000 to $15,000 of extra income, I think you'll find an answer here.

---

**COMMENT**: It's possible that you can earn $30,000 or more via the program, but it won't happen unless you work full time at it and that's not the premise of this book.

---

From speaking to many PEs about their financial situation I learned that most can *get by* on their savings, pension, and social security. What they want is just something extra, to do more than just get by. Perhaps a new car every second year, two trips instead of one a year, membership at a club with better facilities, or dinner out twice a week.

What many need is a simple, dignified way to earn an extra $1,000 to $1,500 a month without killing themselves, taking a large risk, or having to constantly sell, sell, sell. Many want to find a way to make extra money based upon what they know and are interested in. They need the opportunity to control their own schedule and set their own limits. Most importantly they need a vehicle to earn money and not hate the process.

There are three basic entities to working. There is:

Lots of fun

Lots of money

Lots of free time

You have the opportunity to attain only two of these. What are they? You make the choice. The program of starting an info-business and making money by writing can be accomplished, no matter which two items you desire.

As you continue, please remember that the intent of this book is not to entice you *out* of retirement. The intent is to show you how to *enhance* your retirement.

***

Next, I want to talk about an invention that will make your writing business in retirement not only possible, but perhaps even enjoyable. Maybe not at first, but in time you'll wonder how you got through your 55 or 65 or 75 years without one.

It's the computer.

# 3

. . . . . . . . . . . . . . . . . . . . . . . . . . .

# IT'S JUST A MACHINE

## Computer-Phobia Strikes Deep!

Five or six years ago when I talked to PEs, I ran into a lot more computer phobia than I do now. This is not to say that many of you are totally comfortable with the concept of using one of these desktop marvels. But I'm happy to report that PEs no longer have a lock on fear of computers. This gradual lessening of resistance is apparent in comments from PEs. Five years ago I was told "I don't want to ever have a computer." Now, I hear "I wish I could learn to work a computer; they sound neat!"

If you're afraid you can't learn to use a computer, don't worry. Everyone starts out with this fear. I don't think it's any different than when the automobile was first produced or the microwave was introduced.

Initially, people talked about their fear of "breaking" the machine. That was a cover-up of their insecurity. People are still afraid they're not smart enough to master the electronic beast.

The difference is that now people are more honest about their fears, even when these fears are unfounded.

Computers are really not that hard to operate. Yes, there will be new concepts to learn, and yes, you'll make mistakes. But, on the whole, the experience will be pleasant.

---

**COMMENT**: *The modern washer or dryer with its many options and cycles can be more difficult to operate than a computer.*

---

## But I Already Have a Typewriter

You can use your typewriter for your info-business, but you'll work twice as hard for half the results.

Actually, "computer" is not aptly named for what you'll be doing since you will do little computing. What you're really going to do is store data, save data, and recall data. Your computer is going to be one large electronic filing cabinet where you keep all the "stuff" relevant to your info-business.

Your computer will allow you to do two magic things that your typewriter won't: to change and save documents. Your computer will serve as your writing machine, file cabinet, accounting ledger, and printing tool. Your typewriter is only a transcribing machine. It won't help you with spelling, it won't check your grammar, and it won't assist you in finding synonyms and antonyms. With a typewriter, all you get each time you press a key is a tiny letter.

With your computer, you write something, store it on the disk, and later recall it so you can refine or change it for another purpose. If you write an article on how to get the most from the Big Stitch sewing machine, you can later make minor changes in the piece for the Tiny Bobbin sewing machine. With a type-writer, you would have to retype the entire piece. Save and change. Change and save. These are the main reasons you want a computer.

I'm not going to beat this into the ground. I don't believe you can be successful in any business today without having the ability to use a desktop computer. Yes, you can run your writing business without a computer, but it will be very difficult and time-consuming. I urge you to learn a few things about computers and consider buying one.

## The Crash Course on Computers

A computer is not conceptually different from your stereo system. You have the hardware components: the tuner, ampli-fier, tape player, CD player, cables, and speakers. Then you have your programming components; tapes, disks, and the signal from the radio station with the music, news, and weather.

Computers are much the same. The hardware, which sits on your desk, consists of the central processing unit (CPU), usually called "the box," two disk drives (almost always inside the box), a keyboard, a video monitor, some wires, and a printer. The pro-gramming components are called software and consist of the pro-grams and data the computer uses to do something.

The box contains certain parts you should become acquainted with. The first is the chip, the brains of the machine. The sec-ond important part is the memory, where the work gets done. You'll see the term RAM, which stands for random access memory. It's like a giant scratch pad. Memory is measured in millions of characters (called bytes) or megabytes. You'll buy a machine with 8 or more megabytes of memory. A third basic component is the storage disks. One type is called a floppy disk.

These fit in your purse or pocket and are most often used to backup the data in your computer so you can store it in a safe place.

---

**COMMENT**: *Floppy disk is a misnomer. The 3.5-inch disks used in today's machines are encased in a hard plastic shell and are pretty rigid. They don't flop like the old 5.25-inch disks did.*

---

More important is the hard disk, called "hard" because it's mounted in the computer, not portable, and not "floppy." All the programs and data are stored on the hard disk. Hard disks are also measured in megabytes. You'll buy one with anywhere from 150 to 300 megabytes.

You'll hear the term "application." This is a group of programs that do something similar. For example, you'll buy a word processing application. You might buy a spreadsheet application. You'll probably buy a database application. These are just broad categories of "things" that the computer can do. Software belongs to an application. For example if you buy a software program called Word (by a company called Microsoft), you're buying a word processing application. The terminology is not really important, I just didn't want you confused if you hear it at the computer store.

Software is divided into two types: the program and the data. The program is the instructions the computer reads in order to act on the data. Of course, the data is the information that has some use to you. For example, let's use the Microsoft Word program again. Load this into the computer and you're ready to create or act on some data. The data might be the letter you're writing to a magazine publisher asking them to print your article on growing soybeans Or the data might be an article you wrote on soybeans that you're going to change into one about lima beans and resell to a different magazine.

That's all you really have to know about computers. There is hardware and there is software. The hardware sits on your desk. The software is put on the hard disk drive. You start up a program. The hard disk is read and the program is put in the memory of the computer. You then create or change the data. When done, you can print it out. If this is old data, you can also save it back to itself or you can "copy" it to another name so you have the original and the new. For example I could retrieve the soybean article (say it's saved to the name of SOYBEAN and with my word processing software, change every reference of "soybeans" to "lima beans." Then I could save the "new" article to the name of LIMABEAN.

The other parts of the computer are easy. Video monitors vary by size. The ones you're going to be interested in are standard-size color monitors. They usually sit on top of the box.

Keyboards are pretty much the same, though some have a different touch than others.

There are three types of printers out there, but you'll only be interested in laser or ink-jet printers. The output of both laser and ink-jet looks the same. The difference is in speed and features.

A modem is the last piece of equipment you need to know about. A modem is a box that connects your computer to the telephone line so that you can use communication software to dial-out to the world! Modems are priced by speed measured in bits per second. Buy the fastest modem you can afford.

## PC or Apple?

Wars have been fought over less trivial questions. For those who don't know, there are two standards in the desktop computer world. One is the IBM "compatible" machine which uses a chip manufactured by a company called Intel and system software called DOS and Windows, both Microsoft products. These machines are called personal computers or PCs. The other standard is the Apple Macintosh, known as the Mac. It uses a chip by Motorola and system software called System 7 written by Apple.

If you already have one or the other, keep it and use what you have. Either the PC or the Mac will work fine.

If you already know how to use a computer but don't have one, get the kind you know.

If you don't know a thing about computers, don't have one, and are scared of getting one, the choice is easy: get a Mac.

The Apple Macintosh is, hands down, easier to use, easier to set up, and more reliable than the PC. Many people don't agree with me on this and they are certainly entitled to their opinion. However, after twenty years in and around the computer business, and I am confident with my advice.

---

**COMMENT**: *Ease of use is my reason for recommending a Mac. You can set up and use it the first day. The third day you know enough to be dangerous. The tenth day you're a power-user.*

---

Don't take my word for it. Talk to users of both machines. Most people will tell you that the Mac is easier to use, but more software is available for the PC. This is true, but you're only going to buy a few programs; and only one will be used extensively: the word processor. The spreadsheet program, the database program, and the checkbook program are others you'll have use for. The major manufacturers of popular programs produce for both the Mac and the PC.

## What Apple Should I Buy?

Apple has a class of machines called the PowerMacs. It uses a new chip from Motorola called the PowerPC. But you don't need this much power and speed. I suggest you get any of the Macintosh machines that uses what is called the 68040 chip, if they are available. This includes the Powerbook (notebook) and the Quadra line. Look for a machine that is upgradable to the PowerPC chip in case you want to make your computer faster at a later date.

You'll hear all sorts of claims about the speed of the computer. Speed, measured in megahertz or MHz, is a deep and complicated area. Just make sure you buy a machine rated at 20 MHz or higher. For what you'll be doing, speed is not that important. If you were doing heavy graphics work like trying to design the space shuttle, speed would be important. But for doing word processing, speed is not a big concern.

There's a good case for buying a little notebook sized computer. It's portable, you can carry it with you, and store it out of the way. The problem is that the screen is small and the color versions are expensive. If you can make do with a black and white screen, then the cheaper Apple Powerbooks will do fine. Go to the store and play with one. They have a built-in trackball device instead of a desktop mouse (used to point and click on pictures, words.) Some people find working with the Powerbook difficult because the trackball is small. The keyboard is also rather tiny. Because of these drawbacks, you have to decide how important portability is to you.

---

**COMMENT**: *My wife, also a writer, loves her Powerbook. She likes to prop it up on her knees in bed to do her writing.*

---

While the Powerbook comes with an AC adapter, it has a built-in battery that will run for about four hours before you need to switch over and recharge.

I think most of you will opt for the traditional desktop machine. Here you'll be concerned with the "footprint" of the box (will it fit on your desk?). Apple (as do other manufactures) makes its models either small and high, or thin and wide.

---

COMMENT: *I prefer the thin and wide box. I'm not very tall. When I put the monitor on top of the computer, it's not too high for easy viewing.*

---

Go to the store and look at all the sizes and shapes of the Apple machines. There's sure to be one that you'll like.

## What Features Should I Get With It?

Computers are sold like cars. They come in a base model that few actually buy. You pay for add-on stuff such as more RAM memory, or a larger disk, or a CD-ROM drive. Apple makes it easier to buy a machine because they sell most with configurations suited to various users.

Buy your machine with at least 8 MB (megabytes) of RAM memory. This is the scratch pad of internal memory where the computer does its work. Although the more memory you have, the better, an 8 MB machine is all you really need.

The capacity of the hard disk drive is important. Buy one with at least 150 MB (150 million characters) of capacity. Trust me on this. The larger the hard drive you can afford, the better. The most important reason for a large disk is that you'll need lots of storage for your programs and data. Don't let anyone talk you into getting a machine with a small hard drive. You'll be sorry later on. Anyway, large capacity hard drives are not that expensive.

Make sure the floppy disk is 1.2 MB and not the older, smaller 800 KB (kilobyte) model.

If you like, you can get a computer that has a built-in CD-ROM drive. This is the same type of CD you have in your stereo system except the disks have programs and data on them. For example, for about $100 you can buy an entire encyclopedia on a CD-ROM disk. Do you need it? Probably not, but if you can afford it, one would be nice to have. You can always add one later if you want.

The monitor is important. Buy the best you can afford. Apple usually makes a good, better, and best model. The difference is the crispness of the images on the screen. Another consideration is the size. They come in different sizes, like TV sets. Most of you will get by with a 13 or 14-inch monitor. What you'll find is that the larger the screen, the larger the entire monitor. A 15-inch screen is nice, but the entire monitor (with swivel stand) is enormous. Go to the store and check it out.

PCs usually have built-in modems while Macs use external modems. External modems cost more but are easier to install and configure. Modem speed seems to increase each week! Buy one that is rated at least 14,400 bits per second (you'll see the term *baud* used). Modems often come with their own software, but you can use communication programs written by other companies on all modems.

## Put It in Print

The printer is very important to you. If you can afford it, buy a laser printer. Several manufacturers produce them and most are the same quality. You pay for two items: dots per inch (dpi) and pages per minute (ppm). The cheaper printers are 300 dpi at 4 ppm. This is all you'll need. However, some printers on the market are 600 dpi at 6 or 8 ppm and are priced pretty competitively with the 300 dpi machines.

Look for a laser printer that will hold a lot of paper. Cheaper ones may only hold 50 sheets. It's a pain to have to add paper so often.

I also suggest you stick with a major manufacturer, such as Texas Instruments, Hewlett Packard, Epson, NEC, or, of course, Apple. If printers confuse you, buy the best Apple laser printer you can afford and you won't have to worry about setting it up. Apple stuff cobbles together in a snap!

> *TIP*: Make sure the printer can do envelopes easily. Most of them have an attachment you can buy that lets you stack 50 or 60 envelopes. This is nice to have, but you probably don't need it right away. With the built-in manual sheet feeder, you can do envelopes 3 or 4 at a time.

Another type of printer is the ink-jet. Apple makes one, as do the other manufacturers mentioned above. These are about half the price of laser printers and the quality is very good. It's often hard to tell the difference. However, they are slow, very slow. Also, many of them do not have a facility called Postscript. If price is important, then get an ink-jet, but I think over the long run, a laser is a better buy.

The final type of printer type you'll run into is called the dot matrix printer. Don't even consider buying one. Yes, they're cheap, but the output is pretty crude. Words on paper is your business. You want the best output you can get.

## Software Makes Hardware Happen

I can't take credit for this cute (and somewhat risque´) saying, but it's true. Without software programs your computer is nothing but a large paperweight.

Whether you have a PC or a Mac, you have two basic choices. The first is simple, the second is complex.

The complex choice is to buy individual programs that perform separate tasks. You buy a word processing program for writing. You buy a spreadsheet program for doing tables and charts. You buy a database program for keeping lists.

The simple choice is to buy what is called an integrated program, sometimes referred to as an "all in one" program. This is one large program that has the major items that any computer user will need most often. For the Mac there are two major brands. The first is Microsoft Works. The other is Claris Works. Microsoft and Claris are major players in the software world. Although they compete head to head, both products are remarkably similar.

The integrated programs come with a word processor, a database, a spreadsheet, and a modem communications program.

While the word processing part of these packages doesn't come with every feature you would find in a stand-alone program, the program will have everything you'll ever use.

---

*COMMENT: Most software companies take their stand-alone programs, "cut them down" and bundle them into one integrated program. Thus, Microsoft takes its Word software, cuts out some of the more esoteric features, and puts the basic features into the Works program. They do the same with their Excel spreadsheet.*

---

I recommend an integrated program for the first-time computer buyer. You'll save about 70% of the cost of buying several stand-alone programs, and you'll get all the features you'll need for the first year or so.

The other approach is to buy separate programs. This is the approach I recommend if you already have a knowledge of one of the major programs you'll use. Also, if you're the kind of person who must have every whistle and bell possible in a program, then buying the individual pieces will be better than getting an integrated package.

## Name Some Names, Please

As I mentioned above, the two most popular integrated programs are Microsoft Works and Claris Works. There isn't much difference between them (they even copied each other's name.) They each have a word processing program, a database program, a spreadsheet program, and a communications program. Both are good value for the dollar. I would buy whichever one is on sale (sometimes you can get the computer salesman to "throw in" one of these programs when you buy your computer.)

Stand-alone word processing program include Microsoft Word, Wordperfect, Write-Now, and MacWrite Pro. They vary by price in direct proportion to the features they have. My rule of thumb is that if you don't know which one to buy, and can't get recommendations, buy the cheapest one. You can move to a more expensive program later if necessary. Microsoft Word is the biggest seller and probably the most full-featured. It's also expensive. It's what I use. If you buy one of the major brands you really can't make a bad choice.

If you want a spreadsheet, Microsoft Excel is the best choice. Those of you who know Lotus will love Excel. It comes with every whistle and bell imaginable.

Do you need a spreadsheet? No, you could live without one. But if you're already familiar with the concepts of working with these software marvels, you'll want to get one.

If you want a stand-alone database program, my choice is FileMaker Pro by Claris. It's easy to use, and you can run your entire business with it. It comes with several pre-programmed applications such as invoicing, list management, and inventory that you can easily modify for your info-business. You *will* want a database program. Maybe not day one, but after a while you'll want to keep track of things, and a database program is the tool you'll need.

Finally, you may want something to keep accounts for all the money you make. Far and away the best (and cheapest) program you can buy is Quicken. This is a one-write accounting system that works like a check book. Even if you don't want to print your checks on the computer, Quicken can easily keep track of your expenses, income, profits, and losses. The reporting feature alone is worth the money; and Quicken costs less than $100. I suggest you buy it and use it.

---

*TIP*: Later on I talk about opening up a separate bank account for your info-business. Use Quicken to "manage" this account. Remember, the best proof of payment is a check and Quicken really does checks well.

---

There are tons of other programs you can buy. Once you see how easy the Macintosh is to use, you'll undoubtedly buy more software. For example, you might want a good dictionary program (Word processors have spell checkers, but seldom include dictionaries.) There are many time-management programs, sort of like the personal planners many people use. There are graphic design programs by the score. If you get a CD-ROM, you can buy hundreds of reference works. The bottom line is that whatever you might want a computer to do, a program is out there that will do it.

## Try Before You Buy

It's not a great idea to rush out and buy a computer. Before you invest several thousand dollars, spend some small change and take a few classes. I think you'll find them fun. Classes are also the easiest way of getting over your fear of using computers. There are no tests or exams.

Almost every store that sells Macintosh computers has classes from the beginner to the expert level. I'm not talking about a long course. A half day class in Macintosh basics is all you need to learn how to operate the machine. Find a store that has these classes and sign up for one. They're not expensive.

After you have taken the basic computer course, you should take the introduction course to the word processing software you plan to buy, or the course for the integrated program. These are usually two-day classes. You'll learn ten times more through a class than through trial and error at home.

**COMMENT**: *Almost every major program has a "hands on" tutorial that will teach you how to use it. For example, Word has one where you compose, save, change, and print a memo. These are great, but nothing will compare to taking a hands-on class.*

When you see how easy it is to use a Macintosh, your confidence level will rise to new heights. You may wonder how you ever lived without one. It's true. You'll see.

**TIP**: *In several areas of the country, a nonprofit organization called Senior Net holds PC classes and sometimes Mac classes for senior citizens. Check to see if there is a Senior Net chapter in your area.*

## Buy Here, Buy There

Where you buy your computer is not all that important. If you don't move your (desktop) computer often, chances are the machine will never break or need service. Ask around for referrals. Find a store that has classes or has an arrangement with another company that gives classes.

Again, big store or small store makes little difference. Shop them all. Ask questions. Read the ads in the papers.

Most computers come in "prepackaged" configurations. Some stores will buy the bare-bones model and offer to "customize" it for you. Most of the time this is not a problem. However, there are some stores that will use inferior parts and charge top dollar. For example, if the store says that they don't have a model with a 230 MB hard drive but offers to put one in, make sure the store has a good service reputation. The fear is that they will use a cheap disk and charge you for the expensive one.

My advice is to buy a machine that comes configured from the factory. You may end up buying a little more machine than you wanted, but you have the peace of mind of knowing that your machine has not been opened and had parts switched by some misguided service jockey.

> **COMMENT**: Adding parts (like a disk or memory chips) to a computer is a piece of cake. They just snap in. You can do it yourself. While it's true that "parts are parts," don't start messing around with your computer until you know what parts are what!

The question is always raised about buying from a mail-order company. For buying hardware, I say no, a thousand times no. Many times the mail-order firms are not authorized dealers. They get their machines on what is called "the gray market." They make a deal with a large store to buy machines the store orders. This is not illegal. However, only an authorized dealer is supposed to sell new machines. Many stores will not service machines bought on the gray market, if they find out (which is almost impossible.) Anyway, you want to buy where you can get repairs if necessary. Some mail-order firms offer repairs, but you must ship the machine to them and they ship it back (both at your cost). Whatever you might save by dealing with a mail-order firm, you could lose if you need service.

Software is a different item altogether. Knowledgeable computer users buy software from two places: discount warehouses like Price Club or by mail from large catalog companies. Mail-order software is almost always 10% lower than the lowest retail store price. Sometimes you'll see a rock bottom store sale on a software product, but most often the mail-order firms will sell for less. And many times you don't have to pay sales tax.

Retail stores will usually not match mail-order prices. They just can't. You should ask, but don't be surprised if they say no. If you're buying a $40 software package by mail, you might save $4 on the price, but have to pay $7 to have it shipped. No savings here. But when you buy a $299 product (list price) from a mail-order firm for $249, you can save some real dollars.

Where do you find mail-order software companies? Simple. Buy a copy of *MacWorld* or *MacUser* magazines (or *PC Magazine* for those machines) and you'll find multi-page ads for mail-order houses.

---

*TIP*: I usually deal with Mac Warehouse (1-800-622-6222) because they put out a nice catalog each month (which they send free) and I've never had a problem with them. Another big house is Mac Connection. They also publish a catalog. Both often run multi-page ads in the magazines. I can vouch for each of these companies.

---

What I really like about buying software through the mail is that you can usually phone your order by 11 PM and they will overnight it to you by 10 AM the next day. The large firms have a deal with Fed Ex, Airborne, UPS, etc. and the shipping price is very reasonable. The mail-order companies also know what they have in stock. It's a real drag to call a local store, be told that they carry a product, but find that it's out of stock after you get there.

## The Price Is Right

If you shop the stores and read the ads you'll find that the price of Apple computers is pretty much the same from store to store. They probably won't vary by much more than $150.

The important thing to know is that almost every store will match a competitor's price. There is not a lot of profit in computer hardware. Thus, the store must do volume on hardware. There is a bit more profit in software.

Computers are like other products. Stores have sales on certain models at certain times. When one store has a sale on a model, the other stores tend to have one, too. It's a very competitive business.

Outside of price-matching, there is not much bargaining anymore. (Ten years ago buying a box was like buying a car.) The prices are marked and you pay the listed price. Sometimes, the store will throw in a piece of software to make the sale. You might be able to get them to offer you a free class or two in order to close the deal. (Some stores automatically include a free class for first-time buyers.) Shop around.

## Let's Make a Deal

It's important to know what you want to buy. Otherwise, the salesperson is going to sell you whatever the store gets the highest margin on or whatever the store wants to unload.

> **COMMENT**: Most larger stores do not have commissioned salespeople. They get a low salary and a bonus based on volume. You're not likely to face high pressure. It's almost the other way around. Often, it's hard to find someone interested in taking care of you! You may get better service at a smaller store where they use commissioned salespeople. But you'll pay for it.

Make your shopping a two-step affair. Hopefully, you have taken a class and know how to use the computer (at least how to point and click the mouse).

The first day, look around several stores. If you have never been to a computer store, you might feel like a fish out of water. A good store will soon put you at ease. Tell them you don't know a thing but that you're looking for, say a Macintosh with 8 MB of memory, a 230 MB hard disk, a 14-inch monitor, and a laser printer. They will probably ask you some questions about what you're going to do. Tell them about your info-business. Some stores may try to talk you into buying a smaller or larger configuration, depending on what they have in stock (first-timers sometimes get burned that way). But since you know what you want, most will try to sell it to you without any hassle. Have the sales-person give you a written quote. They all have their inventory computerized and do these quotes as a matter of course. Thank them and tell them you have to think about it.

Go home and compare the quotes as well as how you "felt" about each store. Is the store with the best price where you want to spend your money? Pick out the store that you feel is the best in terms of how you were treated and decide to buy there.

Go back the next day and present the bid you got from the lowest store. They will match it 90% of the time. If they can't match the dollars, they sometimes will throw in software or classes to make up the difference. Some will offer (for a small price or as a throw-in) to deliver the computer to your home and set it up.

---

**COMMENT:** For an Apple Macintosh and printer, setting up is simple. It's plug and play. Just follow the instructions step by step. All the difficult procedures are done for you at the factory.

---

Buying a computer is not like buying a home or car. It's a little more complex than buying a toaster, but the principles are the same. Shop. Compare. Purchase.

---

**TIP:** Make sure you fill out and send in the warranty card. This is important because unless your card is on file you won't get free warranty service (usually 1 year.) Also, Apple will send you your choice of several nice gifts (mouse pad, mug, magazine subscription etc.) Also fill out and mail the warranty card for software you buy. With your card on file, you'll be able to upgrade to a new version for a fraction of the new package price.

---

## You Don't Want It Even if It's Free!

In your shopping you're likely to see machines called "word processors." These are souped-up typewriters. Some have a floppy disk, some a small video monitor. One even has a built-in printer. Most are relatively inexpensive; about $500 - $600.

Don't get one of these unless you absolutely can't afford anything else. You're better off with a used Macintosh than one of these new "word processors."

---
*TIP:* You can often find real bargains in used computers. People don't abuse them and will often let them go for very low prices because they've upgraded their system (and need the desk space!). Check your newspaper classified section.

---

Because these fancy typewriters use their own formats, you won't be able to send your material on disk to publishers who ask for your work in electronic format. Also, they are not designed for use in running a business. They are only writing machines. If you were a college student, and *only* had to write papers (no math or science projects) you might get by with a word processor machine.

However I predict you'll be sorry if you buy one of these machines. Very sorry. Anything less than the full-featured computer I described is a waste of money.

# First-Time Buyer Computer Shopping List

**COMPUTER:** 8 Megabytes RAM, 20 Mhz or faster

**HARD DRIVE:** 230 - 500 Megabytes, built-in

**FLOPPY DRIVE:** 3.5-inch, 1.2 MB

**MONITOR:** 13-15 inch color with tilt/swivel base

**KEYBORAD:** Extended with function keys and 10 key pad

**PRINTER:** 300 or 600 DPI laser or ink-jet

**MODEM:** 14,400 baud (or bps)

**SOFTWARE:** Microsoft Works or Claris Works

**OPTIONS:** CD-ROM, Speakers, Multi-Envelope Tray,

# 4

. . . . . . . . . . . . . . . . . . . . . . . . . .

# WHAT'S YOUR LINE?

## How Do You Know What You Know?

Before you rush out and start your own writing business, you should sit down and decide just what your area of expertise is, or is going to be. There are basically two choices you can make. You can use your expertise on something you've done for a living, or you can set up a writing business based on something you know quite a bit about from either your hobby or your education.

There is no magic formula I can give you that will definitively determine what your area of expertise is or should be. However, I can give you some hints.

For a majority of PEs, their life's work will become what we call their genre (jahn-rah). This French word is defined as "a distinct class or category of literary composition." In plain English, it means your area of expertise. Here I use it to signify the broad topic (or combination of topics) about which you're going to write.

---

**COMMENT**: *My genres are business, career, and technology. Because I write about all of these topics, I like to lump them into one genre which I call "the workplace of the future." New genres are being created all the time, such as new age, information highway, home office, etc.*

---

It's very important that you determine your genre. It will define your life as well as your work. It's the subject or group of topics you are, or will become, an expert on. If you've worked for the past twenty years at an occupation that fits an established genre, then you might be set. For example, if you were an electrical engineer, you might consider your genre engineering, electronics, or science.

What is it that you *know*? What are you interested in? What topics could you happily spend the next year or two learning more about? These are important questions that you must answer honestly.

Lots of people never relate their job to their industry. For example, a waitress may not see herself as part of the restaurant industry. A restaurant owner may not see herself as part of the entertainment industry. A dog groomer may not see himself as part of the personal service industry (like beauticians and barbers). Someone who works in a rubber stamp factory might not see himself as knowledgeable about the printing industry.

Often, people are part of two or more industry groups and don't know it. For example, the woman who works as a salesperson in a camera store is part of the retail industry as well as the photo industry.

At the end of this chapter there is a listing of industry classifications as defined by the IRS. Take a moment to see how many different areas you are knowledgeable about.

## I Didn't Learn Anything From My Job.

This is just not true. I don't care if you spent the last thirty years on an assembly line putting nut A onto bolt B, you're an expert in manufacturing. You probably have knowledge of labor relations. You probably have firsthand experience in issues relating to workplace safety, lighting, efficiency, and worker relations. You also probably know about the industry in which nut A and bolt B were used.

If you spent years in sales, either retail or outside, you know much about your industry products as well as closing techniques, advertising, customer prospecting, phone manners, business etiquette, travel difficulties, and time management.

If you spent twenty years as a clerk at the Department of Motor Vehicles, you know about work-flow efficiency (or lack of it), office machinery and how it can help or hinder productivity, manager-employee relations, workplace stress, and, of course, the civil service system.

If you worked the front desk at a hotel, you know about the travel industry, the hotel industry, the psychological makeup of the business traveler, convention planning, office equipment, and customer relations.

If you were a postal worker, you know about issues relating to the U.S. Mail, specialized sorting machinery, working in the bureaucracy, truck driving (if you were a carrier), occupational stress, and perhaps stamp collecting.

If you worked as a short order cook, you know a great deal about food handling and preparation, kitchen equipment, kitchen design, menu planning, working in close quarters, short deadlines, the restaurant business, and of course, recipes.

If you drove a truck, you're knowledgeable about the U.S. highway and transportation system, auto and truck maintenance, the travel industry, driving techniques, safety, loading and unloading methods, tires, weather, truck stops, and probably country music.

If you worked as a home builder, you know about building products, tools, building design, the construction industry, new materials, purchasing, bidding, quality control, hardware, safety, and maybe environmental issues.

If you worked in a wood-furniture factory, you know about wood, trees, tools, finishing techniques, design, heavy machinery, marketing, fabrics, and quality control.

If you worked as a park ranger, you're an environmental expert, an outdoorsman (woman), a cop, a horseman, and perhaps an expert on a particular park or location.

If you owned a printing shop, you know about paper, ink, press equipment, desktop publishing, art and design, work flow processes, business administration, employee relations, dealing with deadlines, business economics, the printing industry trends, and perhaps union shop rules.

If you were a life insurance sales person, you're an expert in finance, retirement planning and, perhaps, grief counseling.

Are you getting the picture?

## Derivative Thinking

A "derivative " is defined as "copied or adapted from others." By derivative thinking I mean a process where you try to arrive at your genre by classifying your knowledge into general (and marketable) topics.

This is exactly what I've started above. Let us take one long example and a few short ones.

You have the skill of typing fifty words a minute, know how to use word processing software, and you worked for the last seven years for a small accounting firm. What can we derive from this? You know about computer hardware in that you have a good idea about the type of screens and keyboards that should and should not be used in an office environment. You're also somewhat of an expert on word processing software. You know which features are important and which are not often used. You might know (or can easily learn) what products work best in different office situations. Would a law office use the same software product (or features) as an engineering company? If you know computers and software, you probably know something about how to train someone else to use them. Or you might know how people should go about teaching themselves the use of the computer and/or software. Since you were a typist and worked in an office, you probably know much about survival in a sweat shop! You might know about getting along with difficult supervisors. You might know something about what makes a good supervisor or a bad one, in which case you know something about management of the clerical labor force. Since you had to read all the documents you typed, you must know about issues relating to the accounting business or one of the firm's client groups. You might know about occupational hazards such as eye strain and carpal tunnel syndrome. Finally, you know the issues that distinguish a good work environment from a bad one. So, your genre could be in the area of: computer software for the office, labor relations, office design and management, accounting industry issues, small office health and safety, word processing training, or new trends in office automation. You could write and sell articles on many of these areas. You could sell articles on how to buy and use word processing software. You could write on health and safety concerns for the clerical worker.

You worked as a loan officer for a bank for the past ten years. Obviously you know the overall banking business. You also know basic loan underwriting procedures. You probably have experience in determining risk factors on different borrowers. You know something about sales. You probably know real estate or small business issues. You might have a background on a zillion government regulations. You might know how to use some specialized loan industry software program. You must know about time management (meeting deadlines), dealing with emotional (rejected) customers, and a host of personal issues relating to banking. Your genre could be banking, small business, sales and marketing, and/or government regulation. You could easily write articles for banking magazines on loan underwriting, software products, and procedures. You could have articles published on how government regulations affect bank loan departments. You could write a feature on "Customer Relations for the Loan Officer."

You spent the last ten years working in a store that sold lamps and shades. You obviously know the lighting industry. You probably also know something about interior design and the importance of lighting in the office or home. Since you were in sales, you know the marketing techniques for your particular market niche. You also know the issues relating to all small retail businesses. A number of industry journals will pay for your articles about the retail lighting business. You could write about new trends such as halogen lamps and lasers. Wouldn't a piece on tips and techniques for selling lamps and lighting products to the interior designer sell to the right magazine? Could you do an article on "Trends and New Ideas in the Lighting Industry?"

You owned an independent video retail store for ten years before selling it and retiring. You must know the trials and tribulations of starting and running a small business. You also know the rental industry. And, of course, you must have a knowledge of the entertainment industry. Video and rental industry magazines will pay for articles about such issues as knowing what quantity of an item to order, when to sell, how to prevent theft, dealing with distributors, and how to select product. Wouldn't an article on profitable sidelines for video store owners (candy, magazines, taping and duplication service) sell to a trade publication? Could an article on the care and feeding of a video store be published?

## I Worked, but I Never Had a Job!

Those of you who never held a job outside the home, can still explore countless areas. The key is finding out just what you know that's of value to other people. This could come from your knowledge of running a house, raising children, gardening, sewing, a hobby, or from your education.

A sixty-two year-old woman in East Lawn, New Jersey, never held a job but knew all there was to know about putting on successful dinner parties because her husband was a banker and clients had to be entertained. She took an interest in researching and writing about how someone can throw together a dinner for six in one hour. She wrote a series of articles called Six in Sixty: Putting on the Ritz in One Hour. They were a collection of recipes and organizational techniques for the man or woman who needed to throw a nice dinner party at the last minute. They get published over and over.

A sixty-seven year-old woman from San Francisco, whose granddaughter suffered from a rare chronic ailment, became an expert in the disease and published many articles about it in family magazines. She makes a nice little income by writing articles for health magazines read by parents who have children with the condition.

A fifty-eight year-old Dallas woman, who had been successful in selling Stanley brushes, writes articles in high-paying family magazines about how others can start their own direct selling business. She also does seminars on the topic.

A seventy-five year-old woman in Virginia, whose hobby is doll repair, earns about $11,000 a year writing articles for magazines sold at craft stores.

A seventy-one year-old man in New York, wounded in World War II, spent much of his life collecting antique radios. He makes a nice little income writing articles for antique collectors on how to find and buy these items. He also sells a video he put together.

One sixty year-old woman in Chicago worked as a volunteer in many local election campaigns. This interest led her to learn all about how computers could be used in campaigns. She now sells articles on how computers and software can be used for candidates seeking election.

So, you see, even without a job history, the opportunities for finding a genre are almost limitless. Even people with what might be considered strange vocations, can find a genre. A woman in Vermont who loves to read, publishes abridgments of bestsellers and sells them by mail order to a list of subscribers who don't have time to read the latest novels but want people to think they did! She charges $6.00 for a twenty-page booklet and sells hundreds each month.

---

**COMMENT**: *I sometimes think that the wackier the idea, the better chance you have for success in the writing business!*

---

## Sure-Fire Success Genres

The following will probably come as no surprise to most of you; I write it only to help structure your thinking process. *If you can find a genre that will help fill people's needs for money, success, self-esteem, health, beauty, knowledge, or entertainment, you'll succeed as a writer.*

For example, you might be a master picture framer. Writing about "how to" frame pictures might be very limiting since few people do their own framing. But writing articles on how to buy a frame for the best price, or a piece on frames of famous art, or using frames to complement room decor, or frame store management, you have adapted your genre to an editor's need for material on these subjects.

Finding a genre that lends itself to the wide dissemination of information to people who can use it to satisfy some need is the key in determining what genre you should pursue.

Choose a genre that has a wide audience with needs that you can satisfy.

---

**COMMENT**: *My knowledge about computer programming and languages has a very limited market. So instead, I write on how computers can be programmed to increase the profits of a company. My genre is not computer science, it's business technology. See the difference?*

---

## If You're Still in the Dark, Make a List

I rely on my gut instinct to come up with ideas. But many people find list making an effective method for organizing their thoughts. So, if you're really lost and don't have a good feel for what you know or would like to be an expert on, try these three list exercises.

For each of these exercises you take a piece of paper and draw a line down the middle. Each list looks at a different aspect of your background. If you spend some time with each exercise you'll begin to realize that you know far more than you think you do. You can write on many subjects, you just have to discover them.

The first list will focus on your special talents and skills. Go back through the past several years and on the left side of the paper list all the things you've done that have given you a special skill or talent. Include your work life as well as things you've done outside your career. On the right side jot down as many article subjects that you can think of that would pertain to each special skill. Use lots of paper and spend several hours thinking about your skills and talents. Save this list. It may become very valuable later on as a source for ideas.

### Special Talent and Skill List

| In this column, list all your special skills and areas of knowledge. Include work-related items. | In this column, list all the possible article subjects you could write about. |
|---|---|
| Real Estate | Financing, neighborhood selection, getting listings, first-time buyer, negotiations, office space . . . . |
| Teaching | Child development, rainy day activities, art, discipline, workload, problem kids, PTA. . . . |

On the next list, outline all the things you like to do. This might include hobbies, daily activities, sports, weekend activities, special subjects you study or follow (like politics, dance, medicine.) Again, take your time and use plenty of paper. On the left side, write down all the subject areas that come into your head about each topic. On the right side, jot down potential article subjects.

## What I Like To Do

| In this column list all your interests and things you most enjoy doing. | In this column, list all the possible article subjects you could write about. |
|---|---|
| Boating | Buying a boat, sailing in storms, boat upkeep, places to go, fishing. . . . |
| Camping | Equipment, RV, campgrounds, hiking, food and cooking, cold weather, desert. . . . |

Finally, make a list of the things that you care about. Many PEs have made a successful writing business on subjects that they're passionate about. This could be world hunger, racial tolerance, animal rights, smoking, highway safety, literacy, etc. Again, write down topics that you would be interested in researching, becoming an "expert" in, and writing about.

### What I Feel Strongly About

| In this column, list all topics you care deeply about. | In this column, list all possible article subjects you could write about. |
| --- | --- |
| Senior citizen issues | Elder housing, health care, travel groups, fitness, beauty, money,. . . |
| Taxes and utility rates | Fairness, time for revolt, wasted money, corruption, agent relations, installment payments. . . . |

After doing these list exercises you should have a pretty good idea of what you know, what you like, and what your interests are.

## Make Your Choice

It's choice time. Decide in what area you will create an information business. You don't want it to be too narrow (such as electron radiology) and you don't want it to be too broad (such as management). There is also no reason you can't have two or three topics, either related or unrelated. The important thing is to *choose an area in which you're really interested.* Not only are you going to spend a lot of time working in your area of interest, but you may wind up as a local, regional, or national authority on the topic. So be sure it's something you like.

If you're a doctor and fed up with medicine, don't choose medicine. The same goes for other burned-out professionals. However, if you are interested in your field (as are most PE professionals), consider making it your area of expertise.

Even if you have some really odd-ball interest, don't discount it. Millions of people are interested in strange things and are hungry for information relating to whatever it might be.

> **COMMENT**: I hate bats, but there are lots of people interested in bats, bat lore, habitat, behavior, etc.

So now you know what you know. Let's talk about making money by writing about what you either like or know best.

The following is an industry classification list as used by the IRS. They assign a code number (not shown here) known as the Standard Industry Code (SIC) to be used on tax returns so their computers can easily determine what business the return is for. The IRS will compare the return to returns from other businesses in the group.

Use this list to help determine the genres you want to concentrate in.

## Agricultural Services, Forestry, Fishing

Animal services
Crop services
Farm labor & management services
Fishing, commercial
Forestry, except logging
Horticulture & landscaping
Hunting & trapping
Livestock breeding
Logging
Veterinary services, including pets

## Construction

Carpentry & flooring
Concrete work
Electrical work
Masonry, dry wall, stone, & tile
Painting & paper hanging
Plumbing, heating & air cond.
Roofing, siding
Excavation, glazing
General Contractors
Highway & street construction
Nonresidential building
Residential building
Pipe laying, bridge construction

## Finance, Insurance & Related Services

Brokers & dealers of securities
Commodity contracts brokers
Credit institutions
Insurance agents or brokers
Insurance services (appraisal, consulting, inspection, etc.)
Investment advisors & services
Other financial services

## Manufacturing, Including Printing & Publishing

Apparel & other textile products
Electric & electronic equipment
Fabricated metal products
Food products & beverages
Furniture & fixtures
Leather footwear, handbag, etc.
Lumber & other wood products
Machinery & machine shops
Paper & allied products
Primary metal industries
Printing & publishing
Stone, clay, & glass products
Textile mill products
Other manufacturing industries

## Mining & Mineral Extraction

Coal mining
Metal mining
Oil & gas
Quarrying & non-metallic mining

## Real Estate

Operators & lessors of buildings, including residential
Operators & lessors of other real property
Real Estate agents & brokers
Real estate property managers
Subdividers & developers, except cemeteries
Title abstract offices

## Amusement & Recreational Services

Bowling centers
Motion picture & tape distribution & allied services
Motion picture & video production
Motion picture theaters
Physical fitness facilities
Professional sports & racing, including promoters & managers
Theatrical performers, musicians, agents, producers, & related services
Video tape rental
Other amusement & recreational services

## Automotive Services

Automotive rental or leasing
Automotive repairs, general & specialized
Parking, except valet
Other automotive services (wash, towing, etc.)

## Business & Personal Services

Accounting & bookkeeping
Advertising, except direct mail
Architectural services
Barber shop (or barber)
Beauty shop (or beautician)
Child day care
Computer programming, processing, data preparation & related services
Computer repair, maintenance, & leasing
Consulting services
Consumer credit reporting & collection services
Employment agencies & personnel supply
Engineering services
Equipment rental & leasing
Funeral services & crematories
Income tax preparation
Investigative & protective services
Legal services (or lawyer)
Mailing, copying, commercial art, photography, & stenographic services
Management services
Ministers & chaplains
Photographic studios
Public relations
Research services
Surveying services
Teaching or tutoring

## Hotels & Other Lodging Places

Camps & camping parks
Hotels, motels, & tourist homes
Rooming & boarding houses

### Laundry & Cleaning Services

Carpet & upholstery cleaning
Coin-operated laundries & dry
cleaning
Full-service laundry, dry cleaning,
& garment service
Janitorial & related services
(building, house, & window
cleaning)

### Medical & Health Services

Chiropractors
Dentist's office or clinic
Doctor's (M.D.) office or clinic
medical & dental laboratories
Nursing & personal care facilities
Optometrists
Osteopathic physicians & surgeons
Podiatrists
Registered & practical nurses
Offices & clinics of other health
practitioners (dietitians, midwives,
speech pathologists, etc.)

### Miscellaneous Repair

Audio Equipment & TV repair
Electrical & electronic equipment
repair
Furniture repair & re-upholstery

### Trade, Retail — Selling goods to Individuals & Households

Catalog or mail order
Selling door to door, by telephone
or party plan, or from mobile unit
Vending machine selling

### Apparel & Accessories

Accessory & specialty stores &
furriers for women
Clothing, family
Clothing, men's & boys'
Clothing, women's
Shoe stores

### Automotive & Service Stations

Gasoline service stations
New car dealers (franchised)
Tires, accessories & parts
Used car dealers
Other automotive dealers (motor-
cycles, recreational vehicles, etc.)

### Hardware, & Garden Supply

Building materials dealers
hardware stores
Nurseries & garden supply stores
Paint, glass, & wallpaper stores

### Food & Beverages

Bakeries, selling at retail
Catering services
Drinking places (bars, taverns,
pubs, saloons, etc.)
Eating places, meals & snacks
Grocery stores (general line)
Liquor stores
Specialized food stores (meat,
produce, candy, health food, etc.)

## Furniture & General Merchandise

Computer & software stores
Furniture stores
Home furnishings stores (china, floor coverings, drapes)
Household appliance stores
Variety Stores
Other general merchandise stores

## Miscellaneous Retail Stores

Boat dealers
Book stores, excluding newsstands
Camera & photo supply stores
Drug stores
Fabric & needlework stores
Florists
Fuel dealers
Gift, novelty, souvenir shops
Hobby, toy, & game shops
Jewelry stores
Luggage & leather goods stores
Mobile home dealers
Optical goods stores
Sporting goods & bicycle shops
Stationery stores
Used merchandise & antique stores

## Durable Goods, Including Machinery Equipment, Wood, Metals, etc.

Agent or broker for other firms — more than 50% of gross sales on commission
Selling for your own account

## Nondurable goods, Including Food, Fiber, Chemicals, etc.

Agent or broker for other firms — more than 50% of gross sales on commission
Selling for your own account

## Transportation, Communications, Public Utilities, & Related Services

Air transportation
Bus & limousine transportation
Communication services
Courier or package delivery
Highway passenger transportation
Public warehousing
Taxicabs
Trash collection without own dump
Travel agents & tour operators
Trucking
Utilities (dumps, snow plowing, road cleaning, etc.)
Water transportation

# 5

. . . . . . . . . . . . . . . . . . . . . . . . .

# WRITING FOR MONEY

## Ladies and Gentlemen, Here's Your Flight Plan

Remember those old World War II air force movies where the pilots sat in the briefing room getting instructions about their mission? Here is my flight plan for your mission.

Nothing is more boring than a discussion on business plans. You don't want to read them and I don't want to write about them. So, I'm not going to spend the usual twenty pages talking about all the considerations you have to take into account when you start a business. We are going to do it very briefly. Since you're not creating a company to build the space shuttle, you don't need a very detailed business plan.

But you do need to think about your writing in business terms because it will help you organize your efforts when getting started. Here are the things you must consider and accomplish in order to be successful:

**The Mission**: Every business must have a purpose. The purpose of your writing business is to make money by creating articles (the product), having them published by others, and receiving payment for them. That was simple!

**Economic Feasibility**: A business must determine whether or not it can be profitable. Goals must be set and some effort must be applied to detailing these goals. I'll do this for you below.

**Market Research**: This is a fancy word for finding customers which I'll also cover below.

**Product Development**: This explains how you're going to create the product. In the next chapter, I'll give you a methodology for writing your articles.

**Product Segmentation**: A business might make one basic product, but change it for different markets. In your writing business, you'll be able to create a basic product several different ways, as discussed in the next chapter.

**Sales Strategy**: Once a business has determined who its customer base is likely to be, this part of the plan details what methods will be used to sell the customer. In Chapter 10, I outline a strategy that will work for you.

**Expansion**: This part of a business plan explains how the business could grow into other areas. I'll pinpoint some targets you might want to aim at once you're established.

## Writing Economics 101

You're going to hear from friends and relatives about how hard everyone thinks it is to make money by writing. This is only a half truth. It's hard to make *a lot* of money from writing.

It's very hard to support yourself in an upper-middle class lifestyle (new car, own house, vacation, a kid in college, etc.), but you're not trying to do that. Your goal is to earn a supplemental income.

> **COMMENT:** *It's not impossible to write full-time and earn a decent living. It just takes a great deal of dedication, research, time, and energy - more than is needed to keep a comparably paid full-time job.*

The first thing you have to do is get out a pad of paper and start figuring out what your financial goal will be. Only you know how hard you're willing to work, how much time you want to put in, and how much money you want to generate. Writing is just like anything else; the more you work at it, the more you'll make.

Instead of starting with a single figure and working down to how much you have to write, it's easier to start with the basic ingredients and build up to what you'll make.

A 1,500 word article should sell for no less than $200. This is a rock bottom figure. True, some publications pay less than this. But you don't have to submit your work to them. Many times you'll get more than $200, but I want to use conservative figures. A $200 article works out to 13.3 cents a word.

> **COMMENT:** *Writers often use cents per word instead of dollars per page because, with the advent of computers, the number of words on a page can vary. In the olden days of typewriters, a page was 250 words.*

To many of you, 1,500 words sounds like a lot. It isn't. Using a computer with Microsoft Word, working in standard 12pt Times type, and using standard margins, you'll get an average of 400 words on a page. Thus, your article will be 3.75 pages. We're not talking *War and Peace* here.

Let's assume you're willing to work twenty to twenty-two hours a week. This will boil down to about three hours of research and two hours of writing per 1,500 word (3.75 page) article. Occasionally the time divisions will be the other way around; more time writing than researching. Whatever the case, you should be able to turn out 1,500 words in five hours. You'll spend about fifteen hours on production of articles and the other five or six hours on administrative stuff (mailing, phone calls, travel, etc.)

I know it sounds daunting, but with a little experience, you should be able to turn out three articles a week. We are talking about 11.25 pages of saleable copy. This is nine hours of research and six hours of writing. Again, this is conservative since many times you'll only have to do an hour of research to write an article, and the piece will only take you ninety minutes to write.

Let's assume you'll only work forty-six weeks a year since you like to take a six-week vacation.

Working at this rate you could write 138 articles a year (46 x 3). But you probably won't. More than likely you'll write three articles a week half the time and two the other half. This works out to about 115 pieces a year.

This is not as awesome as it appears. If you're serious, have good work habits, and truly know your field, it can easily be done. It shouldn't be work: it should be fun.

Will you sell 115 articles a year? No. When starting out, 40% of your work will be rejected and never sell. I believe this is a worst case projection. Once you know the ropes and what your editors are looking for, your rejection rate should go down to a more manageable 15-20%.

Using the 40% rejection rate, you should sell 69 of your articles for $200 each. This will gross you $13,800.

Twenty hours a week for 46 weeks is 920 hours. Divide $13,800 by this and you gross a few pennies more than $15/hr.

If you can earn in the area of $220 for your articles you would gross $15,180.

If you can cut your rejection rate to 20% and sell 92 articles (115 x 80%) for $200 each, you gross $18,400, and $220 per article gets you $20,240.

---

### Worksheet To Compute Earnings

Use this worksheet to help figure what your earnings would be from writing. It is based on receiving $200 per article and a 40% rejection rate. It assumes it will take you 5 hours to complete a piece. Round .5-.9 up, .1-.4 down.

A) Hours I will work each week: _____

B) Weeks I will work each year: _____

C) Multiply A by .75: _____ (writing hours)

D) Divide C by 5: _____ (articles per week)

E) Divide B by 2: _____ (half a year)

F) Multiply D by E: _____ (articles in half a year)

G) Subtract 1 (one) from D: _____ (lower output)

H) Multiply G by E: _____ (other half of year)

I) Add H and F: _____ (total articles a year)

J) Multiply I by .40: _____ (40% rejected articles)

K) Subtract J from I: _____ (actual article sales)

L) Multiply K by $200: $_____ (gross sales)

> COMMENT: *As you build up your inventory of articles, you'll learn how to make slight changes to some which you can resell to different publications. This will increase your income and lower your work load.*

To people who look at these figures and say "no way," I say "bunk." If you apply yourself, utilize your time well, create the type of articles I outline later in this chapter, and have a "good" genre, you can produce 12 to 15 pages a week of information that has value to magazine editors across the fruited plain and purple mountains majesty.

## Buyers: They're Out There Somewhere

After you've played with some numbers and you feel comfortable with the amount of time and effort you plan to put into your new writing business, the next step is to do your market research.

I can't impress upon you how important this is. Many PEs want to jump out there and start researching right away. They figure that they know their field (genre) and have some good ideas for articles (also called product.) They rush to their keyboards, pound out a few products and then face the fact that they have no idea who to sell to or if the product is suitable for the market.

> COMMENT: *Lots of businesses are started by people who leap before they look!*

Depending on your field, market research could take you one week or one month. Your goal is to develop a list of publications or organizations that will buy your information products (articles).

You need to develop a database of customers. It's slow and tedious work, but the bulk of it only has to be done once.

Your first business purchase should be a book called *Writer's Market* [Writer's Digest Books]. This comes out each year and contains a wealth of information about book and periodical publishers. You can't be without it. It can be found at every large bookstore for around $25.

Scan every page of *Writer's Market* for publications that might have an interest in your area of expertise. It's important that you stretch your mind and practice derivative thinking. For example, say your area of interest is personal injury law (maybe you were a lawyer or a police officer.) Would a magazine about hot-rods be interested in a piece on personal injury? Think about it. Or say your area of interest is cooking, food preparation, and restaurant management. What could you write for a camping magazine? Or you worked in the men's department of Sears for five years selling jeans and work clothes. Could you come up with a title of an article that might appeal to an editor of a magazine covering the home construction industry?

In *Writer's Market* you'll find just about everything you wanted to know about most major (and minor) magazines in the U.S., including what type of material they are looking for and what they pay. The above example depicts a listing for a mythical magazine as it might appear in *Writer's Market*.

GREEN THUMB, National Plant Association, 180 Jones Ave., Great Neck NY 11023 (516) 555-1212. Editor: Waren Buttz. 50% freelance written. Willing to work with new/unpublished writers. Bimonthly magazine covering all aspects of food gardening and ornamentals. "We publish not only how to garden techniques, but also news that affects gardeners, like science advances. Our material is for both experienced and beginning gardeners." Circ. 100,000. Pays on acceptance. Publishes ms an average of 6 months after acceptance. Nonfiction: How-to, humor, inspirational, interview/profile, new product, pest control, opinion, personal experience. Buys 80-100 mss/year. Length 500-3000 words. Pays $30-500/article.

> *TIP*: Don't pay much attention to the dollar amounts listed in WM. These are low-ball figures that the magazine hopes to pay you. You can almost always negotiate a better payment. I'll show you how later on.

After you have spent a lot of time looking through *Writer's Market*, it's time for you to pay the first of many, many visits to your library. Go to the largest library you can find. A college library is best, but any large city library will be helpful.

Make friends with the reference librarian. Tell him or her that you're starting a writing business in whatever your genre is and ask for help in locating information on potential sources for sales. The librarian will lead you to a number of reference books, among them *Reader's Guide*, *Ulrichs*, and *Gayles*.

In your search for customers, do not neglect local resources such as corporate and nonprofit organization newsletters, advertising agencies, association newsletters, professional societies, writers clubs, publishing associations, and, of course, your local newspapers.

> *TIP*: Look in the Yellow Pages under Newspapers. You'll find that there are many more papers than you thought there were. Most won't pay much for your work, but if you sell a 500-word piece that takes you 90 minutes to write and get $100, you're making 20 cents a word or $66 an hour.

When you start digging through all this research material, you're going to come up with a wealth of information. There are hundreds of places to sell your writing. Instead of too few places, you're likely to be overwhelmed with choices. That's why it's important that you keep all of this organized, preferably on your computer's database program.

Here is a sample record I would keep for each possible buyer of information.

## Sample Database Record

| Title: | | Freq: |
|---|---|---|
| Publisher Name: | | Circ: |
| Address: | | |
| | | |
| Contact: | Phone: | Fax: |
| Payment: | Terms: | |
| Genre of Pub: | Topics of Interest: | |
| Article Types: | | |
| Notes: | | |
| | Submissions | |
| Title | Date | Response |
| 1. | | |
| 2. | | |
| 3. | | |

**COMMENT**: *This is a very simple record to create with most database programs, especially with FileMaker Pro. Once you have a few hundred records, you'll appreciate having a computer to organize your data.*

Much of this information is available in various directories like *Writer's Market*. However, the best way to research the market is to go to the largest library you can find, pick up every magazine on display, thumb through each one, and decide if there is any remote chance that one of your products might fit in their publication. Sometimes the decision is easy. A magazine on American Indian Folklore is not a likely market for a piece on computer software.

**COMMENT:** *But a computer magazine might buy a piece on how a tribe is using computers to research folklore stories and assist in genealogy.*

A major college library will have thousands of magazines. I suggest you do a two-pass search. First, look at every magazine for ten seconds to see if it offers any possibility at all. If so, make a note. On the second pass, spend more time with those selections, gathering information for your database. Depending on your genre, it could take you a week to a month.

Not only are you searching for possible customers, you're also trying to determine what products they want to buy. Most publications like certain subjects more than others.

An important part of your database is the "Topics Of Interest" fields. Here, put some key words about what type of articles the magazine likes to run. Let's say you write on the home-building industry and have an idea for an article on a new whiz-bang atomic screwdriver. You can easily have the computer search the database for all records that have "TOOLS" in the "Topics" field.

Also enter in your database the types of articles the magazine runs. I'll talk about these extensively in the next chapter.

How many different markets should you catalog? Obviously, the more the better, but you don't want so many that it becomes cumbersome. Somewhere between 300-500 markets would be good, but you might get by with just 200. It depends on your genre. (There are some 9,000 newspapers in the U.S.)

I can't overemphasize the importance of having and maintaining a good database of possible buyers of your product. Your product is of no use if you don't know who is interested in buying it. A good database will make you successful, so devote time to creating one, adding to it, and keeping it up to date.

## Write What You Like

There are about ten million books on how to write magazine articles. None of them are bad. They all attempt to create a methodology to the rather imprecise art of putting information on paper.

I want to teach you how to make money from writing. But, I can't teach you exactly what to write about. While you might be an "expert" in your field, you still have to know (or figure out) what will interest potential readers. My advice is to write on topics that interest you. If you get a few rejections, you made a bad choice. Find another topic. But don't spend week upon week agonizing over a topic. Just do it.

My general guideline is to pick topics the same way you pick a genre. Try to find a writing subject that will appeal to the reader's vanity, health, economic welfare, or intellectual curiosity. For your early topics, stay away from the esoteric. I tell people to ask themselves: What is the biggest controversy or newest innovation going on in my genre today? If your expertise is the printing industry, a major innovation is desktop computers. If you write about the candy manufacturing business, it might be federal mandated labeling. If you're involved with the automotive business, it might be stricter clean air regulations. If you write about sewing, you know that fewer women sew today than fifteen years ago.

Try to come up with titles that appeal to the basic hot-buttons of health, wealth, vanity, etc. outlined earlier. For the printing article, the title might be *"From Disk To Film: Cutting Costs With Desktop Machines."* For the candy article, the title might be *"Ingredient Marketing: The New Label Law Can Improve Sales."* For the automotive article, you might write *"Federal Regs Hit Consumer's Wallets."* The sewing article might be *"Think Again About Sewing: Save On New Clothes That Fit Right!"*

Never forget that the concept is to *sell* your work! Writing can be a fun hobby, but few hobbies pay any bills. Evaluate the saleability of what you produce. Obviously it's a good idea to do this before you write the piece!

People in the business of creating new products often refer to what they call "universal needs." Here is a short list of them:

**Food**: Humans need food to live, thus we have developed an entire culture around food.

**Shelter From The Elements**: We don't have nice thick fur coats like our animal friends, so we need clothes and houses. Thus, we're always interested in information that relates to clothing and shelter.

**Love**: Truly a universal interest.

**Wealth**: Another universal interest.

**Security**: To some, it's a need to belong. To others, it means safety. Because we belong to a species that's fearful of the unknown, we're interested in anything that will help us protect ourselves.

**Work**: We all need some purpose for our existence. To most, this is work, including the need for accomplishment and recognition. We all want to achieve the feeling that we've done the job well, and we all want the recognition of our peers.

While these are the major categories, many subcategories, such as health, creativity, leisure time, self-improvement, etc. abound. If you create articles that appeal to one or several universal needs, you have a saleable piece. Later on, I will talk about having a purpose for your article. For right now, think about how the articles you might write would appeal to the above needs. You'll find that almost any article topic can be slanted to sell to a human need. For example, say you want to write on bees. A 1,500-word article on the life and habits of bees might have a chance of selling to an agricultural magazine. But an article on honey, or one on lethal bee stings, has more appeal to the universal needs (food, security).

I can't say it enough. Understanding the importance of universal needs will have a tremendous effect on the success of your writing business.

## You Can Look It Up!

Writers ask this eternal question: What comes first, the topic or the research? Sometimes you'll get an idea for an article and then do the research. Other times you'll be doing research on one topic and come up with a better topic. Whatever the case, there is only one type of research you want to do: minimal.

We are talking about a 1,500-word article, not a report from a presidential commission or a congressional committee. Nothing will kill your bottom line quicker than spending too much time on an article that is only going to net you $200. It's important that you keep your research time in perspective.

Of course, the best case scenario is for you to write articles that don't need any research. However, outside of opinion pieces, almost every topic you write about will entail some fact finding, be it via interviewing, library work, or phone calling. So, pick a topic you already know quite a bit about so you only have to "fill in" in order to give the piece what is called "current authority."

Let me say this again (and again!): Too much time spent researching will kill your bottom line. Remember, you're not in college doing term papers; you're in business trying to make dollars. Time is money.

It's not just the time in the library you must keep track of, but travel time as well. Does it pay to travel forty minutes round-trip to spend ten minutes in the library finding the answer to one quick question? I urge writers to make use of the phone as much as possible. At least while you're on hold or waiting for a callback, you can be doing something useful. Sitting in traffic is seldom productive.

> *TIP*: *Consolidate research topics so you only make one trip to the library for a number of different articles. Fit your library trips into times when you have other errands to do. This will cut down on wasted travel time. Avoid travel during the rush hours.*

The following tricks of the trade will help keep your research time down to a minimum:

**Reference Service**: Many public libraries will let you telephone the reference desk. They will look up facts for you either while you wait, or will call you back or fax the material. If your library has this service, make use of it.

**Your Own Library**: No writer should be without the basic and inexpensive research books such as the almanac, dictionary, thesaurus, and some form of encyclopedia. Your genre might require specific books. For example, if you write on public relations, you might have some of the better known books on the subject to use for reference.

> *TIP*: *Find a good used bookstore and see what you can find. You don't always need the most current edition of everything. A three-year-old almanac will still give you the population of the United States in 1944!*

**Collect Magazines**: Start a subscription to the major magazines in your area of expertise. Not only is the subscription a tax deduction, but, by saving these, you have a ready reference library. Many magazines publish a year-end index.

**Clip File**: This is sometimes called a "swipe" file. Clip out articles you read that you think could be redone for another publication by using a different viewpoint. Say you write on commercial aviation. You see an article in the travel section of the paper on procedures passengers should follow when their bags are lost. You could rewrite this for an airline industry magazine slanting it toward the procedures passengers expect an airline to follow in assisting with lost luggage. (Rewrite doesn't mean "copy". You can use another author's ideas, but not his or her words.)

**Internet and Commercial On-Line Services**: There are many on-line services that you can dial up with your modem and computer. Granted, it takes a little computer sophistication to use these, but it doesn't require an advanced engineering degree from Georgia Tech! Beyond the well-known commercial services such as CompuServe and America Online, there are a whole host of industry specific databases and computer bulletin boards are available to help with your research. Finally, there's a worldwide network called the Internet. I would venture a guess that there is nothing you couldn't find out by using the Internet. However, you have to be more than a casual computer user to figure out how to navigate through this marvelous information source.

---

*TIP*: *If you're interested, get one of the many books on how to use the Internet and see for yourself what a wealth of information is there for a PE with some advanced computer skills.*

---

**The Telephone**: You've heard the saying that everyone is within seven phone calls of anyone else. I don't know if you can reach the Chairman of The Joint Chiefs of Staff, but you can surely come close enough to get the material you want. Just pick up the phone and call. If you need information on a specific product, call the manufacturer. Need a good quote? Call your source and tell the person who answers (usually a secretary) that you're a writer and need a quick interview. Your source *will* get back to you.

**Get The FAX**: The fax machine is the writer's secret weapon. You may not get someone to return your call, but many times an assistant will prepare and fax information for you. You won't get to the President, but if you fax your questions, the White House staff will fax back answers (get the number from your Representative's office.)

---

*TIP*: There are several directories of addresses, phone numbers, and 800 numbers you can buy. One that I've found useful is The Address Book by Michael Levine, Perigee Books, ISBN 0-399-51793-6.

---

**Use The University**: If you seek information on subjects out of the mainstream, contact the office of public information at the largest university near you. Many have free guides listing campus experts by category. For the chance of getting their name in print, college professors may do much of your research for you! (They have scores of students to do the legwork.)

**The Government Knows All**: The largest publisher in the world is the government. Every agency, bureau, and department has a public affairs officer just sitting at a desk waiting to answer your questions and send you reams of material.

---

*TIP*: Don't call them yourself. Call the office of your congressional representative and tell them what you want. They will know somebody who knows somebody who can get you what you want!

---

**Author! Author!**: Do you need information from someone who has written a book on the subject? Call the publishing company (your librarian can quickly get you the number from *Literary Market Place*) and ask for the publicity department. They will kill themselves to have the author return your call, usually the same day!

**Get Associated**: Get on good terms with the major associations concerned with your field. They will provide you with a wealth of material. You might even be able to get a free "associate" membership, sometimes given to members of the media (that's you!).

Two important points to remember about researching an article are (1) keep your driving time to a minimum and (2) have someone else do as much legwork as possible. There are people far more skilled in research techniques and resources than you are, so let them do what they do best. Your time is better spent *deciding what you want*. Let others (who will be happy to do it,) *get it for you*.

---

*TIP: PEs who have their own info-businesses often hire local college students as research assistants. They assign a topic and have the student come back with copies of three or four articles that contain information on the topic. Thirty or forty bucks to a college student can buy you lots of legwork.*

---

If you have not been to a large research library recently, you're in for a surprise. There are no card-catalogs anymore. They have been replaced by computer terminals. The important lesson is this. Don't be afraid of asking one of the staff to show you how to use them. Don't be embarrassed. Ask! When I go to a different library, instead of wasting twenty minutes trying to figure out how to work the computer terminal, the first thing I do is ask for a quick demo. And I'm experienced with computers and libraries! So don't be proud or stupid. The staff will be happy to show you the ropes. Most of them are pretty proud of their systems.

The best time to go to the library is during the early morning hours before school gets out or classes end (at a large university). Don't even think about going to a university library in the evening. First, it's too crowded and second, the professional staff is gone; you'll be dealing with student assistants (who could probably care less about helping you).

## Notes, Notes, Notes

Contrary to what you might think, there is no generally accepted methodology for doing research. Everyone seems to develop his or her own system. However, several variations are common.

The first is to write the article at the library. You spend time gathering a ton of books, periodicals, and journals, and spread them all out on a table. Surrounded with all your research materials you either write the article longhand or on your notebook computer. I don't recommend this practice because I think it takes too much time. In the first place, if you're using your computer, you can't get up and leave it on the desk because it will be stolen. Secondly, I believe there are too many distractions in a library. Libraries are for research and your den or office is for writing.

The second method is the tried and true 3x5 card method. Actually, 5x7 cards are better. However, I tell people to save the cost and take their notes on yellow legal pads. And everyone has his or her own method for taking notes. Some like the outline method they learned in school. Others write in full sentences. My method is to write the first sentence or topic of each paragraph for the article and under it write notes pertaining to the paragraph. I treat each paragraph as a mini-interview and put in as many facts as necessary to support the paragraph topic.

The third method is often used by people who have a bottomless pocket of change. You make copies of each page of research material that looks like it might be useful. These well-to-do researchers read a chapter of a book or magazine article and take it to the copy machine and run copies of the pages they expect to need later. I use this method because it tends to take less time and keeps me focused on only getting relevant material. (At 10 to 15 cents per copy, you quickly learn to separate relevant material from fluff!)

One bit of advice bears repeating: It's easy to over-research a piece. After all, for a 1,000 - 2,000-word article (three to five double-spaced pages), how much research do you really need? When you read the next section on article construction, you'll see that it's harder to keep a piece short than to make it long.

If you have never done research before then it would be a good idea to take a class or read a book on research techniques. Short classes are often given by college libraries. There are a number of books on the market that have the so-called latest techniques for taking notes and writing research papers. Look in a college bookstore.

> *TIP*: Don't stick with any methodology that doesn't work for you. Look at several books on the subject of research and pick and choose what you feel comfortable with. There is no right or wrong way to research an article. Some ways save time, but most will get you where you want to go.

## Write and Talk, Talk and Write

One of the really big truths is that writing is easy. Anyone can do it and everyone can learn to do it well. After all, why do you think the wages for writing are low? It's because writing is not a difficult skill to acquire or even master.

People always ask: Is it's necessary to take writing classes? Necessary, no; helpful yes, if a class is taken with the proper spirit. No class can teach you how to write. Writing instructors can show you different examples of writing and can critique your work, but you have to develop the skill yourself at your own pace and in your own style.

---

**COMMENT:** *In the film "The Paper Chase," law professor Kingsfield tells his young students: "You teach yourself the law, but I train your mind!" It's also true about writing.*

---

Go to a large bookstore and you'll find shelves of books on writing. If you think you might have difficulty putting ideas on paper, give some of these books a quick look. The problem is that many people try to use these books in place of developing their own style; their own unique "footprint" of words on paper.

There is no word that scares beginning writers more than "style." All writers want it, don't think they can get it, and are terrified that every magazine editor in the country will realize they lack it. You don't need a style; in fact, you might be better off without one! Most articles you're going to do will be straight pieces of prose. You're going to choose a topic and explain it. Most of the time you job is not to humor, sadden, persuade, or even entertain your audience. Your job is to get the information from the page to the brain of your reader. You don't have to write like Nikolai Gogol, John Steinbeck, or Ernest Hemingway. You just need to acquire the ability to express your topics clearly in an organized fashion.

Do readers recognize or make a mental note of the author's style when they read an article in *Vogue*, or *Popular Science*? A few might, but most don't. So why are writers so afraid of not having a "style?" It's because style is what separates great writers from good writers.

Erma Bombeck, Art Buchwald, Ann Landers, George Will, and other contemporary writers who are household names are great writers. They have developed unique and recognizable styles for putting their ideas on paper. However, all you need to be is "good" to succeed in your info-business. You might become a great writer some day. But that's not the objective. The objective is to be good enough to get your articles published and your efforts financially rewarded.

There are always those PEs who have never written a word beyond a shopping list, a shop ticket, or a letter to their parents from summer camp. Many PEs either don't know or fear breaking the rules of grammar. Relax. The rules of basic English grammar and punctuation can be learned. They are outlined in the front of dictionaries, in sections of almanacs, and in numerous writing textbooks. If you find it difficult to master the basic rules (often misnamed *rules of style* ) you can always hire an editor. For $2 to $5 dollars a page you can have a sharp-eyed college teacher (or student) go over your piece and make corrections and suggestions. Do you honestly think that even the best writers always know all the rules of English composition? If you answer yes, why then do magazines hire so many editors?

---

*TIP*: If English is your second language, using a hired editor is a good idea. You might also work in your native language and have it translated. Call the language department of your nearest college or university for referrals.

---

The advice most often given to first-time writers is to "write like you speak." Boy, is this wrong. Sure, if you're writing a book where you're the only "voice" in the work, you can write however you wish. I wrote this book in my speaking "voice".

However, when you're writing for a magazine, you're like a guest in the house. You must conform to the rules of the publication. The rules are usually simple. Your piece should be as sanitized as possible!

What do I mean by sanitized? While there are many exceptions, most articles should be devoid of personality, character, style, or viewpoint. Most editors do not look for personalities as a radio station might. They just want clear, well-researched, and interesting articles for their readership. Most often, they do not look for cute, esoteric, pedantic, scholarly, humorous, or maudlin material. They want the facts written in a clear and concise manner.

Look at the following sample paragraphs:

*The high price of timber has resulted in many building contractors opting for other materials, most notably steel. While long used in the construction of commercial buildings, steel has not been a factor in the home construction industry. As John Jones, president of XYZ Homes, one of the nation's largest builders says, "Steel presents problems with environmental factors. It conducts heat and cold much better than wood." Thus, steel houses may result in higher energy bills.*

***

*That sonic boom you hear throughout the construction industry is the price of lumber rocketing out of sight. The other loud sound is the steel industry cheering. After years of jumping up and down yelling "look at me," steel framing is finally getting a look-see from contractors. But home buyers in cold climates better have thick skins or warm coats. As Bill Smith of ABC Builders says, "A steel house can be colder than an opossum's bottom since metal conducts cold better than wood. People living in steel houses might want to buy stock in their local utility company."*

Which one do you like better? Most people like the second. It contains word pictures and you can hear the author speaking. The paragraph has some zip and personality. The first paragraph is pretty sanitized. It's your basic dry prose. But this is just as likely to get published. Why? Many editors (not all) hate fun! They want the articles in their magazine to conform to a single style. And that style is *no style*! Many editors (not all) lack imagination. They were trained in the classical style of composition and firmly believe that all prose should follow a standard format.

---

**COMMENT**: After "sanitizing" the prose they print, publishers (owners) wonder why magazine subscriptions are down and TV viewing is up!

---

There is some good news in all of this: It's easier to write plain, old, basic prose. After you have done it a few times, it becomes second nature. However, writing with zip and flair takes some doing. Since many editors do not seek anything that might liven up their publications, you'll get a lot of practice writing plain old standard material.

So, you're not going to write like you speak. Most of the time you're going to write like everyone else writes. It's not particularly hard, but it's not particularly creative either. Look at it this way. In the time it would take you to put together one really bright and clever 1,500 word piece, you could do three articles in the terse style I call "editor's delight."

# 6

. . . . . . . . . . . . . . . . . . . .

# WRITING SMART, NOT HARD

## Writing Articles Is Like Making Cookies

I said it earlier and I will repeat it again. One of the really big myths perpetrated by the trade press, professional journalists, and everyone who has ever received a byline is the concept of how hard it is to put words on paper that people will read. If you want to believe that those people who turn out story after story, article after article, day after day, week after week are all Rhodes Scholars, that's up to you. The truth is that article writing is a craft, not a gift. And like any craft, you can learn it. You may not be as good at it as some people, but you can be good enough to get published.

To me, nonfiction writing is much like wood working. Given the right tools, the right approach, the right materials, and the right instruction, almost anyone can become accomplished enough to build a nice desk, chair, or dresser. It may not happen overnight, but it is possible to attain adequate writing skills in a relatively short time.

---

*COMMENT: Fiction writing is different from non-fiction. Being able to craft a story and characters into a book that people will read for generations is a talent, a gift. The Twains, Poes, Hemingways, Alcotts, and Steinbecks of the world are not like you an me. They have talent. You and I only have skill.*

---

In the last chapter I talked about writing in general. In this chapter, I will give you a bare-bones writing methodology that you can follow.

My concept is simple. Each of the several types of articles that you can write, without exception, uses certain building blocks. Let's look at the parts of a nonfiction article and you'll see what I mean.

## The Lego™ Approach

Almost all of your articles can be constructed using tried and true building blocks, much like a child builds something with Lego™ blocks. Just about every piece you will write has the same components.

**The Lead**: This is the hook, which consists of a few sentences or a short paragraph that grabs the reader's attention. Every article you write should have a lead even though it's the first thing an editor is likely to change. If you can't come up with a great lead, chances are that the editor can. Editors may not know anything about your subject area, but they are universally skilled in creating leads for almost any topic. The kind of lead you use will depend on the subject you're writing about and your intended audience.

*The Question Lead*: Say you were doing a piece on smoking at the worksite and wrote, "*Are you a secret smoker, living in fright because you're afraid your non-smoking boss might find out?*" This is a question lead. It gets the problem out in front of the reader and helps identify the audience. This lead, which is particularly effective for self-help articles, is a favorite of most editors. You can't go wrong using this lead unless you're writing to a very sophisticated reader, who may think it somewhat juvenile.

*The Dialogue Lead*: "*I won't tolerate smoking on the premises or employees who smoke; you're fired!*" *said my boss to the woman at the desk next to me.* Dialogue leads are great when your topic revolves around characters and people. The suspense factor is used to heighten the reader's interest and state the topic of the article, all in a few sentences. Editors love dialogue of all kinds, especially dialogue leads. These leads can be employed at almost any level of sophistication. For example: "*We may have a severe waste disposal problem here,*" *said the company president.* "*If we do, you're history!*" *replied the chairman of the board.* The dialogue lead is usually a sure hit.

*The Shock Sentence*: In this lead, you make an outrageous statement to shock, scare, or even humor your reader into finishing the piece. "*In the city of XYZ, you have greater odds of being killed by violent crime than of getting a traffic ticket.*" Often, these leads are followed by a disclaimer such as "or so it seems." Take a look at the supermarket tabloids and you'll see the "masters of shock" at work. However, many editors believe that shock leads are overused and they often blue-pencil (delete) them.

**The Quotation Lead**: In this lead you work a famous quote or saying into the opening paragraph. *"Ask not what your country can do for you, but what you can do for your country" were words that sparked patriotism and social involvement of young people in the 60s. Do these 60s kids, now 90s parents, still feel the same way?* This lead uses both a quote and a question.

**The Anecdote Lead**: This is a short, pithy story that leads the reader into the main body of the article. *I never thought of myself as being addicted to anything. But on the advice of my doctor, I kept a record of how much I spent on cigarettes for two weeks. As the dollars added up, I realized I was a tobacco addict and needed help. I didn't know where to start.* This would lead the reader into an article that tells how to find help to quit smoking.

**The Case History Lead**: If you're doing a profile of someone (especially an exposé), the case history lead can give a maximum amount of information in a minimum of words. This lead gives the bare facts necessary for the reader to understand the problem, which is the body of the article. For example, a piece titled "Great Advances in Computer Technology: How They Occurred" might start like this: *Bill Gates, as a young man, loved to tinker with things. He was always asking* *"what if?" It was early in 1978 when he decided that a better way for programming tiny computers was needed. The young college dropout spent many late nights pondering the possibilities of designing a new computer language, then settled for improving an old one.* This type of lead is another that is often overworked. Use it for articles that have some high drama content, such as the discovery of a new vaccine, the solving of a crime, or the ninth-inning home run.

**The Descriptive Lead**: This works well in articles that center around a specific place or locality. It's often used for travel articles or pieces about the physical home or workplace. An article on crime in small towns might start like this: *I live in Happy Valley, a small town with tree-lined streets and clean sidewalks. Down the block from the main post office is the hardware store where men congregate each morning to talk politics and drink coffee. The ice cream store around the corner is crowded with high school kids around 3 PM on school days. No one thinks about crime in Happy Valley.*

As you plan an article think about the lead that you might use. The lead is really important. It's like the oft-mentioned "first impression." Without a decent lead, no editor is going to get past your first paragraph. Coming up with a good lead is not easy. But, it only has to be good enough to hook the editor. He or she may change it to hook his/her type of readers, something they will know more about than you. If your first few sentences are dull and unimaginative, your article is going to land in the wastebasket (File 13). If you were an editor reading several submissions about the 50th anniversary of D-Day, which one are you likely to continue reading?

> *On June 6, 1944, the largest flotilla of armed men and materials left the shores of England for the beaches of northern France. History labeled it D-Day.*

***

> *"Keep your heads down, you idiots!" I heard the sarge yell as our landing craft bumped to a stop and we plunged into the cold water off of Normandy. We didn't think about making history. We were just trying to get to dry land. Maybe because I listened to the sarge, I lived beyond what history books now call D-Day.*

**The Premise:** This is the second building block of your article. It may not be evident to you, but every article has a premise - or central point (or points) the author has to make about the subject. This important paragraph or group of paragraphs usually follows the lead.

You've hooked the reader's attention by a clever opening. Now you have to explain what you're going to explain! Often the premise is nothing more than a statement upon which the rest of the article is will be built upon. For example:

> *There are thousands like me - secret smokers who are addicted to tobacco and want to quit. We're embarrassed: we don't know where to turn for help.*

***

> *Fifty years is a long time, but I couldn't help but notice how much Normandy beach remained the same. I found it easy to relive that fateful day.*

***

*While you may not hear the frequent din of police sirens as you would in a large city, the same crimes that we associate with the inner city, occur with increased regularity on Main Street. But, imaginative police techniques are helping smaller towns quell the rising tide of violence.*

\*\*\*

*We tend to think that the great innovations of science and medicine occur in a lab. However, in the computer industry, great ideas are often the result of a single person working late at night on his or her kitchen table.*

\*\*\*

*Running a small business, such as a quick print shop, is similar to managing a baseball team.*

\*\*\*

*Midsize banks must stem the outflow of their core deposits to competing mutual funds, or they will find themselves in a difficult competitive position relative to their large brothers and sisters.*

The premise is often the very first line you'll write after the lead. They're easy to recognize. When your friend asks, "What are you writing about today?" you can answer in one, two, or three easily understood sentences.

> **COMMENT**: *Hollywood has a buzz word for premise: high concept. The kind of high concept that the movie and TV biz likes the best is one that can be put in a title, like* Honey, I Shrunk The Kids, *or* The Terminator, *or* Planet Of The Apes. *It's easier to get a script read with the title like* The Texas Chain Saw Murders *than* Howard's End. *Maybe that is why it took so long to get a movie like* Schindler's List *made.*

Sometimes the premise is part of the lead or is so self-explanatory that it's unnecessary to state it. This is especially true in articles on technical subjects. However, there *is always* a premise to every article. If you don't have a premise (or don't stay focused on it), your article will wander all over the place, make little sense, and will be quickly rejected. People (most editors) don't like to read things they don't understand. We've all read articles in which we couldn't figure out what the author was trying to say, probably because the author never formulated a premise.

You should start with a premise and make sure everything else in the article revolves around it. The lead gets the reader interested in the premise. The body, transitions, and conclusion support (or deny) the premise. A good premise is necessary to a good article, but a good premise alone is not enough.

**The Body**: This part of the article will contain the most words. It's the solid backup information that supports the premise. This is what you research. You look for quotes, statistics, anecdotes, history, theory, fact, conjecture to support your premise. The body of the article will prove to the editor and reader that you know your subject well.

After you get some experience, you'll find the body the easiest part of the article to write. It's harder to come up with a highly marketable premise and really tight lead. But once you do, unless you're writing on something absolutely state of the art, you should have tons of supporting (or contrasting) material on your premise. You just have to find it, consolidate it, organize it, and write it.

A retired biologist from New Jersey, who writes on the pollution of oceans, told me that his writing is just the opposite of how he "did" science. Instead of looking at events in nature and developing a theory, he now starts with a theory and tries to find events to fit the theory.

A retired math teacher in Virginia who publishes booklets on quality control in manufacturing said that when she writes, she "draws the curve, then finds the data! That's not how we did it in high school physics, but I think it's a good way to approach a writing topic! Figure out what you *want* to say and then find what you need to support it."

**Transitions**: These are the fourth ingredients of writing. They act like mortar to bricks. They hold ideas (thoughts) together. Unless you're writing a very short piece, you'll need transitions to provide crosswalks by which your reader gets from one idea to another.

Sometimes a transition will take the form of several sentences. The purpose is to cement the major ideas of the body together into a coherent chunk of information easily digested by the reader's mind.

The transition prepares the reader for some new point or subject. As you read, be on the lookout for clever transitions. Here are some common ones:

1. Another aspect of this problem is. . . .

2. In talking with several experts on the subject. . . .

3. According to the latest survey figures. . . .

4. Taking the other viewpoint. . . .

Like leads, transitions are scrutinized by editors. Editors with even minimal experience are experts in using and suggesting transitions. Many editors look at your transitions to gauge your writing experience. It's something you get graded on. Editors know that finding a great lead is hard, but they expect writers to bridge the gaps between points smoothly so reading is easy. Don't underestimate these little phrases of transitions.

> **TIP**: Sometimes you don't need a transitional phrase. If you're starting a new subtopic and have a section heading (like in this book), the heading serves as a transition. The reader knows you're going to discuss a new subject by the presence of a heading.

**The Conclusion**: This is the final wrap-up of the subject and summarizes what has been said. The conclusion is often the most creative part of the piece. Many authors will use the conclusion to interject their own viewpoint on the subject. This is where you can agree (most often) or disagree with all the verbiage above it.

> **COMMENT**: There is a political reason to put the author's viewpoint at the end. If the editor disagrees with you, he or she has at least read the entire piece and may be impressed with everything but the final bit. If you include your viewpoint at the beginning and the editor disagrees, your piece might end up in the cylindrical file without an entire reading.

Here is the beginning of the conclusion to an article about smoking at work:

> *While the debate rages over whether or not to ban smoking in the workplace, there is overwhelming evidence that using tobacco products can be hazardous to your job. If you smoke and want to keep your job, consider getting help in order to become an ex-smoker. You'll feel better, and probably work better too.*

The author's viewpoint is not only that smoking can cost you your job, but that smoking is generally unhealthy and that you should quit.

---

**COMMENT**: *You should also hope that the editor who reads your piece on the hazards of smoking is not a two-pack-a-day user!*

---

## Aim, Then Fire

Your piece must have a purpose and you must understand what it is. In books on writing, the concept of "purpose" is usually discussed early on. I put it here because I want you to get an idea of what a good article consists of before I muddle your mind with this important topic.

There are three main functions an article can fulfill. Some articles purport to do all three, but short articles seek to accomplish only one of the following:

**Inform**: Most pieces you read (and will probably write) are designed to impart some information. The reader spends time with the piece with the expectation of coming away with more knowledge than before.

**Persuade**: A persuasive article is written in the hope that readers will take some type of action such as writing to a legislator or calling a toll-free number.

**Entertain**: This article's purpose is obvious: to elicit an emotional response (laughter, tears, reflection, dismay, etc.)

Let's take a simple example: speed bumps. That's right, speed bumps. For some reason (hopefully because you think you can sell it) you decide to research a piece on what are called traffic undulators.

If you decide to write a piece to _inform_ the reader, you might research the facts and figures about construction, maximum speed of crossing, costs, pros, cons, etc. You then write a nice article titled "Those Pesky Speed Bumps: All You _Never_ Wanted To Know!"

If you're a speed bump fanatic and believe the world would be better off with bumps at every intersection, the purpose of your article might be to _persuade_ people to take your position and write letters to the traffic department requesting speed studies of their local streets. You would write an article listing benefits of having bumps placed strategically around the city (business would benefit, accidents would be prevented, lives saved, insurance costs lowered, etc.) You title it "Speed Bumps Can Save Your Child!"

Finally, if you think you can sell a "fun" piece on the topic, you write a nice little article about all the things that have happened to you, your car, passengers, cargo, etc. after hitting these bumps at too high a speed. You can have an _entertaining_ anecdote about how, on a blistering hot day, a dozen eggs flew out of the box, cracked open in the back of the station wagon, and fried before you got home. You title it "Things That Go Bump In Your Car" or "Unsafe At 10 MPH."

Do you see what I mean about purpose? Before you even think about what lead you're going to use, or even your premise, establish your purpose for writing the piece in the first place.

---

*COMMENT:* Once you get some experience, you'll research one article and create two others from the same research. If you can make three sales from one basic research session, you improve your bottom line by 60%. Always keep in mind how you can leverage your time to get the most sales from the research you do.

---

## Product Segmentation: Just Like Ford

I'm sure you've noticed how the auto manufacturers make "look alike" models with different labels. For example, Ford takes a basic Taurus model, dresses it up with a different interior and perhaps a few minor features, and calls it a Mercury Sable. This is sometimes called product-market segmentation. What it really means is customizing the basic product to sell to the buying market.

---

*COMMENT:* GM used to take one model and produce various cars for all its labels. They once took the poorly made Chevy Cavalier, dressed it up, and called it a Cadillac Cimmaron. Nobody was fooled; they bought BMW's instead.

---

There are seven basic article body styles you can choose from, depending on your market.

1. The Personal Experience Piece
2. The Interview Profile
3. The How-To
4. The Like-It-Was Article
5. The Visit-To Piece
6. The Editorial Article
7. The Journal Article

## The Personal Experience Piece

This is sometimes called the "I" format because it's almost always written in the first person. This type of article must have a high degree of *reader empathy*. When you write about a personal experience, it must be applicable to the reader. It must be on a topic that the reader has faced or could face. Authors frequently use this format when writing about a crisis they handled or about a dramatic event they experienced. The basic concept of this piece is that the reader will take away a lesson on how he or she should or could handle a similar situation.

When I say that these articles are about dramatic events, I'm not necessarily talking about flying the space shuttle or surviving a bomb blast. Most personal experience pieces are about everyday events that occur in the course of the workday at the store, plant or office; or on the weekend at home. What makes the drama is the interpretation that you give the incident or experience.

*TIP*: I call this the "spotlight effect." If you shine a spotlight with enough intensity on any event, it becomes dramatic. Look at how the news media can take an ordinary story about a guy accused of tax fraud, and build it up into the event of the decade. A good writer can create an interesting and dramatic story about running to the store for a quart of milk!

Once you've decided to write on a certain event from your past experience, you must answer two important questions to determine if this format is going to work:

1. Who is the reader? Make a mental note of his or her age, education, economic position, interests, beliefs, etc.

2. How will your experience help the reader? Determine what the reader will take away after reading your piece.

If you can't get a clear picture on both issues, you'll waste your time writing the piece. Every editor to whom you send the article will ask these questions as she reads your piece. If she doesn't see the answers, you'll see a rejection slip.

As I said earlier, if you use the personal experience format, you must include a high degree of *reader take-away* (writer lingo for *what the reader learns* from your article). Thus, you should spend more time determining the lessons you learned, new viewpoints you received, and how your life was changed so you can concentrate on making sure that there will be ample reader take-away. Many interesting articles are submitted that don't hit home on the issue of reader take-away. Editors are smart. This is what they look for when they get a personal experience submission. Spend as much time describing your *reaction* as you do the actual situation. For example, if you were a teacher and wrote "Per Diem

Substitute Teaching: Eight Hours In Hell," don't spend 1,500 words on all the crazy (terrible) things that happened to you, and only 200 words on what you learned. There won't be enough reader take-away, and the editor will reject the article. What is important to the reader is not that you almost got knifed by a fourteen-year-old punk, but how you handled it and how you were affected by it.

A personal experience article can take one of three formats::

> **Humor**: Editors love a humorous piece that also teaches a lesson. While I will cover humor later on, remember for now that anything with a great amount of humor has a high possibility of editorial acceptance, if it's really clever and not trite.

> **Action and Conquest**: You don't have to be the pilot of a plane with engine trouble. You can write a gripping story of being a passenger in a jumbo jet during a terrible storm. The action doesn't even have to be physical. If you ever made sales presentations, were there times you felt utter frustration, nervousness, anger, the thrill of winning, the agony of losing?

> **Mind Games**: This format usually details how some action or event changed your viewpoint on some important subject. In this type of article you describe the "blackness" of your life and how you overcame whatever was causing it. Worrying about an impending layoff, overcoming the death of a co-worker, recovering from an on-the-job accident are all examples of articles that describe a psychological state and how your "view of the world" changed.

Writing the personal experience article is not difficult. After all, you're writing about something that happened to you (or someone like you). There usually isn't a lot of outside research required; most of the work is in organizing the events and making sure there's a sufficient amount of reader take-away.

Editors look for pieces with "strong reader identification." This is almost as important as reader take-away. Readers identify with what's going on in your piece when they can put themselves in your place. Something in your article must stir a universal reader response. The reader must say to him/herself "Wow, I've been there. I know what the writer is talking about!"

One way to achieve this identification is to use dramatization. Instead of just telling what happened, borrow some tools from the fiction writer and tell a story. Instead of saying that the fourteen-year-old boy reached in his pocket and pulled out a knife and the teacher (you) dared him to use it, create some dialogue and set a scene. Show, don't tell:

> *Joseph wasn't the biggest kid in the class, but I could tell that he wanted to be. When I told him to raise his hand if he had something to say, he got up and reached in his coat pocket. "I'll let this do my talkin' from now on," he said as he brandished a five-inch hunting knife.*

> *"You have a choice, son. You can take your best shot. But if you do, you better kill me. Otherwise you can sit down and be quiet. Now, what's it going to be?" I asked calmly even though my heart was ready to jump through the window!*

Anyone who taught school can identify with the character, the incident and the response. They can put themselves in your place and decide what they would have said. This is reader identification.

My last point about the personal experience piece concerns a common statement: "I never had any experiences anyone would want to read about." This is not true. It is just the opposite. If you look closely, hardly a day goes by when you don't have some experience that could become a personal experience article. It all goes back to "thinking in derivatives." You've had many events happen to you. You only have to tap the well for ideas to flow. Besides your work or career, things happened to you in adolescence, school, marriage, parenthood, travel, illness, crisis, etc. you can transform into marketable articles. Find a way to relate your experience to this question: *In what way will my experience help someone else?*

---

### Tips For Personal Experience Articles

- Consider all your experiences for articles.

- Write from your heart. Show how you changed.

- Don't tell, show. Dramatize. Use dialogue.

- Read other personal pieces. Imitate style.

- Make sure there is reader identification.

- Determine the reader take-away before you start.

## The Interview Profile

I think writing about your own experiences can be the easiest type of writing. But if you're one of many people who don't feel ready to write about their own life, you might want to write profile articles about other people.

One nice thing about this type of article is that you don't have to think much. Your subject does it for you. Of course, you have to find a subject. Where are they?

Everywhere. And they can't wait to cooperate. You just have to find one that will "sell."

List the people who are the movers and shakers in your genre. They can be local, national, or international. In your readings, pick out names of people who have done something unusual or who are controversial. Look for people who have overcome obstacles, have made a contribution to your area of interest, or who have some new ideas about your genre.

Believe it or not, your most marketable article will be on a non-celebrity. If you're in the computer industry, no one wants to read another piece on Bill Gates. If you're in finance, Warren Buffet has been covered *ad nauseam*. You want to find the man developing some kind of whiz-bang software in his kitchen, or the woman using tarot cards as a method for selecting stocks.

Read the small articles in your industry journals. You'll often come up with names of people doing interesting things.

Ask yourself these questions: *What have they done (or are doing)?* and *Why is it interesting?* Get two good answers and you have a definite prospect for a profile piece.

Don't let death of a subject stop you! Some of the best profiles are done on long-gone pioneers of some industry.

---

**COMMENT**: Who was the "best" insurance salesperson? What was the personality of the person who invented the transistor like? Who was responsible for opening the first dry-cleaning business in the U.S.?

---

Sometimes the spouse or child of your intended subject is a better prospect for an article. Everyone knows Ross Perot, but what's his son or wife like? This stuff sells!

When you research your industry stars, look for a new angle or twist. If during your research on Donald Trump, you discovered that he attended military school (he did), you might develop an article about his experiences at the school (New York Military Academy) and what the school is like today. (It's hard to imagine "The Donald" as a disciplined spit-and-polish high school cadet!)

---

**TIP**: I suggest you initially concentrate on live non-celebrities. These articles take less research time and, if done right, have a better chance of getting ink.

---

Once you have a subject in mind, make contact and ask for an interview. You have to decide if you're going to do a face-to-face interview or a phone interview. I suggest you do phone interviews even on local subjects because there is less travel time. However, many writers believe that much of the fun in doing profiles is in meeting live with the subject.

There is no one correct way to get an appointment. Most people will be glad to find an hour or so to talk to you *at their convenience*. Find the work number of the person and call his or her office. Don't call working people at home unless you can't reach them any other way.

Tell the subject that you're a writer interested in doing a story on him that you hope will be published in such and such magazine. (Tell them you're not working for *60 Minutes!*)

There is no need to say that you've never had anything published, if that is the case. After you've seen some ink, you can tell them some of your credits, although few really care.

Trust me on this: Most people - even presidents of large companies, well-known engineers, inventors, writers, top sales people, and other luminaries of your genre - will be so excited about the prospect of having a profile done on them that they will bend over backwards to cooperate.

You may have initial contact with the person's secretary. This is no problem. Secretaries know their boss would be stupid to turn down free publicity and they will make sure he or she gets the message.

> *TIP*: Nothing will make your phone ring faster than leaving someone a message saying you're a writer and want to do an article on him or her to be published in XYZ magazine.

Ask your subject when a good time would be for him or her to spend an hour or so with you, either by phone or in person (if local). Don't be surprised if subjects want you to call on them at home for an evening interview. Try to make the appointment several days in advance, so you have time to prepare.

Many profile writers ask their subjects to send (fax) resumes, or other items to help get a good perspective on the person.

Always, always, always ask the person to send (or give) you a black-and-white publicity photo, if they have one. If you plan to do the profile in person, tell your subject that you're going to bring your camera. People want to know in advance so they can wear a nice suit, do their hair, etc.

Also, tell them you may bring a tape recorder. Few will object. If they do, decide if you still want to do the piece.

*TIP*: Buy yourself a nice little tape recorder that you can keep in your brief case. Learn how to use it. Don't put it right in front of the subject. Some people are tape-shy! Put it on a table off to the side. For phone interviews, you can use an answering machine that has a record function. Or you can get an attachment to connect your recorder to the phone. Check out Radio Shack.

While I suggest you use a tape recorder, it's up to you. If you do use one, be sure to take notes as well. Tape recorders have a nasty habit of breaking down at inopportune times.

Before the interview, do your homework. You should know a lot about your subject. Prepare a list of questions that you plan to ask. You may not ask them all but should have them just in case. Memorize the first few questions so you can get the interview rolling without sounding like an amateur by saying, "Let's see, oh yes, here it is, the first question is. . . ."

Your job is to find interesting items from the life, times, accomplishments, thoughts, cares, and beliefs of the subject so that you can craft a salable article. Writers often determine in advance what material they want from their subject. Remember, the piece must contain reader identification. Think about this before you meet or talk with the subject. Try to determine beforehand what's *really* interesting about this person. Design your questions to bring out these points. Also remember that you'll have to pry the *really* interesting information out of some subjects. Not that they'll try to hide anything from you, they just don't think they are interesting or don't know what will make an interesting article.

Many writers look for an emotional angle. Rather than looking to uncover some new fact about the subject, they seek to report how the subject feels about a certain topic. For example:

*Dr. Smith gets emotional when he discusses the state of health care in rural areas. He is despondent when discussing the past, but flashes with anger when he talks of today's bureaucrats and policy makers who keep people in poor mountain areas from receiving the medical treatment they deserve. "My patients are poor, sick, and mostly old. They live in out-of-the - way places. They don't vote or write letters, so they're forgotten. I hate politicians!" he says with fire in his eyes.*

Readers (and editors) respond to emotion. Facts are fine. Emotion is better. A profile that displays the range of emotions (humor, fear, anger, despair, etc.) your subject portrays will get you published over and over again.

If you do an in-person interview, take note of the surroundings. Readers are interested in how notable people arrange their offices, decorate their living rooms, etc. These items turn editors on. For example:

*Dr. Smith's office is an idyllic sanctuary within the busy clinic. The walls, bathed in warm red paper, are complemented by antique oriental rugs and the old English leather highback chairs we sat in. It's a quiet, peaceful room; not where you would expect to find a man well known for his fiery temperament. He may be regarded as a drill sergeant in hospital corridors but his office decor would suit a quiet English professor.*

When you start your interview, warm up the subject for the first three or four minutes by engaging in some small talk. This will relax both of you.

> *TIP: A good way to learn interview techniques is to practice on a friend or neighbor. After your first few interviews, you'll get the hang of it. No matter what professional journalists would have you believe, it's not that hard.*

When you interview someone, it's important to keep the subject focused. People will often wander off the subject and want to talk about things that are fascinating to them but not to anyone else. A Florida woman once interviewed the chef of a fancy restaurant. "He rambled on about how a microwave oven works. I knew my editor wanted readers to know how the chef uses it to prepare gourmet vegetables. It was a long interview. Maybe I can sell some of the information I got to a magazine on electronic cookware!"

Your subject may answer a question then plead with you not to use his response. **Never use material the subject asks you not to use.**

> *TIP: Before you begin the interview, tell your subject to use the term "off the record" before he or she says something they don't want used.*

When you're ready to write the piece, review your notes and play back your tape. If you did your homework and tried to find points of reader identification and reader take-away, it will come together easily.

Start with a lead. Dialogue leads work well with profile pieces. Determine what your premise is and what you'll use to support it. But don't look too deeply for a premise. Often the premise is "this is an important, exciting, interesting person that will be fun to read about."

You've probably read thousands of profile articles. With practice, you'll have no trouble writing them yourself.

---

**Tips For Profile Articles**

• Choose an interesting subject.

• Determine what you will highlight in the article.

• Do your before-interview research.

• Create questions that will get answers.

• Don't use off-the-record material.

• Capture subject's emotions.

---

# The How-To Article

The how-to is by far the most marketable article type you can write. Unfortunately, it's the one that usually takes the most time to either research or get down on paper. The physical how-to is also not the easiest piece to write. By physical, I mean the article that instructs someone how to do some manual operation. How to program a VCR or fix a fax machine may be simple operations for you, but putting them on paper with diagrams, drawings, and photos is not an easy task.

I suggest that, in the early stages of your writing business, you concentrate on what I call the mental how-to article. This usually revolves around the concept of achieving some business or vocational goal. For example, "10 Ways Sell More Cars" or "How To Use Long Distance Cold Calling To Maximum Effect" or "How To Select a VCR For Your Business" or "How To Find A Competent Fax Repair Person."

We're in a post-industrial service economy. Most of us don't do as many physical activities as we did years ago. We don't grow and preserve our food, change our oil, mow our lawns, roof our houses, trim our trees, program our computers, write our own ads, etc. We hire people to perform such services for us. You have two choices. You can write to the audience that provides the service or you can write to the audience that needs and hires the service.

---

*TIP: Think about it. How many people out there actually program computers? But how many businesses hire outsiders to do this task? I always advise writers to target articles to the "need and hire" audience rather than to the "hands-on" audience.*

---

**Do It Yourself**: This is the most marketable how-to. PEs who have manual skills can sell their skills over and over again. If you were a house painter, you did more than what people commonly associate with painters, spreading paint on surfaces. You knew how to mix colors, prep different surfaces, use rollers, compressors, brushes, build scaffolds, etc. You can put together many how-to articles for those starting out as painters, or for the suburban do-it-yourself guy or gal.

Whenever you write a do-it-yourself piece it's important to use clear concise language. Write for an 8th grader! Use short sentences. Don't include too much information in any one paragraph. A long piece is better than a short one. The editor will cut what's not needed.

Make sure you tell the reader where to find the materials and what they are likely to cost. Even if you're writing for a professional audience (like other painters) include the supply costs and sources. There are lots of beginners out there.

Include photos. Learn to use a camera if you're not already adapt at taking pictures. You don't need expensive equipment. Any of the newer cameras with built-in zoom lenses (for close-ups) will do. Include photos for each step of the procedure. The editor will decide what photos to put in the piece.

---

*TIP*: Use black-and-white film and send glossy prints, not negatives. Some publications prefer slides. Some writers take two shots of each scene using two cameras, one with slide film and one with B&W.

---

Remember to ask the questions about "why" someone should want to do the project. Consider the concept of reader take-away and the universal needs I mentioned earlier. Your best approach is to take some skill you did professionally and apply it to the popular media. If you were a plumber, roofer, electrician, chef, gardener, lineman, or in any occupation that required manual skills, you simply redirect what you did professionally toward the everyday reader. Don't be afraid to do a little research and expand your skill so that it's applicable to the common person. For example, say you were a telephone lineperson. Most people are never going to put up their own poles and string line. But you probably know (or can quickly learn) how to wire a home with twisted pair (the industry jargon for telephone cord). Show editors how their readers can easily string line for a new phone and fax line, and you've made a how-to sale.

---

*TIP*: The basic article can be resold in different markets. A resale opportunity using the how to wire a home with twisted pair example would be how to wire an office where special fireproof wire and equipment is needed.

---

**The Help-Now Article**: This is what I call those how-to articles that are non-physical in nature. These articles are directed toward showing the reader how to achieve some intangible.

You can't pick up a magazine anymore without seeing at least one help-now article. Nearly every mass market publication, industry specific magazine, newsletter, or journal will have some article designed to help their readers *do*, *acquire*, *understand*, or *avoid* something. Read those four words again. What do you know from your life that encompasses one of those terms?

Everyone has knowledge that will help someone. A 65-year-old former loan officer regularly writes articles like "Ten Ways To Help You Get That Loan" or "Getting Credit After Bankruptcy." A woman in New York who taught high school biology for 22 years writes how-to pieces explaining complex scientific concepts to kids. She is published in many teaching journals as well as local papers. A retired bartender writes articles for restaurant trade magazines about how managers can use new bar technology (special cash registers, drink dispensing machines, etc.) to increase profits. A former radio announcer and producer has articles published in entertainment industry magazines about how local stations can produce talk shows, find guests, get sponsors etc. Read the first sentence of this paragraph again. It's true.

If it's not, you can always find a source of information. A woman in Ohio worked her entire life in a tire plant. She was not interested in writing about tires. However, soon after retirement, her best friend suffered permanent hair loss. The ex-tire worker found that this was a subject hardly written about. She consulted experts and became an authority on women's hair loss. She has had her work published around the world. From wigs, to makeup, to how to tell your lover, she has written articles on how women can cope with hair loss.

The help-now article is easy to write. In your lead, state the problem clearly. Hit the reader (editor) between the eyes with it. Don't dance around. Look at an example that could be titled "Bringing Guests Back To The Hotel Dining Room."

> *By all accounts, receipts at high-end hotel dining rooms have dropped almost 25% in the past two years. This has had a devastating effect on many hotels throughout the industry.*

The next section outlines possible causes of the problem. Don't assume your reader (editor) knows why the problem is occurring. Spell it out.

> *Surveys have shown that people are eating lighter fare. . . . They have less time to enjoy long business lunches as they did several years ago, and the tax laws have changed how much can be deducted. . . . Many guests don't want to change clothes to have dinner, especially after a long trip.*

Finally, outline the possible solutions to the problem. Don't skimp here. This is the meat of the article.

> *One well-known hotel in Chicago abandoned their dress code and urges guests to dine in their best restaurant in sport clothes; no tie required. . . . Several hotels have changed the menu from heavy French foods to lighter northern Italian dishes. . . . A hotel in Atlanta offers a two-for-one night each week.*

Good how-to articles take more time and work than other article types, but they are not all that difficult. A little practice is all you need to find your own formula for putting these highly marketable pieces together.

---

### Tips For How-To Articles

- Know why your audience will read the piece.

- Use simple language.

- Double-check your facts and figures.

- Use photos.

- Quote knowledgeable authorities.

## The Like-It-Was Historical Perspective

The nostalgia article is often harder to write than the types because it doesn't automatically appeal to any basic universal interest. This piece is also more difficult to sell. You often have to *convince* an editor that his or her readers *are* interested in nostalgia. Finally, nostalgia articles are typically longer than the 1,500 to 2,000-word pieces I've been describing.

Some PEs are terrific at writing like-it-was articles and have sold them to newspapers around the country. Others make the common mistake of writing only half an article!

If you write a wonderful piece about what it was like to work in the airline industry forty years ago, you might sell it. But you've left out half of the audience: those who were not around 40 years ago! Thus, you must find a way to link any like-it-was piece with how-it-is-now.

Instead of a nice march down memory lane, create a link to the present. In other words, your article should become a historical perspective.

---

**COMMENT:** *Instead of pure nostalgia "like-it-was" articles, I recommend "see how far we've come" pieces that link the past to the present.*

---

If you want to write nostalgia articles, span a range of time to help the reader appreciate the how and why of change. This is especially true when writing for industry-specific magazines or journals. Few editors of automotive engineering publications are willing to run a piece on how ball bearings were made fifty years ago. However, they will take a good look at it if the article takes an "editorial" position. This is your second task. As the expert (or the reporter quoting some expert), you must convey to the reader that things are better now (ball bearings are more reliable, better made, last longer etc.) or that we are headed for disaster (ball bearing failure, due to poor manufacturing processes, causes many problems in today's cars.)

Like-it-was articles lend themselves to wide markets and re-sale opportunities. Even obscure topics can sound interesting. For example, few people are interested in how radios are manu-factured today. But many would be fascinated to learn how early radios were mass-produced, what materials were used, etc.

---

**COMMENT**: *In a way, nostalgia does meet a universal need. Most of us receive warmth and comfort from reliving the past.*

---

Again and again, writers have taken an off-the-wall topic, researched it using a nostalgia angle, and sold it to widely read magazines such as *Smithsonian*. Feature editors of large papers love to run such articles, especially if you tie the piece to some local angle (was there a radio factory in the region at one time?)

One reason like-it-was articles are hard to write is because the author must paint vivid word pictures for the reader to get a feel for what it was like way back when. In short, the author must be more talented than the PE turning out profile pieces.

Photos can really help your nostalgia pieces come alive. There are several photo services where you can, for a small fee (roy-alty), buy rights to use a photo in your piece. Sometimes your local newspaper has its own photo service. If not, someone at the paper can probably recommend one.

---

**TIP**: *National photo services such as Bettman News Photos in New York City charge fees in the $50 to $80 range. Make sure you raise your price for articles with photos.*

---

It takes longer to get good at putting together nostalgia ar-ticles. You should read and clip the like-it-was pieces you find in your daily reading. Study the leads, the structure, and the language of the articles. Note how the author makes connections between past and present. Also note how the author uses transitions. Gracefully taking your reader from one time period to another is a difficult task that you will have to learn. But others have, so you can too.

Many PEs end up doing nostalgia pieces as derivative works from other articles they've researched. For example, a retired cattle rancher in Denver did some research on current technology available for feedlots. In the course of his investigations he came across material on how feedlots operated before the advances in technology. By talking with other ranchers he came up with an interesting then-and-now piece. He sold the articles to different magazines, then sold each magazine the other article! He also got the like-it-was piece printed in several newspapers. It was a human interest article to many readers of the region. It took him twenty hours to research and write both pieces, but he made four sales for $150 each and another four sales for $75 each, totalling $900. That's $45/hr. ($900/20=$45) and there are more sales he can make.

---

### Tips For Like-It-Was Articles

- Use vivid word pictures.

- Establish a then-now link.

- Use your own photos.

- Use photos from a photo service.

- Think "human interest."

## The On-Location Piece

Much literature (and myth) on the writing business touts the fringe benefit of traveling and taking tax deductions. This part is not a myth. The myth is in assuming that you'll sell the article. The travel article is one of the hardest pieces to sell. Why? Because so many people visit so many places and write about them. Writing travel articles is a hard way to make money because the cost of your trip will usually be higher than your income from any articles you sell.

Writers used to be advised to find out-of-the-way places and create must-see articles. Well, I believe everyone has been everywhere that anyone might want to go! So if you think you're going to visit London, or Paris, or East Tennis Shoe, Nebraska, and sell an article about what you saw and did, then I want to talk to you about taking a look at a bridge in Brooklyn, New York.

Forget the travel article. In its place, substitute the on-location article. Within your genre, there must be many places you can visit that relate to your area of expertise. The article that explains what-goes-on at a particular location is far more marketable than the standard travel article.

Before you pack up and go somewhere, do some thinking. No matter what you write about, there are some locations that are important. Within those locations are institutions that should be visited. And within those institutions there are activities going on that should be reported. You just have to determine the locations and institutions.

For example, let's say you used to work in the advertising department for a distiller of spirits. You probably know the booze business inside and out. What geographical locations are important to the industry? Obviously, wherever major ingredients come from (grain, sugar, barrel wood, etc.) as well as where the major distilleries are. Kentucky might be a destination. So might Scotland. Since Scotland sounds more exciting than Kentucky, let's go there! It will be part business, part vacation.

Think of several topics that you might write about. You'll get other ideas when you arrive and start visiting, but you need some good titles to pique the interest of your hosts. How about some of these topics:

> Making the Single Malt Scotch
> The Magic of Scotland's Wood Aging Process
> Tasting Scotch For A Living

Find the address and phone number of several distilleries that you could visit, perhaps by calling the British embassy.

> *TIP: If you've never made an international phone call, all you need to know is in the beginning of the phone book. Call your long distance operator (dial 00) and find the cheapest time to call the country you want. Fax during the cheap period.*

Keeping in mind the time difference, call during *their* business hours. You may have to get up in the middle of the night, but it's only for a few minutes. When you get someone on the line (who speaks English!), ask for the fax number of their public relations department and who the PR director is; that's all.

> *COMMENT: You could do all of this by mail, but almost all international correspondence is now conducted by fax. Mail takes too long. If you don't have a fax machine, use one from a mail service like Mail Boxes Etc.*

Compose a short one or two-page letter saying you're a well-known US writer on distilled spirits and would like to do a story about their organization. You can mention titles you have in mind. Tell them when you want to visit, how long you'll be at their factory, what resources you might need, and mention anything else you think will be useful, like suggestions where to stay. You can tell them where you plan to sell the piece. There is no need to send clips of your work or tell them what a great writer you are. Fax this off when rates are lowest.

They will probably fax back a letter within a day, falling all over themselves with offers to help you find lodging (they won't pay for it, sorry) and to give you directions on how to get to their place (assuming it's in the middle of nowhere!)

Will you make money on these articles? Considering the cost of travel, probably not. Let's say that you get five sales at $250 each, which totals $1,250. If your airfare was $650 and you spent $100 a day for 7 days, you lost $100. But you got an almost-free trip to Scotland. How is it almost free?

Uncle Sam is going to let you write off most of the trip cost. You'll be able to deduct around $1,000 from your other earnings which means you'll pay less tax. Whatever the amount of tax that you don't pay is your profit. Let's assume you end up paying $400 less in tax. You spent $1,350 on the trip. You got $1,250 in sales. You're out $100. But you saved $400 in taxes. Thus, you have $300 in your pocket and an "almost-free" trip to Scotland.

The on-location article is often a mix between the profile and the personal experience. You have to write in such a way that the reader can see what you saw. These articles are big on description. You must describe the most interesting things you see to get the editor's interest. Few editors are likely to be interested in the beautiful grounds surrounding the Scottish factory. Editors are more likely to want a description (and photo) of the dark underground maze of tunnels where the barrels are aged.

However, it's important to include some geography into the article. After all, you're describing a faraway and maybe exotic place. It wouldn't hurt to include a few words about your visit to a local pub near the factory where you had a nip. Just remember that geography is not the focus of the piece.

Even if you're not going far away, include some local color. Say you live in Tampa and write on robotics. If you make an appointment to visit Disneyworld in Orlando to research an article about how computers make everything move, add some color about the Magic Kingdom to liven up the piece. You want to convey to the reader that you were actually there, live and in person, and that you did not write the article from a company brochure!

Remember to use word pictures. Don't say it: show it. Look at the difference in two descriptions of a glassblowing shop:

> It was dark, smoky, and somewhat dank in the cellar where Carl created his handmade works. While the oven is two thousand degrees, it did not seem to affect the temperature of the windowless room.

***

> We were led down the brick steps to what we thought was a dungeon. Moisture from the cold stone walls penetrated our clothes. A haze of gray smoke met our eyes as we descended the last few steps, making it even harder to see Carl standing near the soft glow of the oven. Although the oven was hot enough to melt glass, the heat did not touch the misty chill that enveloped us in a room that had never seen sunlight.

Maybe this is a bit overdone, but you should *get the picture!*

The lead is even more important in an on-location article than in the others we've looked at. You have to get the editor to read about what occurs in a place he or she has never been, might not like, or might not find interesting. You must hook your editor in a few sentences. Does this lead for a piece on a high-speed printing factory hook you:

> *Faster than a speeding bullet, a 120-page book flew out of the press. Then another and another. I stared in amazement. John Jones, the shop foreman smiled, "Welcome to our San Diego plant. You're not in Kansas anymore!"*

Be sure there's plenty of solid information in the body of your article. After all, there was a reason you visited wherever you went, so make sure the editor knows why you went there. Make sure the reader comes away with whatever you learned. Word pictures are nice, as are long descriptive paragraphs. But make sure there is plenty of meat. If you went to a glassblowing shop, you might highlight why handmade glass is better, stronger, clearer, than machine made glass. If you visit a new printing plant, you want your reader to understand the new technology you witnessed.

An easy way to accomplish the above is to constantly ask yourself during your visit, "Why is what I'm looking at important?" If you keep that one question in mind and take notes that support your answer, you'll have plenty of material for a good on-location article.

Always look for the new, different, and better. That's what editors want to parade in front of their readers. New, different, and better; these are the keys to selling visit-to articles.

> ### Tips For On-Location Articles
>
> - Find an interesting location and institution.
>
> - Do your research.
>
> - Capture the important information.
>
> - Write a great lead.
>
> - Take lots of pictures.
>
> - Write in vivid word pictures.

## The Editorial Article

This is a good writing product to market. Yet many people don't consider themselves competent enough writers to put their *own thoughts* down on paper. But, in reality, these are often the easiest and most profitable articles to write. Easy, because they require little or no research. Profitable because editors don't receive as many of these articles as they often would like; especially articles that are humorous.

What are you angry about? What do you feel strongly about? Whatever your genre, there are issues that divide the members of your reading market.

Many editors of industry magazines love controversy. They are forever searching for the piece that has the potential to strike a nerve with an audience, such that the issue makes it to the mainstream media. Every publication looks for articles that stir up the pot and get people talking about the pros and cons of an issue, and, of course, the magazine that reported it.

There are basically two areas you should look to for possible editorial articles. The first are people issues. Ask yourself: What are people doing in my field that drives me nuts? For example, how about the software project manager who calls employees during the night and on weekends to ask questions? How about bank loan officers who have a "bad attitude" toward customers? What about printers who promise work by Friday which they know darn well won't be ready until Monday? What about the buyer who takes on a line of products just to fill space in a store when she plans to return most of the merchandise? People are always doing things that are either stupid, wasteful, immoral, illegal, or sleazy. And editors love to get articles about these people. Why? Because there's a great deal of reader identification involved. We all know someone who drives us crazy.

Often these pieces take a how-to premise; there is a special way readers can or should deal with individuals with whom they have to work. This is a reader take-away. However, the main reader take-away is the good feeling readers get in knowing they are not alone. Others have to work around jerks too!

The second editorial piece is situational or issue-oriented. What policies are being adopted in your genre that you don't agree with? What changes are taking place in your area of expertise that you feel are harmful, hurtful, or just wrong? What about banks that replace full-time tellers with part-time people so the institutions doesn't have to pay benefits? What about the restaurant that asks for a credit card number when you make a reservation and charges if you cancel? What about airline ticket policies? What about computerized sales calls? What about schools that pay administrators a zillion dollars while teachers take a cut?

*TIP: If there aren't things that bother you about your genre, you might not be all that knowledgeable about it. Sorry, but positive pieces don't sell as well as dirt. Nobody cares that Lever Brothers is using recycled paper. They'd rather hear how the treasurer of a local charity embezzled the bingo proceeds.*

As I said earlier, editorial pieces are not hard to write, as long as your thoughts are organized and you present the topic in a cool and rational manner. This is not talk radio. You don't have the opportunity to rant and rave (unless you do it with wit and humor) about some issue. You need to approach this type of writing with the same building block style as the others. Explain your premise, lead the reader into the situation, and perhaps explain what can or should be done about the issue.

Finding topics is not difficult. If you're peeved at something, others probably are too. Ask around. Make some calls and see if your topic interests others in your genre. Sometimes they'll give you a quote that can be used in the piece.

*TIP: One of the best ways I've found to come up with editorial pieces is to start with the headline "Why I Really Hate _____." Fill in the blank and all sorts of ideas will flow into your head. If you have to think hard, you're not passionate enough about the topic to write on it!*

I maintain that either you can write humor or you can't. It's a gift. I don't believe any book or school can turn you into a humorist. If you have the gift, the world is waiting to read your articles. Many editors love to receive clever, witty, and just plain funny editorial pieces from writers. It's not that they don't get enough submissions, they just don't get enough good ones.

Humor pieces tend to follow two simple formulas: The first is to write about a situation that you were involved with and work it into a "think piece." For example, if construction is your genre, you can probably write about "The Plumber (or painter, or carpenter) From Hell." By taking a humorous look at plumbers, you can expound your theory that most plumbers must be watched, can't be trusted, don't know what they're doing, charge too much, or are truly saints (take your choice!)

The second approach is to set yourself up as the "goof." If you were in the restaurant business as a manager, write about the night everything went wrong and how you tried to handle it, but didn't, couldn't, or wouldn't! These articles create reader identification. Laughing at yourself is an excellent way to get a point across.

I seldom recommend that PEs have their articles reviewed by family and friends mainly because outsiders don't usually know much about your genre. However, humor pieces should be previewed to give you an idea of whether you're funny or not.

---

*TIP*: You might think your piece is the funniest since "Who's On First?" Don't be surprised if friends consider it about as funny as their VCR programming instructions. Humor is hard to write.

---

### Tips For Humor and Editorial Articles

• Keep a journal of situations that annoy you.

• Don't be overly aggressive. There are libel laws!

• Is there enough reader identification?

• Test humor articles on family and friends.

• Is there a how-to-fix-it possibility?

• Think: "Why I Hate _____."

## The Five W's

The final article type is not only the easiest but probably the one you'll write the most often. This is the plain vanilla journalism article. There is a simple formula to most journal articles: What, Where, When, Who, Why.

If you spent any time in college, you wrote term papers using this formula. If you were in a management position, you wrote company reports using it. If you contributed to a newsletter for your church, club, organization, or charity, you wrote this kind of article.

There is no magic to turning out basic journalistic prose. All it takes is a little study and a little practice.

Here's my magic sixty-day course in journalism. Buy the *Wall Street Journal* each day for two months. Read the entire three front page stories. Even if you aren't interested in the content, look at how the Journal's writers answer the five W's. While these articles are longer than those you'll probably write, they are (in my opinion) the best writing of its type available in the country. Just study for the first month. During the second month, each day after you finish reading the Journal, write a 1,500 word story about nonsense. Make up a story about anything; don't do any research, don't spend more than an hour or so writing, and don't think too much! Just write. You can make your story as wild as possible. Just write.

---

*TIP*: I tell people to write a WSJ type article about visitors from space landing in their town. Another favorite of mine is a story about the discovery for the cure to cancer. Finally, there is the subject about a limited nuclear war between Chad and Botswana! Just write!

---

Continue reading and writing for thirty days. Most people become fairly good at getting the important points down on paper in a sequence readers can understand. You'll find that it's not hard to write the journalistic article.

> **COMMENT**: *Whenever you need guidance, ask yourself: "How would the WSJ cover this?"*

Depending on your market, the basic journalistic article can be harder to sell than others because there is far less reader identification built into the piece. The charter of a newspaper is to present the facts clearly, concisely, and without bias. Journalists don't care if readers become involved or motivated. While I disagree, many editors feel reader identification is not why people buy newspapers. Thus, knowing how to write as a WSJ newsperson does not guarantee that you'll see any ink. Having the skill is one thing. Finding a topic that interests an editor with a checkbook is quite another. However, if you're privy to a "newsy" item, knowing how to get it all down (covering the 5 W's) is surely a plus.

The countless books on how to "do" journalism are all pretty much the same. I've never read a bad one. Feel free to get one from the library, but I believe your time would be better spent by following my sixty-day cram course.

> **COMMENT**: *If it was really hard to write as a journalist, print reporters would be better paid! What is really unfair is what blow-dried TV news "readers" often get paid compared to those who write the copy!*

One important item to be aware of when you study the WSJ or any newspaper is how reporters weave several of the article types into their pieces. In a long news article you'll see parts of the "profile piece," parts of the "personal experience piece," perhaps parts of the "how-to piece." Good journalism is a craft, not an art. You can master it. Many before you have. It just takes some study and some practice.

Sixty days won't qualify you to apply for a job at any major paper, but you should be qualified to sit down and write a 1,500 word article on most subjects in your genre that your average magazine editor will accept (if the topic is good).

---

*COMMENT: What separates real journalists from part-time or would-be writers is speed. If need be, a top writer can turn out a 1,500 word one-draft article on a breaking news story in 30 minutes, 10 minutes under a 40 minute deadline. You try writing 50 words a minute! Good luck!*

---

### Tips For Journalism Articles

- Include the 5 W's.

- Do your research.

- Use quotes.

- Write on a 10th grade level!

- Study the WSJ.

- Use short sentences, short paragraphs.

## Attitude Is Half the Battle

Writing is a confidence game. You can't really do it unless you *believe* you can do it. I don't even think you can learn it unless you truly believe you can learn it. In my opinion, every creative endeavor needs a supportive environment. This is why I'm not a great fan of writing classes held in most schools and colleges.

Many teachers of writing take the attitude that it's hard work and, unless you've suffered the pangs of anxiety or have paid your dues via depression, rejection, self-doubt, and perhaps starvation, you're not worthy of calling yourself a writer.

This is why so many schools and classes are bad environments for learning how to write. They become critique sessions with everyone more eager to heap scorn and ridicule on you. Who needs that! What learning writers *do* need is praise and adulation.

That doesn't mean that you can't come away from a writing class or seminar with good ideas and perhaps new skills. However, often you will leave feeling lousy about your abilities, your chances for success, and the craft in general.

People who enjoy writing are good at it. Plain and simple. You're not going to enjoy something when everyone is putting your efforts down.

---

*TIP: There are many, many fine writing instructors who care about their students and who maintain a supportive classroom environment. If your town or city has one or more, they will be easy to find. Ask other writers. They will know who is good and who isn't. The writer's grapevine is pretty accurate.*

---

I urge PEs to have their friends and families read their work with only one question to be answered: "Is this piece, in your opinion, good enough to be published?" Don't ask why, or for tips, or for help. All you'll get is criticism, and you don't need that. If you get a "yes" answer, great! If you get a "no," go back and try to figure out why without getting a long critical diatribe from someone who probably doesn't know a verb from a noun!

In any book on writing you'll read stories of first-time writers who had their first pieces published. It happens all the time, but not as often as these books would have you think. The point I'm making is that you need to believe that what you put on paper is good. Then you have to read it as if you, yourself, were an editor.

---

*TIP: Put your piece away for a few days before you pick it up to read. Make believe you're the editor of the magazine to which you're submitting your work. Read it from his or her perspective. If it's good, you'll know it!*

---

After you've written your first article, remember this: 99% of the people you know have never even *attempted* to write a publishable article, much less *completed* one. You're special! Take the attitude of a winner. Don't let doubt and depression get you down, even after your fifth (or fiftieth) rejection. This is a new craft and there are things you have to learn. If you follow the styles and building blocks presented earlier, you'll eventually succeed.

Think of it this way. Tens of thousands of people do write and sell their pieces. They may not make a million dollars, but they do all right. You can be one of them!

They've been published without the help of this book! You're ahead of the game!

And it *is* a game. Like other games, it has rules. In the next chapter you'll read about the rules, customs, tactics, and strategies used to sell your work.

You're going to learn how to *win* the game.

# 7

. . . . . . . . . . . . . . . . .

# THE BIG SELL

## The System is Against You

Writing is not one of our highest paid occupations. Why? Perhaps, because so many people *can* do it (not necessarily well!). I believe that the laws of supply and demand have the same effect on the writing business as they do on every other business. Editors have a multitude of vendors to choose from and try to get the most for the least. An editor buying articles for her magazine is no different from an office manager buying office supplies for his business. Both look for the lowest cost supplier consistent with the quality needed.

The low pay problem is compounded by the fact that many writers virtually give their product away in order to see their names in print.

Do understand one thing: In the writing and editorial business, money is tainted. For some reason, authors and editors are supposed to be above the lowly method of commerce called buying and selling. An editor says she "acquired rights" to a manuscript. The writer didn't sell his piece of work; it was "accepted."

---

**COMMENT**: *Nurses and teachers once had a non-mercenary attitude toward their professions. Fortunately, both groups woke up and found they could demand better pay for their work. Most writers still need this attitude adjustment!*

---

The reality is that writers sell, and editors buy. The curious thing is that the buyers set the price at which the sellers have to sell and the sellers accept this as a fact of life! Instead of a writer saying "this article will cost you $350," the editor says "we will only pay $100 for an article of this type." The editor gets no argument, just grumbles.

You see, writers rarely consider themselves business people. They think of themselves as artists. They're above the daily grind of grubbing for money. And because of this, they nearly starve to death!

I bring this up as an introduction to the nuts and bolts of selling your work to the information (print media) world. It's probably unlike any business you've ever been associated with. Money is not important and time is not important. Thus, writers don't get much for their efforts, and it takes them forever to close a sale (sorry, I mean "get an acceptance!").

Over the years, a traditional set of procedures has been developed that writers follow in order to make sales to editors. Most of these work against the writer, mainly because the "rules" were made by the editors. Take a look at two traditions still prevalent in the business. Fortunately both are changing or fading away.

The first is the issue of multiple submissions. Traditionally, writers only sent their work (or a query, which I'll discuss later) to one publisher at a time! That's right, one! And, writers can wait up to three months for an answer of acceptance or rejection! Traditional editors have an unwritten rule that if they find out that a writer made a submission to another magazine, they will not consider the piece (now) or the writer (forever). What a crock!

The second tradition is called "paid on publication." Once your piece is accepted, you don't get paid until they publish it, which could be six months later. They could decide months later not to publish it, which means your piece is taken out of the market. Or the magazine could go out of business. Either way, you get the shaft! Great system, huh?

If you really don't care about making sales or getting paid, fine. You can follow the traditional ways. But don't cry when an unscrupulous editor takes advantage of you.

## You Want Omelets? Break Some Eggs!

I must have read three dozen books on how writers should go about selling their work. All could have been written by the same person! They pretty much say the same thing.

Here is how the old song goes. The writer comes up with an idea for an article for a specific market segment. The writer decides for which magazine or paper the article would be best. The writer then sits down and composes a one-page letter telling the editor what the article is about and why it should be published. This is called the *query letter*. The writer sends the query letter and waits weeks or months for a reply from the editor. If the editor thinks the idea is good, she gives our guy the go-ahead to develop the article. Sometimes there will be an advance or a kill-fee arrangement, but most often the work is done on speculation (a.k.a *on spec*). The writer sends the piece off to the editor. Again he waits weeks or months for an acceptance or a rejection. If it's rejected, he queries the second choice magazine and starts the whole waiting process over. If the piece is accepted with payment upon publication, the writer waits for a check. Sometimes it doesn't come for months after publication, but there's nothing he can do about it!

This system is great for editors, but lousy for writers. Fortunately, change is in the air. Writers are waking up to the fact that they're being victimized. The system is becoming more equitable. What I'm going to tell you is not exactly revolutionary, but my advice is on the forefront of change and is likely to be criticized by more traditional members of the literary profession.

Basically, you're going to ignore the traditional single submission policy. In addition, you're not going to waste time with clever query letters. If you want to *sell* an article, *send* an article.

But before you're ready to send a piece, you have to do some research on what to write about and where to send it.

## What and Where?

I talked earlier about selecting a genre and a writing topic. What I didn't mention was the concept of scope. A common mistake PEs make in topic selection is taking too broad a view. If you want to be published, narrow your focus as much as possible.

The eternal question is whether you should initially spend time thinking of a topic or researching the market. In truth, I don't think it makes that much difference. You have to do both anyway. As I'll point out later, spending time on these two processes will result in far fewer rejections.

Here is how I do it. I prefer to carefully search for a topic idea. I write a one- or two-sentence "high concept" blurb. I then consult my database to determine which magazines might want my article.

But other writers work in reverse order. They go to the library, spend considerable time looking at the last couple of issues of selected magazines and try to glean a topic that might appeal to these markets.

No matter what you do, narrow the focus. Let's say you write on business matters. A topic such as credit card fraud is just too broad for the short pieces you will be doing. Take one facet of fraud, such as how merchants should handle cards reported stolen when they call in for authorization. You could break this down further by concentrating on how store clerks might be able to recognize stolen cards by the behavior of the customer. Your article might be "Stolen Card Users: Body Language Gives Them Away." If you write on medical issues, an article on warts is too broad. Say you find some study that suggests that eating broccoli prevents warts. Keep breaking down the concept. Will broccoli prevent all warts? What age groups are affected? How should the vegetable be cooked? Why do doctors think this occurs? By the time you're done, your topic might be "New Research Shows Baked Broccoli Can Prevent Warts in Teenagers."

Whatever your area of expertise, make sure you limit the scope. Remember that editors look for topics that fit the niche market of their magazine. Your job is to provide those topics.

In deciding where to send your work, there is no substitute for actual market research. Go to the library and peruse all the magazines and newspapers you think might be interested in the piece. Spend time with each publication. Consider how it's organized, make notes of the visuals, see who the advertisers are. Check the length of the articles, the slant of its editorial policy (you don't want to send a article on hunting to an outdoor magazine with an anti-hunting slant).

---

*TIP: If you can come up with an article that can be tied to a magazine's advertiser(s), you have a winner. For example, if you do an article on outdoor furniture and mention (at length) some company that advertises in* Lawn Furniture Gazette, *you can take it to the bank!*

---

When you do your research, make mental notes on how you might slightly change an article to make it more marketable to a particular magazine. For example, if you do a piece on the "History of the American Rose," a magazine involved with decorating and flower arrangement would want a piece slanted toward the decorative. Another magazine might want a slant on gardening, protection from bugs, etc. Two-thirds of each article would be the same. However, you would spend 500-700 words discussing either the decorative possibilities of roses, or protecting them from insects, weather, etc.

---

*TIP: You can easily get two articles for the "price" of one by slanting the same material toward two different publications. Look for these opportunities.*

---

Many PEs make the mistake of thinking that if they send the same article out to a hundred magazines, they are likely to make at least one sale. What they don't know is that editors are looking for pieces at least slightly tailored to their particular magazine. This piece of advice alone will make you more sales than anything else you will learn. *Find a way to tailor each article to the magazine you're sending it to.*

When I said that you should abandon the old notion of single submissions, I didn't mean that you should shot-gun the piece to every media that could possibly use it. This is foolish and will accomplish nothing other than help the post office overcome its deficit.

---

*TIP*: Amateurs write a piece, make fifty copies, and send it to every book (slang for magazine) listed in Writer's Market that could be interested. The pro selects one, five, or ten really good bets and tailors the piece for each one.

---

## Who and How?

You should be familiar with one section of every piece of print media: the "masthead." It lists who's who at the magazine, along with the address and phone number. You can learn a lot from the masthead besides names, but it is the names and address that you want to note.

A good rule of thumb is to not send your article to the top name on the masthead. You especially don't want to send it to the managing editor, because the managing editor is usually responsible for the nuts and bolts of the whole magazine, ads, printing, budget, etc. You want to find the editor who selects pieces like yours. On smaller magazines, the editor or senior editor selects all the material. However many magazines have editors for different departments of the publication.

I suggest that you call the magazine and ask to whom you should send your piece. The receptionist might way, "Just send it along and someone will read it." Right! It will end up in the *slush pile* (you'll see this term often in writer's magazines) with other manuscripts with no specific name on the address. Often the person who answers the phone (perhaps an intern English major from the local college) will not know who does what at the magazine. Ask to speak to the editor by name or his/her assistant (get the name from the masthead or *Writer's Market*). When you get someone on the phone, don't go into a long dog-and-pony show. Just say "Ms./Mr. Jones, I'd like to submit an article on _____ (travel, trucking, banking, computer communications, etc.) Can you please tell me who to address it to and their phone and fax number?" Say thank you, and get off the phone.

---

**COMMENT**: *Sometimes the editor will answer and want it sent to him or her or will connect you to the proper person. This is great. Make some small talk, but don't go into much detail. Reference the conversation in your cover letter.*

---

I take a totally different viewpoint than others on what you should send once you've decided where and to whom to send it. My advice is to forget the query letter and instead send the manuscript along with a short "pitch letter."

I believe that, for most authors, query letters are a waste of time. The literature on the subject of selling words has instructed authors to spend a ton of time on the query letter in hope of enticing the editor to give you a green light to write and submit an article. If you were writing long pieces that take weeks of research and entail significant expense, the query letter is a good idea. But for PEs who are going to submit short pieces, I say go ahead and send the entire work.

A query letter in which an unknown writer says she can write an article on such and such a topic comes across to many editors as just so much blue sky. (In the computer industry it's called vaporware!) The editor doesn't know you, doesn't know if you know his publication, and doesn't know if you can even spell CAT without being spotted the C and the T!

Sending the entire article shows the editor your merchandise. He or she has something to judge you by as opposed to a clever query letter promising the world.

Look at it this way. If the subject is of no interest to the editors you'll get a rejection notice. But, if the subject is good and you only send a query, you'll get a letter or a call back saying that you should write and submit the piece. When the editor reads it a week or so later (longer if the piece was not already written), he might have lost his initial interest in the topic.

When you send the manuscript, even if the subject is not of immediate interest to the editor, she might glance at it for no other reason than it's there. Editors are people too! They get curious, and think "What the hell, I'll read a few paragraphs." If the work is good, you have a chance of selling it right then and there. If it's bad or of no interest, you'll still get rejected. So, you're no worse off than if you just queried.

Editors may pay lip service to the concept of "query first," but by and large they read almost everything addressed to them, so long as it's presented well. Here and there an editor might be less than pleased that an author (lowly creatures that we are!) did not query first. But, if the work is good and the editor can use it, (in fact, needs it), he will not make a big deal about you breaking the "query first" convention.

It makes sense. When you send a query, you're asking an editor to make a judgment without most of the evidence. The editor only has the "nature" of the topic to consider. Will it work or not? However, when you send the goods, you give the editor a chance to expand the horizons of his publication. You're giving him something to ponder. The editor can see, feel, smell, taste, and experience your product. If it's any good, perhaps he will be inclined to accept the piece "on a lark." That's unlikely with a query.

The big criticism I receive is from editors who ask, "Do you honestly believe someone can write an article for my magazine that's the exact topic, slant, structure, style, and content that I would want without some advance information?" The answer is "Yes!" It's done all the time. If you study your market, I mean really know what types of articles the publications you submit to most often print, you can develop a marketable piece without help from an editor. Believe me, if you spend a few hours looking at back issues of a particular magazine, you'll learn what a publication wants.

> *TIP:* If you can't get a sense of what a specific publication is looking for, than don't submit to them. If you don't know your market, you can't sell into it. It's that simple.

The truth of the matter is that most editors don't really know what they want, except within very broad limits. On the phone, they probably won't tell you more than you can easily gain by reading a few issues of their magazine. One fact of life in the publishing business is that most editors move from job to job every two years. Few editors stay on their jobs long enough to be able to tell you how to develop an article that they would buy.

> *COMMENT:* If you ask an editor about what slant you should take, she will likely tell you to read the magazine and develop your piece along the lines of similar articles! Many editors don't know the history of their own publications.

As I said earlier, if you read the writer's magazines, you'll hear editors howl about wanting queries only. But believe me, editors sometimes face deadlines when some author couldn't (or didn't) produce the manuscript after his query was given a green light. That editor will be very glad to find your piece in his file and you'll get a call ASAP asking if the article is still for sale. (Many editors keep good material they rejected on file for several months.)

## Make Your Pitch

Instead of sending a query letter that begs the editor to allow you to send your merchandise, send the manuscript along with a *pitch letter*. This is different from a query and is easier to write.

Half the pages of books and magazines on writing are devoted to showing authors how to write query letters that will get them writing assignments. And every year, the writers of these articles try to outdo themselves with cuteness, hype, or manipulation. The more I read clever query letters, the more I'm convinced that authors believe they can get an editor to take a bad or inappropriate piece by writing a great sales letter.

---

**COMMENT:** *Twenty years ago, when people were not bombarded with so much hype and exaggeration in advertising, a clever query may have sold mediocre pieces. Today, all of us are deluged with direct mail pitches to the point of numbness. I know editors who never read query letters that sound like they were written by a used car salespeople.*

---

Now don't get me wrong, the purpose of the pitch letter is to sell. However, you don't have to hit the editor over the head with heavy hype to do it. Writer-PEs often make the mistake of composing letters that are too long. They tell the editor, at great length, what the piece is about, how it was written, why it's so good, and why the editor should buy it.

Editors are not stupid. The vast majority are perfectly capable of determining if a piece is good or bad, right or wrong for their editorial content. However, when faced with lots of good material, many have trouble deciding what to buy and what to pass. You need to help them make this decision.

Since you are sending the manuscript, there is no point in wasting ink (toner) describing the piece in detail. What you want to emphasize is why the editor should buy it. And the "why" is always the same basic reason: because readers will benefit from it. Remember the concept of reader take-away? This is what you're selling, benefits. You're not selling the content of your work (the topic and style) or the features (charts, photos, sidebars). You're selling the benefit(s) the editor's customers will receive by reading the piece.

You don't need to hype the piece. The article should sell itself. You do need to convince the editor that buying it is a wise decision. Is this hard? Not if you understand the concept of reader take-away. In the final analysis, this will convince the editor to buy. Your piece might be topical, interesting, and cleverly written. But if the editor doesn't think that readers will find it useful within the context of the whole magazine, he or she will pass. By the same token, your article might be rather mundane, poorly constructed, and not the most topical subject in the genre. But if you sell the editor on its benefits to the reader, you'll get the green light.

---

**COMMENT:** If you sell the editor on an article's benefits, even if the piece is poorly written, he or she may buy it anyway and assign a junior editor to polish it up.

---

How do you write a pitch letter? That's like asking how to propose marriage. There are thousands of ways to do both. Writing a pitch letter depends on your subject, your audience, and your personal writing style. However, each pitch letter should have these basic elements:

**The Opening.** Write a few sentences describing the piece. I don't believe in clever opening sentence "hooks." Editors have seen them all, and you're not likely to come up with one they haven't seen previously. I often use a few simple sentences to describe my topic: *The information superhighway is the marketing medium of the future. It's also a most misunderstood medium. My article "How To Profit Over The Internet" addresses both of these issues.* I've always believed that if you can explain your topic in three quick sentences, it's narrow enough for a short piece.

---

*TIP*: A formula I like is what I call the "syllogistic opening." In simple terms: this plus this, therefore that! I like to use two sentences that relate to my topic and tie them together with a third. Read the above example again.

---

Whatever you do, please don't write: *The enclosed article is about how businesses can use the information highway. I think you'll find it interesting.* This is what a seventh grader would write and editors seldom buy articles from seventh graders! Be imaginative, but stay away from cute.

**The Sell**. This is the heart of your pitch letter. It doesn't have to be long, it just has to be convincing. Tell the editor what the reader will gain by reading the article. *This piece outlines steps a business should take to prepare for the new marketing methods. Executives will learn what technology investments have the best chance for profit. Mid-level marketing managers especially will benefit from the discussion on positioning their products to take advantage of on-line marketing opportunities. Technical management will be able to determine if their company's communication infrastructure will lend itself to these new opportunities. Most importantly, readers will come away with a clear understanding of what the information highway will and will not do for their business.* This is short, sweet and to the point. Notice that I don't go into a long dog-and-pony show on what the article is about, what it covers, or how easy to it is to understand. I stick to the basic reader take-aways. As I always tell writers, sell the benefits and you sell the article.

---

*TIP: You might want to look through the many books out there on how to write query letters. Just remember, you're not querying; you're pitching. By now you should know the difference.*

---

**The Threat.** I get a lot of criticism for this part of the letter, but I believe it works and works well! In a direct and polite way, I tell the editor that I'm making multiple submissions and often to which other publications. *I'm always up-front with my editors. This piece is being simultaneously sent to several other publications including Compuclown, Infogeek, and Megatwit. If you would like first rights to the article, please call or fax me ASAP.*

This brings up the topic of rights (which I will talk about in the next chapter). What you're selling here is usually called "first North American serial rights." This is fancy wording for the opportunity to publish this before anyone else.

---

*COMMENT: Note that if this had already been published and you were looking for a resale, you would state this and probably send a clip of the original article. Editors in non-competing markets often buy pieces that have been successful elsewhere.*

---

The purpose of "the threat" is to motivate editors to act and act now. If they don't move on it, they might lose it. By including the names of other magazines, I increase the pressure for the editor to make a decision. Editors know that good articles do not stay in the marketplace for long.

Some people think that I'm doing a hard sell by using "the threat." Not true! I haven't lied, or even stretched the truth. I have stated a fact of business life. I'm telling my customer they have an opportunity. If they don't take it now, perhaps someone else will. I don't know if this is a threat or a motivator. All I know is that it works if done correctly.

---

COMMENT: *Sometimes you'll get a rejection saying the magazine doesn't read articles sent as part of a multiple submission. Don't believe it. It got read, if for no other reason than to see what the competition was getting!*

---

**The Price**. I suggest that your pitch letter include a statement telling the editor what you want for the piece. Always ask for $50 more than you're willing to take and never ask the price listed in *Writer's Market*. Also, if you're making multiple submissions, don't use the same price since some magazines are probably willing to pay more than others. I also include the word-count in the statement on price. A price of $200 for 1,800 words sounds better than $200 for 4 pages. And 11.1 cents a word sounds even better! Finally state that you'll only sell the article if you receive payment "on acceptance." *The cost to Megatwit Magazine for the 1,765 word article will be $225 (12.7 cents a word) payable to the author upon acceptance.*

Some people don't like to put the price in the pitch letter. But if you don't, be prepared to bargain your terms upward, because the editor is likely to make you a low-ball offer.

You still may get a low-ball offer by stating your price, but since you've kicked up the amount, there is room for negotiation. Some writers go so far as to include a four-word statement after mentioning the amount: *This price is firm.*

If your work is any good, the magazine is not going to nickel and dime you for $50 or even $100 dollars. However, if you're asking $800 from an editor of a small circulation magazine, don't be surprised when he or she comes back with a figure of $150. If you don't come down, they will have to reject it.

---

*COMMENT: Price rejections don't usually happen unless you're way, way out of the ball park. The managing editor (the one in charge of the money!) will call or write you and try to work a deal.*

---

**The Qualification Statement.** You should include in your letter a short paragraph telling the editor why you're an expert on the subject as well as any other qualifications you might have. This is not the time to be modest. Say anything and everything that might convince the editor that the piece was done by a knowledgeable writer. It's not necessary to write a resume, just put down some convincing facts. If you've been published before, let the editor know. Here is some wording that I use, which you can modify for your own experience. *Having worked in the computer industry for the past 17 years, I'm a recognized expert in data communications. I believe you'll find this article representative of my experience. FYI, I enclose a clip from my recent article published in Compunerd.*

Never, never, never tell an editor that you're a beginning writer. If you write a professional looking pitch letter, you'll look just like the seasoned pro whose letter the editor just finished reading. This is another reason you should just send the article instead of relying on a clever query letter to sell your piece. If the article is good, the editors won't know it's your first piece. If they ask, tell them you've been published in "in-house" publications. It doesn't count for much, but it's better than saying you've never been published or that you're a first-timer.

---

*COMMENT: Think about this. You're only an unpublished writer once . . . never again.*

---

**The Last Word.** Don't end your letter with some trite phrase about hoping the editor will like your work and that you look forward to hearing from her. Instead, be dramatic. Say something, anything, that will get the editor to pick up your piece and start reading. *"Selling On The Network" is the kind of information business readers are searching for. It's perfect for Megatwit Magazine.* I've known writers to challenge an editor. *You should read this now. It's the kind of work you're looking for.* Some writers will politely play one magazine off against another. *Infogeek has bought my work before. I believe Megatwit will be equally interested in considering my material.* Or, you can play another game. Instead of making multiple submissions, tell the editor that if you don't hear from her by a certain date (make it 48 hours after you think she will get the piece), you will send it to the competition. *I believe Megatwit is the publication most suitable for this work. If I don't hear from you by the close of business on April 1, I will submit to Infogeek.*

I purposely do not include a sample pitch letter because I don't want tens of thousands of readers copying it. If everyone uses the same letter, it will not have the desired effect. Use the building blocks that I've presented and compose your own pitch letter. You can be creative, but stay away from cute. Remember, the main purpose of the letter is not to sell the piece, but to get the editor to read it NOW.

---

**COMMENT**: *You usually can't sell a poorly done article even with a great pitch letter. Editors are not stupid. You can get them to read it but not buy it. The work must stand on its own merits. With the right sales pitch, good work should sell. (Even with a bad sales pitch, good work will sell, but not as quickly!)*

---

## What Will You Take for It?

You'll have to decide what you want your bottom line to be. Except in rare instances, I don't believe any writer should ever make or accept any offer below ten cents a word.

I'll give you a few general guidelines about the publishing business, but remember that every situation is unique. You can charge more to magazines that publish to a large city audience than to those that have a rural or small town readership. The coastal markets generally pay more than the heartland. Most often, nonprofit organizations cannot pay as much for your piece as for-profit magazines. Newspapers usually pay less than magazines do.

Every edition of *Writer's Market* has a chapter on rates. This is a general compendium, but it's very helpful. Be sure to take a look at it. As I mentioned earlier, the rates you see in individual listings in *Writer's Market* are usually low-ball figures.

Here are words of truth you won't hear from anyone else: Most editorial editors could care less what an article costs. The business side of their publication is not important to them (except for their own salaries!) That is the role of the managing editor (sometimes called the executive editor) or publisher. Editorial editors do realize that the more the magazine makes, the bigger their salary. Editors of all stripes know that writers are vain. The biggest secret, the plain unspoken truth, is that editors know that many (maybe a majority of) writers will gladly trade dollars for a byline. Editors sincerely believe that they can get your work cheap! They have before with other writers.

## The Clip Myth

Writers cause their own low-pay problems. They believe that by collecting a string of writing credits (clips), they can someday trade these in for big-time writing assignments that pay *mucho dinero*. Well, that doesn't happen. What does happen is they spend years virtually giving their labor away for peanuts.

Another myth in the business is believing that publishing a piece in this month's magazine will significantly help you get published in another magazine next month. As I said earlier, each piece stands on its own merits. If it's no good, it won't get ink.

But writers refuse to believe this. They have been fed the party line for so long that they believe it. Here is the phone conversation that takes place thousands of times a day: "Ms. Smith? This is John Jones at *Rocks and Soil* magazine. We want to accept your article, but $250 is beyond our budget. We know that since *Rocks and Soil* is one of the leading gardening mags, having a piece published with us will really help you build your career. We can offer you $75." Ms. Smith figures that, yes, she'll be able to send a clip from *Rocks And Soil* off to other magazines who will accept her articles for big fees. So, she takes the $75. A few months later, she sends a piece off to *Weeds and Seeds* along with the clip from *Rocks and Soil*. *Weeds and Seeds* tells her the same thing and she figures that, yes, *two* clips will *really* get her going. So, again, she takes five cents a word.

> **COMMENT**: *Editors play all sorts of mind games on writers. They seem to sense that writers are the worst business people on the face of the earth!*

There is some truth that having a portfolio of clips will make it easier for you to get published. The key word is easier - not automatic! Editors are not interested in what you did yesterday, last week, or last year. What do you have for them now? Is it any good? What will it cost them? PEs on a retirement pension probably don't have to get top dollar for their work. But they should not let editors take advantage of them.

## Don't Give It Away

I don't care if you have a million dollar a year pension. You should not give away your work. Decide what your bottom line is for a piece and stick to it. If you worked ten hours on a 1,500 word piece and you think you should get $30/hr., then charge the $300. It works out to 20 cents a word, definitely within the range of many publications.

One of the best ways you can determine what to charge is to join a local writers group. Almost every community has one or more of these (some are for fiction writers, others for nonfiction people). Ask the librarian how to contact one of these groups. Go to the meetings and network with the members to learn what they are charging.

> *TIP*: Ask other writers who are more serious about the business side of writing what they charge. Remember that many still take low pay because they believe in the clip myth.

When it comes to negotiation, keep these ideas in mind. If an editor tells you she can't pay what you want, you're in a position of strength. The magazine *wants* your work. There are two things you can do, but you can't do both!

You can stick by your guns. If you priced the piece correctly, and you tell the editor that you firmly believe the article is worth your price and that you won't accept less, half of the time they will cave in and meet your price. They'll usually say something like, "I have to check with the managing editor." An hour or a day later, they call back to tell you the good news.

If you think you need to bargain, ask the editor what she had in mind. *However, once you do this, it will be next to impossible to get your original price.* You have opened the door to negotiation. A smart editor will ask you what is the least you would be willing to take. A smart writer will counter the question by asking the editor what is the most the magazine would be willing to pay. Never be the first to mention a figure. There are no rules, standards, or conventions to negotiating a price. A good editor who does price negotiation every day will always beat a writer who doesn't often enter the negotiation pit! That's why I advise people who don't mind bargaining with editors to price their work a few dollars above their bottom line.

---

*TIP: I try to price my work correctly and I don't negotiate. Take it or leave it works best for me.*

---

Some editors will read you the clip myth. Some will give you the magazine's editorial policy on payment limits. Some might even try to intimidate you by saying that you're missing a chance of a lifetime to get published in their book. But down deep they know that if the work is good, someone else will buy it at a price close to what you're asking (if it's reasonable). So, if you're willing, come down a few dollars, but don't give it away.

---

*TIP: If the editor persists in offering less than you believe your article is worth, say this: "Ms. Editor, I understand what you're saying. But if your magazine wants the piece, I'm going to assume that Infogeek will also, so you can understand why I can't take your offer."*

---

## Forget the SASE

A sacred cow of the writing world has been the SASE (self-addressed stamped envelope). Again, I advise against convention, mainly because it doesn't serve much purpose for you. Also, why should you pay the magazine's postage?

Writers include a SASE to get their work back. In the days when work was done on a typewriter, when copying fees were high, and when writers only made single submissions, it made sense to get the manuscript back. Modern technology has made the SASE obsolete. Since you're only sending four or five pages which can be run out on your computer in a matter of minutes at roughly two cents a page, you don't need the piece back. Plus, you save by not having to pay the postage.

The SASE was also done as a convenience for the editor. Writers would have a reply form that had many reasons why the material was being returned. Do you want to know that the piece "is not of interest at this time"? Yes, you do. But since you're sending the piece out to many markets, the information is not all that valuable. I have no problem including a fill-in form with your articles so editors can give you feedback on why they are not buying it. But unless you pay close attention to those reasons, I don't think it's worth your postage. Many magazines have their own rejection forms and many don't get too many articles so they can afford the postage.

You might want to include a one-page reply form that has the name of the magazine, the title of the article, and a request for the editor to use the remaining space for any comments. I wouldn't give them boxes to check since the comments are more important, especially if they jot down a few lines on how the piece could be improved. Many editors will write a few lines telling you why they can't buy it and how it could be improved.

*COMMENT: Most editors who see a piece of work they like but can't buy for some reason (maybe they bought a similar piece yesterday!) will be happy to write a short note on your form encouraging you to submit another piece.*

If you have a fax machine or fax service (much advised), request that the editor fax the form to you. Having a fax number is helpful because many editors will compose a "positive" rejection on their computer and fax it from the computer without printing it out. I'm believe the fax machine is more important than the telephone.

## Fax, Don't Call

It used to be standard practice to wait a few weeks and call an editor to whom you sent work. This is changing. With the downsizing (a.k.a. layoffs) that has occurred in the industry, magazine staffing has been pared. Many editors handle work for more than one department of a magazine, or work for different magazines within a conglomerate. Editors are busy, and don't have time to talk to everyone who submits work. Thus, voice mail was invented! So, you can call, but you may not reach a human.

Instead of calling, compose a quick note and fax it at night to the editor's office. True, it might require a quick call and get the fax number, but the secretary can give you that; you don't need to reach the editor. When the editor comes in the next morning, perhaps the first thing she will see is your note and perhaps she will call or fax you about your submission.

## A Done Deal

When a magazine or paper decides to buy your piece they may call or fax you. Some will just send you a form letter in the mail along with a contract to sign. Some just send you a check with a note.

If you get a call from an editor (usually an editorial assistant), don't go crazy on the phone. That's the mark of an amateur. You've worked hard to show you're a pro, so don't go on and on thanking the editor for taking your work. Simply say something like: "I'm glad you liked the piece, Ms. Smith. When can I expect the contract?" Don't be cold, but don't gush! Remember, to the editor it's just a business deal. It should be that to you also. Do your victory dance after you hang up.

> **COMMENT**: Vince Lombardi once said to a young player who would wildly jump up and down in the end-zone, "Son, try to act like you've been there before!"

Don't expect a check to arrive the next day. Most publications buy articles one to three months in advance of publication. While you should insist on payment upon acceptance, there's not much you can do if payment does not arrive before the pub date. However, many magazines pay their writers in a timely fashion. Also, you'll probably have to sign the contract they provide (see next chapter). Once you return the contract, they will usually cut your check at the beginning of the next month.

> **TIP**: I write a thank-you note after I get a check from a publication, not before.

## Rejection

A billion words have been written on how to handle rejection, what to do about rejection, how to channel rejection into productive activity and so on. I have nothing against your reading and understanding different theories and methods writers use to cope with having their work turned down. However, I suggest you spend time learning how not to be rejected in the first place.

> **COMMENT:** When I took boxing in college, the coach gave me these words of wisdom: He said, "You can spend equal time learning how to take a punch as opposed to learning how to avoid taking a punch. What's the better use of your time?"

Rejection is a fact of life in the writing business. It's going to happen and there is little you can do about it. Assuming you wrote a good piece, a rejection is nothing more than an editor telling you she can't use this article right now. If the same article is rejected by 15 different magazines, then I venture to say that it's not a marketable piece.

I see brilliantly written, factual, well conceived pieces that are a joy to read, but don't sell. Why? There are two reasons: (1) The topics are poorly selected. (2) The writer does not sell the editor on the value of the piece.

This is what avoiding rejection (and making sales) is all about. You don't have to write Pulitzer Prize material. You don't have to be a talent like Bombeck or Rooney. You can sometimes write poorly (that's what editors are for!), but you must come up with material that is topical and you must convince editors to buy.

With all the emphasis on style, construction, point of view, and other technical aspects of the craft, I'm convinced that most analysts of the writing business miss the point. Editors don't reject articles, they reject topics. Why? Because most pieces submitted by writers are on topics that have been published to death. If you're going to get a piece published about how the law enforcement war on drugs has been a failure, it better be prizewinning material because it has been done, and done, and done! But come up with a good piece on making drug possession a capital offense and you probably have a winner (whether they agree or disagree, readers would be interested!). When was the last time you read a piece about publicly executing all drug users who commit crime? Probably not recently! Editors are tired of running articles about drugs as a sickness needing to be treated. Write a piece on drugs being a crime that requires harsh punishment (as Arab countries practice) and you have a sale, probably multiple sales.

The best way to avoid rejection is to come up with ways to avoid rejection! It sounds silly, but it's the absolute truth. And the best way to avoid the rejection of your writing is to read. That's right, read. See what's out there in your field of interest and do something different. Maybe not *totally different*, but different enough to sell an editor on the "newness" of the piece.

---

**COMMENT**: *One of my favorite quotes is from John D. Rockefeller: "Take something common and make it uncommon."*

---

I said above that if your article is rejected by 15 editors, it's either poorly done or not marketable. Sure, *Gone With The Wind* was rejected umpteen times then finally accepted. But that's the exception, not the rule. One thing to remember is that today's rejection can become tomorrow's acceptance. It often happens that an editor will buy a piece he turned down six months ago.

This is usually because the author was way out "in front" of an issue that later became popular. For example, a few years ago writers who submitted articles on "total quality management" received rejections left and right from the business press. Then TQM boomed and editors scrounged their files for TQM pieces to fill their pages.

> **COMMENT**: It's hard to be way out in front of an issue anymore because there is so much media (print, broadcast, cable, on-line). Editors are always on the prowl for the new and different to fill their pages or air time. The competition for material is murder. Writers with a knack for recognizing trends have a terrific advantage.

One strategy writers use to avoid "total" rejection is to hold back their marketing efforts. They will write a piece with the idea of sending it to 10 markets. But, they only send it to five. The reasoning is that if all five reject it, perhaps one editor will write a short explanation on how the piece can be improved. The writer then "fixes" the piece and sends it to the other five.

Rejection is a particularly sensitive issue in the writing world because of the personal nature of the product. If you go into a shoe store, try on 10 pairs of shoes and buy none, the salesperson will not take it personally. After all, he didn't design or make the shoes. However, writers design and craft the product they sell. How-to books instruct writers not to take rejection personally. I disagree only because I don't think it's logically possible to separate yourself from your product. A single rejection is a rejection of your article. Twenty rejections is a rejection of you as a writer.

If you've done your marketing research, send out a piece to ten good prospects, and come up empty, you did something wrong. Maybe you thought the topic was more marketable than it was. Perhaps you sent an interview piece to a magazine that never does interviews. Perhaps the piece did not cover the topic thoroughly enough. Whatever the reason(s), learn something from the experience. Figure out what you did wrong, why the piece was roundly rejected.

Don't dwell on the rejection; focus on your future acceptance! Decide which type of writer you'll be: one who is always *finishing* projects, or one who is getting rejections. The first writer never makes a submission because he is scared of rejection and thus, his projects never get completed. The second writer gets sales along with rejections.

In other words, finish the article, send it in, and see what happens. Don't be a hostage to doubt, indecision, and fear. Don't be a wallflower! Take action! Do it!

---

**COMMENT**: *I have an award that hangs in my office. It was given to me when I managed a large project for a client. It proudly says: "Alan Canton - Often Wrong But Never In Doubt!"*

---

One thing you need to remember is that the number of rejections per article is not important. It's the number of sales per article that you care about. Let's say you're pretty slow or don't want to work too hard. In one month you turn out five pieces and send each to 15 markets. One article bombs, but each of the others are accepted. Look at the results:. 15 rejections for the bomb, 14 rejections and 1 acceptance each for the other four = 4 acceptances and 71 rejections. But, you sold 4 out of 5 articles, which is an 80% success rate. Let's say you got $220 for each sale. You made $880 with an out of pocket expense of $39 (75 submissions at $0.52 each for postage). You net $841. If you can do this each month you'll net $10,092 for the year. We're talking 5 articles at 8 hours each. So, $841 divided by 40 hours is $21 and change per hour. Think about what you would be making if 25% of your sold articles sell again in another market.

The important thing is not to give up. Rework your products and send them to different markets. Sure, you're going to get a few bonehead editors who send your articles back because you didn't query first. (Some people rework and reprint the pitch letter and send it as a query with an apology). You're going to pick up lots of rejection slips. But if you stay with it, you *will* make sales and you *will* make money. So don't give up, take action!

---

**TIP**: *Canton's law of taking action: If you have a good idea, do it. It's always easier to apologize later for not doing it "right" than to get permission in the first place.*

---

## We Don't Want That, We Want This!

It may happen earlier than you expect. You've sent article after article to *Retail Footwear News*, but no sales, just postcard rejections. Then, out of the blue, the editor calls to say that they have another subject in mind. Would you be interested in doing it? They've read your other work and think you can do this job. They can't make assurances, but they will "give it every consideration," if you write the piece. Should you do it?

Obviously you should, but with reservations. It's important to find out why they rejected your other articles. If the editor called you, she is familiar with your work and should be able to explain why your previous articles were rejected. Tell her you need to know so that this piece won't suffer the same fate.

As long as the request is within your skill level and you feel confident that you can bring it off, take the assignment. It may be an easy one as the editor is likely to tell you exactly what she wants covered, whom to speak with, and what slant to take. You should feel pretty good about yourself. Of the ten billion people she could have called, she called you.

Fax her a letter and an outline of the proposed article to be sure you agree on the assignment. This is also a good time to mention or repeat what you expect to be paid, and when you expect to submit the article.

---

*TIP*: Some editors give assignments and demand exclusive rights, not first time rights. Unless you're positive you could never sell the piece to anyone else, don't take the assignment. But if you have an entire file drawer of article ideas, and feel that you can safely burn one, then go ahead.

---

If you accept an assignment that will take a lot of your time (say 20 or 30 hours over several weeks instead of the usual 6 or 8 hours), try to negotiate what is known as a kill fee. This usually pays you half your rate if the editor cancels the assignment in mid-flight. Kill fee arrangements are most often done on long, big-dollar articles that take the author months to produce. Unless you're well known to the editor, you probably won't get a kill fee, but at least ask for one. It makes you sound professional.

## Develop Your Market Nose

No matter what your genre, always ask yourself the eternal question: "What can I write about that people want to read?" When you read an article in a trade magazine, try to figure out why the editor accepted the piece. If you can get into the head of the customer, you have a great chance of providing what she needs.

When you see a story on TV ask yourself if you can adapt something from it to your genre. Perhaps you see a segment on the news about baby boomers thinking about retirement. Does this relate to your area? Probably does, but how?

Talk to people in the industry or interest area you cover. Call some local person in your field and ask what is hot in the business. Whenever you see something new or different, think about which market might publish information about it.

Keep your mind active and you'll soon develop a kind of radar for what will and what won't sell. Later on, your radar will be fine-tuned enough to distinguish between an article that is a sure sale and one that's just a good bet.

Be conscious of everything going on in the world around you and it will all come to you. Your open and inquisitive mind will reap you greater rewards than all the writing talent in the world.

# 8

. . . . . . . . . . . . . . . . .

## THE WRITING BUSINESS NUTS AND BOLTS

## The Business of Business

No matter what business you're in, certain basics are common to all ventures. Entire books have been written about how to set up a business and if you were going to start a retail or service business needing lots of equipment and many employees, you would be wise to get one of these books. But for the typical writing business run from home, you can learn all you need to know from the pages that follow.

Even the simplest of businesses can be made complex! You can over-computerize, over-record-keep, and even over-plan. Some compulsive people need to know to the last detail how their business is doing, even if the information does them little good. I urge you to adopt the KISS method (Keep It Simple, Stupid!).

People waste more time on process than they invest in substance. What's the difference? I call process all those activities that are necessary, but that do not directly contribute to your bottom line. For example, paying bills is process. Going to the store to buy paper is process. Spending two hours learning how to use a software program is process. Spending thirty minutes recording just the right answering machine message is process. Talking to anyone wanting to sell you something is process.

In the writing business, writing is substance. Time in the library doing research is substance. Talking to an editor is substance. Reading back issues of a magazine to decide if it's a good market is substance. Substance activities bring in money are must-do activities. Process activities support substance activities.

It's important to make good use of your time if you want to have something substantive to show for it (that is, money.) Otherwise, you end up like many writers who have the most wonderful accounting system, the world's greatest database program, a state-of-the-art fax-answering machine hookup, and a beautiful color-coded filing system. They raise process to an art form, and never have any sales!

Why does this happen? Simple. Process is easy because it's directed. In other words, you know how to accomplish the process activities. For example, to pay your bills you first do A, then you do B, and finally you do C. It's a no-brainer. People like spending time on processes because it's familiar; it's what they did most of their working lives. Most jobs are a small part of a large process.

Most substance activities, on the other hand, have no rules or formats. Substance is creative. There are no starting or stopping points. Sitting in front of a blank screen and putting down an outline for an article is a far different activity from sitting at the computer and entering figures into your accounting program.

People avoid substance because ego is involved in the final outcome. There's little fear of failure in balancing books. But creating a new article is the ultimate test: Will I succeed in selling it? We avoid thinking about rejection and failure; we would rather take a nice safe path: doing a process activity.

> **COMMENT**: This happens to a lot to salespeople. They spend less and less time looking for new customers (substance) and more time selling to past customers (process). Or they spend most of their time on other process activities like updating their address book, reading product literature, or attending company meetings.

While I think it's important for you to follow the advice in these pages, you shouldn't get carried away. Most of what follows is process. While they may be necessary activities, it's important you keep your efforts in perspective. Don't over-complicate your business. Don't take on new processes that you either don't understand or which will have only marginal impact. Spend your time wisely. Keep it simple, stupid!

## A Single-Engine Business

Every business has a form or classification. You can choose a partnership, a corporation or a sole proprietorship (a.k.a. sole prop).

Almost all of you can forget the corporate form of business unless (and only if) your accountant or tax advisor says it would be to your advantage. Never, never, never become a corporation without consulting someone who knows what they're talking about. I won't spend time on the corporate format because I think it's usually a bad choice for most PEs. It's a paperwork nightmare and a pain in the butt at tax time.

> *COMMENT: You may see ads saying "incorporate in Nevada and escape taxes." This is a half truth. These ads are run by companies (sometimes law firms) that make money (fees) by forming corporations. Talk to your own advisor.*

The partnership form is OK if a friend wants to share the work and be in business with you. Be aware of one aspect of partnerships called "joint and several liability." This means that all the partners are liable for damages or collections even if only one partner obligated the business.

For example if Smith and Jones go into business and Jones signs a contract to buy $5,000 worth of computers, Smith is also liable for the debt. Not half of it, but the whole debt. Thus, if the business goes under, the store can sue either partner for the debt, since they are jointly as well as individually liable. Make sure that you and any potential partner understand that a creditor can come to either of you for total payment.

> *COMMENT: Most partnerships don't break up over money, but over differences in personality or business direction. Smith wants to do A and Jones wants to do B. Crash!*

If you plan to form a partnership, have a lawyer draw up a simple partnership agreement. Also, take a look at *The Partnership Book* by Dennis Clifford (Nolo Press, ISBN 0-87337-141-0).

The vast majority of writing businesses are sole props. What this means is that there's no legal or tax difference between your personal and your business property and income. Even though you may have a separate bank account for the business, the IRS and the law treat the business as just an extension of you! Thus, you're liable for all debts of the business. The sole prop is the easiest to set up, but there is no protection from liability.

---

**COMMENT**: *Don't be concerned with this. Writing businesses have little liability. So long as you don't libel someone, you won't be sued.*

---

## What's in a Name?

There's always much debate about whether writers should do business under their own name or under what is called a fictitious name. Since you'll be a sole prop, it makes no real difference to the IRS or state tax people. Most writers do business under their own names

In favor of using a different name, writers say it makes them look more professional to editors, and using another name provides flexibility to branch out into other business areas. For example, say you write on religious topics and do business with the company name "The Final Word." It would be easier to also do seminars or publish books under this name, than as Jane Doe.

To do business under a separate name, set up a bank account under that name and keep all business expenses and income separate from your personal account. Tax-wise, there is no difference; it's just a question of accountability. The IRS has a habit of classifying some individual businesses as a hobby and not allowing deductions for expenses. However, when you show that you actually operate as a for-profit business (using a business name is court-approved evidence of your intent), you can stand up and say: "This is a real business with a name, bank account, stationery, etc."

On the other hand, people who do business under their own name simply open another checking account at a different bank and use it for all business purposes. By keeping good records, the IRS will not classify you as a hobbyist. Also, when you file for your business name, you become "a public record." You'll get notices from every government taxing agency under the sun wanting you to fill out forms for their files. Even the telephone people may come after you because it's not legal to answer the phone with a business name if you're not paying business rates.

So where do I stand on the fictitious versus real name issue? I don't think it makes much difference. However, I think you gain just a little more by doing business under a fictitious name. I think any extra defense you can have against the IRS is important. I also think that a letterhead with a business name sends a more professional message to an editor than one with just your name. Thus, I recommend you think up a name for your writing business. But if you prefer to do business under your name, it is no big deal.

If you decide to get a business name, take this advice: be inventive. Some words relating to writing have been used in business names to the point of nausea (a zillion info-businesses use "wordsmith" in the title). Stay away from concepts like "electric pen" or "magic keyboard." They've all been used. Also, many editors equate "cute" names with amateurs.

> *TIP*: Here is my suggestion. Make your name refer to your genre. Use the word "group" or "editorial". For example, if you write on gardening, how about "The Green Writers Group." ? If you write on banking, how about "Bank Street Editorial" ? When the editor of Compunerd gets your pitch letter with the company name of "The Byte Writers Group," she'll feel she's dealing with a consummate pro.

To officially use a business name, you must file for it with the county in which you live. In most states you go to the county recorder's office, fill out a brief form, pay a small fee, then receive several copies of the forms stamped by the clerk. You then have to advertise the name in a newspaper once a week for four or five weeks. Usually, the office where you fill out the form has some drop-boxes from different newspapers in which you can put one copy of your form along with a check. The paper will take care of the rest. Their fee should be approximately $30 to $50.

One copy of the form is for the bank. You must give it to them in order to get a checking account in your fictitious business name.

If you have questions about how to get a "DBA-doing business as" name, ask a new accounts person at your bank. They will know the procedure well since they're always opening new business accounts with people who have just gone through the DBA process.

## A Space of Your Own

Have your own space for your writing business. In spite of the common reference to the guy who runs his business from his dining room table, it just doesn't work. You need a place where you can set up your computer and keep all your necessary odds and ends together. It's best to have your own office. If this is not possible, set up a desk in the corner of a room and do your business from there. You're going to end up collecting a mountain of stuff, so you need room for file cabinets and several bookshelves. You must also have several electrical outlets and a telephone jack.

You'll spend a lot of time in your office (or corner) so make it as nice as you can. It doesn't cost much to turn a spare bedroom into an office. You can buy used office furniture (look in the Yellow Pages) and an electrician won't charge more than a few hundred dollars to install additional outlets or telephone jacks if necessary.

---

*TIP*: I recommend you put your desk near the window. When you get a case of writer's block, looking out the window into the real world can help free up your creative energy. (Some writers prefer a windowless environment to avoid distractions!)

---

## Office Things

Go to any office supply store and you'll see a ton of stuff you can buy for your home office. Fortunately, you don't need much to get started. I'll briefly cover the important items you should have.

**Computer:** I beat this into the ground in an earlier chapter. This business requires a computer and good word processing software. I don't care if Andy Rooney uses a thirty-year-old beat up typewriter. You're not going to be effective unless you have and can use the premier writing tool of the day: your computer. End of sermon.

**Phone:** If your regular phone line is frequently in use, order another line for your business. Call the phone company and they will give you all the details. If some wiring must be done, it's less expensive than you might think. The phone company can do it or you can have someone else install what you need (most electricians can do this). If you want to legally answer the phone in your business name, then order a "business" line. The rate is slightly higher because there is no flat fee for local calling. You pay in the area of a penny a minute for each call. If you make a huge number of local calls, your bill could get pretty high, but since most of your business calls will be long distance (the penny does not apply) having a business line won't cost much more.

> *TIP: What a business line really gets you is a listing of your business name in directory assistance and in the Yellow Pages. Forget the Yellow Pages, but being in directory assistance might be important if you do commercial writing.*

If you're going to buy a new phone, shop around and try out several handsets. You may spend a lot of time on your phone, so find one that is comfortable to hold that does not hurt your ear. You'll be surprised at the difference in phones. Many phones, especially the so-called designer models, are really difficult to hold for long periods of time. While redial and hold features are nice, I don't believe phones with all those memory buttons are really worth the extra cost. Cordless phones are also an option for your business office, but some have poor sound clarity.

Speaker phones are basically a waste of money because callers can tell you are on one and will often request you not use it because it's hard to hear. Unless you need one for conferences, don't invest in the speaker phone feature.

You might also consider call waiting. I don't use it, but people who have it seem to like it. Make sure you learn how to disable call waiting. Than turn off call waiting when you don't wish your outgoing calls to be interrupted or when using a modem. An incoming call will usually disconnect you when using the modem.

Finally, if you do a lot of phone interviews consider investing in a headset. News reporters use these all the time. While the subject is speaking, the reporter can pound the key board taking notes or quotes. A company called Plantronics makes a good quality headset.

**Answering Machine**: You can get an answering service, but they're quite expensive. You'll also have to invest in call-forwarding. I advise that writers invest in a good quality answering machine. Never get one with a single tape. Make sure it has one tape for the outgoing message and another for incoming messages. Some machines allow you to record two outgoing messages to select from. Make sure the machine has a voice date-time stamp. Newer machines have voice help features you use when you retrieve your messages from a remote location. Also, make sure your machine can be turned on remotely. Many times I leave my office and forget to turn on the machine. I can call it from the car, enter a code, and it will turn on (or off). I also like the feature that allows me to change the outgoing message remotely.

Some people like the phone/answering machine combination. I advise against it because most of these units have fewer features than stand-alone answering machines do.

Some new machines on the market are all digital; there are no tapes. These are pretty neat but are also rather costly. Some only have enough memory for a limited number of calls, but that number keeps increasing as new models come out. Also, prices seem to be going down, so take a look.

Don't buy a cheap machine. Get a brand name machine with as many features as you can afford.

**Fax**: If you stay with the writing business, you'll eventually get a fax machine. To start out, you can get by with a fax service provided by many "mail" stores, stationary stores, as well as answering services. However, find a service close to your home since you go there often.

My advice is to buy a fax machine and use it as your desk phone. True, it takes up desk space, but it's handy.

> *COMMENT: A fax machine is just a regular telephone hooked up to a special modem connected to what is called a thermal printer. It's not very high-tech by today's standards.*

Fax machines come with a million different possible features. Make sure the machine you buy has these two important ones. The first is a page cutter. The cheap machines don't have this. They don't cut the paper from the roll until after the call is done, as opposed to cutting each page. Having a scroll of 7 fax pages (and they do curl up like a scroll!) is extremely inconvenient. The second feature is called a telephone answering device interface, or TAD. It's not the same as a phone/fax switch. The TAD allows you to connect an answering machine to your fax. When a call comes in, the answering machine (if you remembered to turn it on!) takes the call, but the fax "listens in." If it's a voice call, the fax machine does nothing. But if it's a fax call, the fax machine intercepts it, prints the fax and sends, a "hang-up" message to your answering machine. All the newer machines on the market today have this important feature.

By having a TAD, you can get voice or faxes anytime day or night. This means that you don't need a separate line for your fax. If you are in the office when the phone rings and you hear a beep, just press the start button on the fax machine. If you're out, the TAD takes care of everything. However, remember that while you're talking on your phone, nobody can fax you (they get a busy signal). This is the drawback of not having a dedicated phone line for your fax. Unless you expect a large volume of faxes, your business line can double as a fax line.

The TAD works about 98% of the time. However, some older fax machines that might call your machine do not work correctly with the TAD on your machine. If this gets to be a problem, can buy other switching hardware. Ask at your office supply store.

A nice feature on some fax machines allows you to turn on the fax-receive function from another extension. If I'm in my living room when a call comes in and I hear the beep or squawk from the sending fax machine when I pick up the handset, I can press three numbers on the phone and the fax machine will start receiving. I don't have to run into my office and press the start button.

Almost all fax machines double as a copy machine. You put in a page, press the copy button, and out comes a copy. It is great for single copies, but too slow for multiple output.

Fax machines come in two basic configurations: thermal or plain paper. Plain paper faxes use regular copy paper instead of rolled fax paper. They are expensive and are designed for large offices. If you can afford one, by all means get one, but all you need is an inexpensive thermal (roll paper) fax with a paper cutter.

---

**COMMENT**: In case you're interested, I use a Brother Intellifax machine. I like the Brother line because they make a special high-quality (and high cost) heavyweight paper for the machine.

---

Finally, you can get a modem with software that will fax directly from your computer. This is great for sending faxes, but not so terrific for receiving them. There are a lot of technical reasons for this that you really don't want to know about. My main objection is in leaving a $1,800 machine on 24 hours a day. Some say it is OK. However, I believe differently.

So, consider buying a stand alone-fax machine. It will probably become one of your most valuable and profitable investments.

> **COMMENT:** *When you consider the cost of paper, envelope, stamp, and time to stuff, it is far cheaper to fax, especially at night.*

**Paper Goods:** You'll want to have a nice letterhead as well as business cards. There are several ways you can go.

You can find a graphics designer (ask any quick printer or Kinko's) and have your letterhead designed and printed. You can have matching cards done also. Unfortunately, this can be rather expensive.

You can order from several catalogs that have pre-designed logos and styles. These are also expensive, but probably less so than having a letterhead custom made.

Finally, you can do what I do. I use a simple design for my letterhead that I do myself on my laser printer. Once you learn how to use your computer, the entire world of graphic design is open to you. I make my letterhead look dignified, much like a lawyer or doctor. You can be more creative if you prefer. I just find that a simple design works for the business market I write to. Below is a sample.

---

# The High-Tech Writers Group

*From information to knowledge. From knowledge to wisdom.*

123 Any Street
Your City, ST, 99876
123-456-7890

---

If you like logos, then by all means, use one. You can have a desktop designer make you one that you can import into your word processor and use on all your letters.

Because I design my letterhead on my word processor, from time to time I like to change the saying below the title. I have a number of letterhead styles, some plain and some fancy. Being able to change styles is a nice part of doing it yourself.

Business cards are just as important as your letterhead. However, no law says they have to match. Mine don't. I get them from a catalog house and change styles each time I run out.

---

*COMMENT: I'm convinced that letterheads and cards are overrated. Yes, you want to have nice materials, but no editor (or other business person) is going to make a definitive judgement on you based on your business card or letterhead. Sometimes too much "flash" can work against you.*

---

If you're going to use color, stay away from red because it does not fax well (it turns clay gray).

As for paper, use any color you want. However, I suggest you stick with a good white or ivory bond. If you use a laser printer, make sure the paper won't jam the machine. Most lasers will take most 20-pound papers. However, some textured papers don't take laser toner well.

If you order your letterhead from a catalog and you get one of those simulated engraved inks (raised lettering), make sure it is laser printer and fax machine safe. Some melt under the heat of a laser or fax machine. The catalog should tell you what inks are laser-safe.

**Postage:** There is no getting around the fact that postage meters are handy. Years ago they were quite cheap. However, the rates have gone up a lot. You can't own the meter: you can only rent it, and rent is based upon usage. The more you mail, the higher your monthly rental is. If you do the minimum mailing, your monthly rate is probably going to be around $15 to $20 a month. It sounds reasonable, but I don't believe $180 a year for a meter is a great use of funds. I use stamps.

You should also get an account with an overnight carrier like Fed Ex or UPS. Just call their toll-free number and request one. They will send you preprinted air labels with your company (or your) name on them.

Some of you might want to get a post office box. These come in handy if you travel a lot, if your mail comes late in the day, or if you don't want people to have your home address. An alternative is a box from a mail house like Mail Boxes, Etc. But be careful. What happens when you've given your address to lots of people and the mail house goes out of business? Some large franchise mail houses have this covered; the mail gets forwarded to another store for a few months. However, the mom and pop outfits don't have such backup.

**Where To Buy**: The best place to buy office supplies is the large warehouse stores or the discount chains like Office Depot. I prefer the discount chains because you can get their charge card and they will bill you. This is good for tax reasons. They also deliver. Finally, they will match the price of the warehouse store.

---

*TIP*: *Most chains say they will match any advertised price. However, the warehouse stores don't advertise. But talk to the chain-store manager and they will usually take your word for what the price is at the warehouse. I do this on big ticket items like laser cartridges which run $60 to $70.*

---

The most expensive place to buy office stuff is at the grocery story or the small independent stationary store (like the local

Hallmark). And never ever buy office supplies over the phone by credit card from someone you don't know. There are many dishonest people out there.

Some office supply catalogs have good prices, but like all mail order, you have to pay for and wait for delivery. However, if you live in the middle of nowhere, these catalogs are great.

## Service, Please

Your writing business is likely to use a number of services. You don't need all of them to get started, but be on the lookout for services that will give you more time to write.

**Copy Service:** Even though copy machines have come down in price, I don't advise you to buy one. Instead, find a good copy house in your area. Some nationwide franchises (like Kinko's) have good service. Many larger companies also have graphic and design services, which might come in handy. Some office supply stores have very low prices on copies to lure people into the store. I use Office Depot.

---

*TIP*: When you submit an article and photos, instead of sending the negatives or prints, have the pictures scanned and printed on a laser printer and send those. Tell them in your pitch letter that you'll send originals if they want to buy the piece.

---

Some services will allow you to transmit your work by modem and they will print it out and make umpteen copies for you to pick up, saving one trip.

**Quick Printer:** Every once in a while you're going to need a quick printer to do flyers, or leaflets. Now that the costs for image copying have come down significantly, you will not use a quick printer for many items. Still, you never know when you'll be asked to give a speech and the organization will want you to supply 1,000 flyers to send out with their newsletter. I use AlphaGraphics.

**Computer User Group**: Just about every town has user groups for the IBM PC and the Apple Macintosh. Join the right group. You will be provided with phone numbers of people willing to help you if your computer goes crash in the night!

There are also groups within groups, called SIGs (special interest groups). For example, many Macintosh user groups have a writers' SIG.

Even if you don't go to the meetings, join the group so you can tap into the wealth of knowledge of experienced computer users who will help you and answer questions. You can also call in to their on-line bulletin board which almost every user group has. They're invaluable for getting answers to questions, learning new ways to use your computer, and finding out about free or low-cost software. Most users groups have hundreds (some have thousands) of these programs that you can download to your computer using your modem.

---

*TIP*: There is a ton of almost free software written by hobbyists who sell the programs via user groups. These are called shareware and the cost is often $5 or $10 for some really incredible programs. I use one called Easy Envelopes that does what it's named for. Another shareware program called Zterm has become a standard in the Mac world for modem communications.

---

**On-Line Service**: An on-line service is like a super information service. Many of you have heard of Compuserve Information Service (CIS), Prodigy or America Online (AOL). They have just about any generalized information service you might want, from reference books to stock quotes. One of the big attractions of the on-line services are the forums. These are just big bulletin boards where people who share special interests, post and answer messages to each other. They can also chat on-line. Almost all the services have writers' forums.

Which one should you choose? Try them all! Most have free trials. When you join a user group, ask about having someone sponsor you into one of these services. You'll get free time and they get a few hours at no charge if you decide to join. I've used both AOL and CompuServe. They are about the same.

Most of these services charge by the hour of connect time. Others have a flat fee for unlimited use of certain parts of the system and charge connect time for others. For example, a service might charge $10 a month for unlimited use of news, weather, sports, encyclopedia, movie reviews, and a few games. However they might charge $5 an hour for using the forums.

Every writer should belong to at least one of these information services. If nothing else, people can send you e-mail via the service. E-mail which may be new to many of you, will one day replace the fax machine (which has just about replaced the post office). I can dial up my on-line service, compose a letter to you (if I know your e-mail address), and send it. It is delivered almost instantly to your "mail box" on your information service. Most services either don't charge for e-mail or give you 40 or 50 messages as part of the basic rate.

---

**COMMENT**: *E-mail is not limited to just one service. All services are connected via the Internet. You can send and receive e-mail all over the world virtually for free.*

---

Many editors will allow you to submit (upload) your articles via e-mail. This saves postage and time and is another reason to subscribe to an online service. Find one you like and join it.

**Research Assistant**: You probably won't want to use a research assistant right away, but be on the lookout for one anyway. Let's say you write on agricultural subjects. You might look for a bright young agriculture major at your local college or university (contact the department chairperson). If you pay this person $10 an hour for several hours of research on a given topic, it allows you to turn out more articles, which should increase your income. It's even possible to get the research done free if the student can get academic credit for the effort.

You might also look for home-bound mothers of young children who can get out for a few hours a day to do research for you.

---

*COMMENT: You could also hire these people to ghostwrite articles for you. It's done all the time. Ghost articles are expensive, as the writer expects to get the same kind of money you would get. However, sometimes you'll find someone who needs an extra hundred dollars and can write a 1,500 word article for you almost off the top of his/her head.*

---

Some people will do research for you for free if they get to share the byline. Often college professors have long academic (that is, difficult to understand) journal articles on subjects that you can rewrite into something for a general magazine or paper. Offering to share the byline and giving the professor final review rights might get you a piece with hardly any research costs.

## Sights and Sounds

It's not a secret; it's a well known fact. Yet it's ignored by the vast majority of PEs writers. Photos sell stories. Say it again, and remember it. Photos sell stories!

Editors love pictures. Some editors like pictures better than the text. Always try to include a photo or two with your articles.

Do you have a camera? If so, you might get by with it until you need better quality. If you're looking to buy a camera, don't spend a month's income on one until you know what you will need.

For most of you, a simple PHD camera will work fine. What is a PHD camera? It stands for "push here, dummy!" What you want is a single lens reflex (SLR) camera that has auto-everything and a zoom lens. A zoom lens fits on the camera and gets longer or shorter, depending on your preference. You just twist the lens (or hold down a button) and your subject gets closer or farther way. There are a million ranges of zoom lenses. Most writers find that a lens that zooms from 35mm to 70mm is fine. The higher the number, the further away you can shoot and enlarge the subject. The smaller the number, the closer to the subject you can get for those close-up shots. You can get a lens that zooms from 50mm to 200mm, but it will be pretty heavy, and quite expensive. A 35-70 should do fine.

---

*TIP:* Some writers always take their cameras to an interview and ask difficult questions while taking a picture. It puts the subject at ease. For some reason, people will open up while you're shooting film.

---

Make sure your camera has a built-in flash. Since many of your pictures will be taken inside, having a built-in flash saves time in having to mount a flash unit. A built-in unit is not as bright as a stand-alone unit, but it will be fine for most of your photos.

The automatic point and shoot SLR cameras that you can buy for a few hundred dollars are terrific. The camera senses the available light and does all the focusing. All you have to do is zoom in or out, depending on how you want your picture to look then PHD!

> *TIP*: The nice thing with SLR cameras is that what you see in the viewfinder is what your picture will actually look like.

As for film, most often you'll buy slide film. You can tell slide film because it has the word "chrome" on the end of the name. Check the different one-hour photo places in your town. Most don't develop slide film, but you'll find a few that do, if you use a certain type of slide film. Call around to see what film they recommend.

For black and white, check the Yellow Pages under Photography or ask at your local camera shop. You may want the shop to do what's called a contact sheet of your black and white work. These are large sheets with very small prints of the pictures from the roll of film. It's cheap to develop a contact sheet. From it, you can pick the best photographs to print. This will save some money since you won't develop each print individually.

> *TIP*: Call your local newspaper and ask to speak to one of their photographers. Ask them to recommend places to have your film developed. They might also recommend equipment, vendors, and classes.

Learning how to compose photos is not difficult. Like anything else, it takes some knowledge and some practice. There are always courses on photography available at your local university or junior college. Some photography stores offer classes also. Try to find one taught by a working photo journalist. Again, ask at your favorite camera store. There are also many books on the subject of learning to use your camera. Get one on the basics of photo journalism and read it. However, you can't learn from just a class or book. You have to go out and snap pictures. Take lots of them. It is the only way you'll really learn.

The final piece of equipment you might want if you take a lot of pictures of interview subjects is a tripod. It cuts down on camera movement. You can buy a very lightweight aluminum tripod that travels well.

If you do lots of interviews, you'll also want to get a small tape recorder. There are all makes and models out there. Make sure you get one that is rugged and that has some type of voice activation. I'm not making an endorsement, but many writers say that Radio Shack has good equipment.

Also at Radio Shack you can buy a specialized attachment that lets you tape your phone interviews. They sell a cheap little suction cup device, but it does not work well. Instead, invest in the gizmo that connects directly to your phone line.

Many answering machines will allow you to record conversations, but some machines have short durations such as five minutes. You'll find a small pocket recorder more useful.

---

*TIP*: *Always tell people that you're taping their phone interview. It is common courtesy as well as the law.*

---

## Contracts and Rights

As you sell your writing, you'll receive contracts of all kinds. While some magazines work by verbal agreement, many have long and complicated documents that require half a dozen initials on multiple copies before they will take your piece. It's important to look at the big picture when you're reading a contract. Forget about the inconsequential issues. *Just concentrate on what you have to gain or lose by signing the contract.* Also, remember that contracts are almost always negotiable. When you get a contract, decide which points are important to you and which are not.

Most often you are not selling your article; you are selling someone the right to use it. You own the piece and you have total control on all rights, unless you sell the article along with all of its rights. Obviously, you want to keep as many rights to your work as possible so that you can resell your articles.

The reason rights are sometimes not mentioned by editors in their letters of acceptance is because the Copyright Law of 1978 says that writers are selling onetime rights to their work unless they and the magazine agree otherwise. Thus, there is often an understanding that the author is only selling the editor the right to publish the story once.

There are several kinds of rights you have. Don't try to memorize them. Just be aware of the differences so that when you see them mentioned in a contract, you know what you're giving up (or not giving up).

> **First Serial Rights**: This means you're giving the magazine or paper the right to publish the article for the *first time*. These are the rights most publishers want; they want to be the first magazine to print your article. Often you'll see the term "First

North American Serial Rights," which allows the publisher to print your article both here and in Canada. Most often you'll sell first serial rights.

**One-Time Rights**: This differs from the above in that the editor has no guarantee he will be the first to publish the work. A cousin to this is Simultaneous Rights where a publication is buying rights to a piece that may appear at the same time in another magazine.

**Second Serial Rights**: Obviously, you're reselling the article to a second magazine.

**All Rights**: If you sell all rights, you no longer own the article and can't resell it anywhere. You should get more money; some authors charge double since they believe they can usually sell almost any piece at least twice.

---

*TIP: It's permissible to sell all rights if you never plan to resell the piece. Some magazines insist on all rights, but most don't. I usually have more ideas for articles than I can possibly write, so if I have to give one up "forever," it's no big deal as long as the price is right.*

---

**Foreign Serial Rights**: If you only sold First U.S. or North American rights, you can resell the piece to a magazine published outside the U.S that publishes material that has already been in print in the U.S. This can be a good market, but the pay is usually not too good. However, it can be "found" money.

There are other rights such as syndication rights, subsidiary rights, and dramatic rights. If these rights are applicable to a piece of your work, contact an attorney who is knowledgeable in publishing or entertainment law.

## Copyright

You should be aware of a few basic facets of the copyright law. This law exists to protect your writing, and it recognizes you (as creator) as "owner and grantor of all the rights, benefits and privileges" that come with ownership. The intent of the law is to protect you, the creator of an original work.

The law gives you the right to print, reprint, and copy the work, to sell and distribute copies, and to make what are called derivative works (translations, novelizations, dramatizations etc.) of your original work. The law gives you control over these rights and helps assure that you'll be paid for your work.

The minute the work is created - whether it is on paper or disk - and you indicate authorship, the work is copyrighted. The protection lasts your entire life plus 50 years.

You don't have to register your work with the Copyright Office to receive protection. However, doing so can offer certain legal advantages in case someone infringes on your copyright. If you wish to register, request information and forms from the Register of Copyrights, Library of Congress, Washington, DC 20559. Just follow the instructions, enclose copies of the work and the fee, and send it off. In about 6 weeks you'll get a notice of copyright with a registration number from them. This is an important document, so keep it in a safe place. You can register a group of articles (for one fee) by placing them in a notebook and giving them a single title, such as "Articles By Joan Jones." Also, you can register a work at any time, before or after publication. Remember, the work is protected as soon as it is created. Registration merely establishes a legal framework of the creation date in case someone claims the work is not yours.

So, should you register? My advice is to only register books, very long articles, or articles you might someday turn into a book.

Whether or not you register, you should display a copyright notice on the bottom of the first page of your article when you send it out. The format is the symbol © (you're allowed to hand draw this if you like, but most computer fonts have the symbol), *or* the word "Copyright" along with the year date of the first publication and the name of the copyright owner. Either Copyright 1995 Ellen Jones or © 1995 Ellen Jones will do the trick.

---

**COMMENT**: *Since 1989 it is no longer mandatory to display a notice of copyright, and failure to do so does not result in loss of protection. However, display it anyway so there will be no confusion over who owns the work.*

---

Ideas and titles cannot be copyrighted. Facts are also not copyrighted. Only the actual expression of ideas or information can be copyrighted. Thus, you can't copyright the idea and title of a story on how to sell steel to the British government and you can't copyright a list of government import/export documents necessary to the transaction, but you can copyright an article that results from your research along with the expression of your ideas. Others can come along and write an article on the same topic, use the same title, and list the same forms. They can also express their idea the same way you did. But they can't copy your exact words and put their name to them.

Finally, a copyright can be sold or transferred. You can sell all rights, but still retain ownership via the copyright (although it isn't much good). It is best to never sell your copyright unless someone makes you an offer you can't refuse.

## Work-For-Hire

This is a special area of the law that you should be knowledgeable about. Work-for-hire is work that another party commissions you to do. There are two types: (1) writing done as a regular employee, and (2) commissioned work specifically noted as "work-for-hire" at the time the commission is granted and accepted. These words must be in the agreement according to the Copyright law. If you see these words, understand that you are party to an agreement that will result in the loss of all your rights for any work you create.

You'll only see work-for-hire clauses when you query an editor with an idea for a piece and she accepts it with the provision that you do it as work-for-hire. You can't sell an already existing article as work-for hire because it's already protected by copyright the split second it's created in tangible (readable) form. Some editors, when they make an assignment, have the writer sign a work-for-hire form as a routine part of the contract. Lots of writers have been burned by not knowing what they were actually signing.

Under work-for hire, you don't own the copyright or any right! For a fee, you forfeit any potential income you might make from resale of the work. You can't sell it because you don't own it!

---

*TIP*: I advise you to only sign work-for-hire arrangements for articles you absolutely know you will never ever want to see again! Better yet, don't sign them at all!

---

## Finances

One great thing about a writing business is its simplicity. There is no inventory, no employees, no formal government regulations to follow, and little in the way of established structure. There is no one right way to run the business. Some people are fanatical about keeping every "t" crossed and "i" dotted, while others pay minimum attention to the details of running the business.

After speaking with many writers, I honestly believe that simplicity is the key to happiness. But so is good record keeping. You have to fill out a Schedule C at tax time. The better the records you keep, the easier that task is.

One of the best ways to keep good records is to keep your writing income and expenses separate from your personal ones. Whether or not you get a fictitious business name from the county, it's a good idea to open a separate checking account. It is not necessary or even legally required to have a separate account, but doing so will provide a clear trail of income and expenses at tax time.

You may not want to bank at the same place you have your personal account because the fees for a business checking account might be too high. However, if you have a good-sized balance at your present bank, you can often talk them into giving you a no-fee business checking account in return for keeping your personal business with them. Banks know that if you go out looking for a business account, some other bank will make that offer if you transfer you personal account to them.

*TIP*: Some banks have very favorable checking account fees for small businesses; however, most want you to keep a balance of $3,000 to $5,000 to escape a fee. Take some money from another account and keep a balance so you don't need to pay a fee. Why give the bank $10 a month ($120 a year!).

Another good idea is to use a separate credit card for all your writing business purchases. This way you have the credit card statements to serve as receipts and the checks you write to the credit card company as proof you actually spent the money!

*COMMENT*: I use an American Express Corporate card (even though I'm not incorporated) for my business expenses. While this card costs twice what other cards charge for yearly dues, I find the quarterly and end-of-year reports that AMEX provides worth the price. Also, AMEX is not a credit card because you must pay the balance each month; you can't pay over time like VISA.

I mentioned in the chapter on computers and software about getting a bookkeeping and check-writing program. The most popular program is called Quicken and a sixth grader can easily learn how to use it. You might not use all of its features, but for writing checks, doing simple profit-and-loss statements, and just keeping everything in balance, it can't be beat for the price.

*COMMENT*: Once you've started doing all your check writing and financial record keeping on your computer, you'll never go back to a manual system. Trust me.

If you do plan to use a manual system, a company called Dome makes an excellent single entry ledger book that you'll find useful. They also make an auto mileage log book.

One great feature of a program like Quicken is that it allows you to assign each check you write an "expense category." Thus, at any time you can easily see how much you've spent for any given category such as phone, postage, or travel. At tax time, you don't have to add up hundreds of receipts or canceled checks. All the figures for your Schedule C are right there on the computer. You can print them out and take them to your tax advisor.

When it comes to taxes, make sure you keep receipts of all kinds. Get yourself one of those accordion folders that are organized by either month or category and stuff all the receipts you get into the folder. This is especially important for items for which you pay cash. Make sure you keep your credit card receipts, especially those for gasoline.

You should also keep a log of all miles you drive for business purposes. Keep the log in the car and make an entry each time you get out of the car. It's a pain, but it can save your bacon if you get audited and your mileage deduction is questioned.

> *TIP*: Pay attention to taxes. Think about this: The biggest expense every person has is not his or her house or car; it is taxes. Learn how to work the tax system to your advantage.

I think it's a good idea for all those who plan to start a business to see an accountant or tax advisor, especially if they're not familiar with business finances in general, and small business tax ramifications in particular. An hour or two with a professional can get you on the right track so you not only stay out of tax trouble, but you indeed use the tax law to your maximum advantage.

Do remember this about the tax code: generally, to be considered a business (by the IRS) you need to show a *profit* (not income) in three out of the last five years. Otherwise, you're classified as a hobby and you're only allowed to deduct expenses up to any income you made.

---

*TIP*: The question of hobby or business is not black and white; there are many shades of gray here. Consult a professional.

---

The general rule is that any expense you incur that's related to producing income for your business is deductible, with a few limitations. (The tax code is always being changed with respect to business meals and entertainment.) There is also a deduction you can claim for a part of your home used exclusively and regularly for business. This is complicated, and everyone says it raises a big red "audit me" flag. However, most IRS home-office audits are done on people who have outside jobs and use a home office in the course of that job. (For example, an anesthesiologist who did all his work in a hospital but kept a home office to do his books and billings was not allowed a home office deduction.)

Of course, you'll have to file an itemized return to take advantage of any deductions you might have. Because of this requirement, I believe that nobody should ever do his or her taxes manually. Either take them to a professional or use one of the many computer programs that do taxes

---

*TIP*: I use a program called MacInTax. It's easy to use and finds deductions that you might overlook. It will also import figures from Quicken (since both programs are made by the same company.)

---

I'm not a tax advisor. While I'm pretty knowledgeable about tax matters (you will be too after a year in business), I do have occasional questions. I don't ask the IRS questions because they often give the wrong answers. (Even the IRS can't understand the tax code!) Find yourself a good tax advisor and trust his or her judgment.

One last point on taxes. As I said earlier, you will have to file a Schedule SE for self employment taxes. This is the percentage that would be taken from your pay if you were employed by a company. Now that you're self-employed, the percentage is figured against your *net profit*. Thus if you gross $15,000 and net $9,000 after expenses, you will pay self employment tax on this figure.

---

*TIP*: If you don't want to be concerned with any record keeping, bill paying, or tax stuff, you can find a (home based) bookkeeper who will probably do the whole thing for you for a reasonable monthly sum. Check around. It's deductible!

---

## Manuscript Format

There are no hard and fast rules about what your manuscript should look like when you send it to the editor. However, there is a general format based on common sense as well as convention. The important thing is to get the editor to read it.

First of all, don't use a cover sheet or title page. And don't staple pages together. (Editors hate stapled pages!) Use a paper clip.

In the upper left hand corner or centered on the first page is your name, address, phone (fax) number and Social Security number (so they can cut you a check and report it on a 1099).

In the upper right corner (or below the other information),

put the word count (your word processor will give you this number), the rights you're offering for sale (if other than First North American Rights), and your copyright notice.

Center the title in capital letters about one-third of the way down the page. Double space and put "by." Double space again and type your name.

Drop down two double spaces, indent, and start the article. Always double-space the piece and use at least 1-inch margins all the way around.

**Use an easy to read type font. I like Times, 12 point. Use a font with a serif as it's easier to read. Helvetica looks nice but it's hard on the eyes. Do you think this paragraph (Helvetica) reads as easy as the others? Most people don't.**

On every page after the first, put your name and the page number in either the upper right or left hand corner (Jones -3). Some people repeat the title below the name-page number. Drop down two double spaces and continue the manuscript.

---

*TIP*: You can configure your word processing software to create a manuscript page by using what are often called "style sheets." As I said earlier, you really can't do this business well without a computer!

---

John N. Jones
123 Your Street
Your City, ST 99999
Tel/Fax (999)555-1234
SSN: 123-45-6789

Word count: 1,678
Copyright 19xx John Jones

**THE EMPLOYEE TRAP**
**Make Sure Your People Are Really Contractors**

by

John N. Jones

This would be the first paragraph of the article. The amount that you indent is up to you. Some people indent the equivalent of two letters, and others like to indent .25 of an inch. It won't make much difference to the editor.

Don't forget to leave a nice margin. Also, you should put your name and page number on all pages but the first.

As I said, there is no actual standard as to what your manuscript should look like. Just make sure it is double spaced, the pages are numbered and that you put "the end" at the end so the editor knows there are no more pages.

## Photos

When you submit photos, make sure they're correctly iden-tified. Editors will want either black and white (often 8x10 glossy) or 35mm slides. Very few will take color *prints*.

On all your photos and slides, print your copyright notice along with your name and address. Also put a number on the slide or back of the print that corresponds to the caption. If you write on the back of a print, don't press too hard. It's better to write on a label and stick it on the back of the print. For slides that come in a plastic frame, you'll have to use a label (and write very small!).

Captions should be written on a separate sheet. However, if you have only one or two prints, type the captions, snip them and tape them to the back of the print.

Never ever submit original negatives.

## It's in the Mail

The usual advice given to authors is that all material six pages or less in length should be folded in thirds and sent in a regular #10 business envelope. I suggest that you use a 9x12 manila en-velope and not fold your work. Many editors don't like to get articles folded because they never seem to unfold and lay flat on the desk.

Always mail your material first-class. If you really want to make an impression, send it by air express.

---

*TIP*: The rates for 2nd day air express are dropping to around $5 for as much as you can stuff in the cardboard envelope. If you send it air express, I guarantee it will be read. It's just human nature to open something that someone else thinks is urgent enough to spend extra money to expedite.

---

Put prints into a manila folder or slap them between two pieces of cardboard to keep them from being bent or damaged. You can buy special mailers for prints from some photography stores.

To mail slides, put them into protective vinyl sleeves and send them the same way you send photographs.

Many editors are willing to receive submissions by fax, but don't fax them unless you are positive that it will be OK. First of all, many editors don't like to read fax material because it's hard on the eyes if they don't have a plain-paper fax machine. Second, thermal fax paper is hard to write on. Finally, editors don't like having their fax machines tied up by writers sending unsolicited material. The only time to break the rule is if you have an article on a fast-breaking story that a newspaper might want. But, make sure it's really urgent. Of course, if you do fax things, try to do it after your time zone's business hours when the rates go down, or early in the morning before they go up.

More and more editors will accept work via e-mail files. Make sure you know what format the article should be in. Most will accept MS Word or WordPerfect files. Some only accept what is called ascii files.

As I mentioned earlier, I don't recommend that you send the traditional SASE (self-addressed stamped envelope.) If the editor likes the article and wants to buy it, she will get in touch with you on her dime. If she doesn't want it, most editors will still spring for a stamp and send a rejection form or letter. If you provide an editor with your own form that she can fax, you'll be looked upon as a high-tech pro.

## File It, Don't Lose It

There are countless file systems that writers can use. Some people file by subject, some by magazine, some by date. You name it, there's a way to file it! I suggest you keep it simple and create a folder for each article and put copies of all correspondence (various pitch letters) in the folder.

---

*TIP*: Earlier I mentioned that it's a good idea to tailor your pitch letter to the magazine to which you're submitting. Don't waste disk space keeping a copy of each letter. But keep a paper copy so that if they call you, you can remember what you said.

---

You should also create some folders for the different topics that relate to your genre. These will become clip files where you'll put ideas you find in other magazines. (In the trade it's called a swipe file.) For example, if you write on the fast-food industry and see an article about a new french-fry machine in some trade magazine, you might clip it and put it in a folder called "equipment." You not only create your own research library, but when you get enough different articles in a folder, you can synthesize all them into an article of your own.

Some people (myself included) are pack rats when it comes to saving old magazines. Try to fight this. When you decide to put a magazine aside for future reference, you think you'll remember why. But two months later you won't. If you do decide to keep magazines instead of individual clips, be sure to put some

Post-it Notes™ on the stories you might want to refer to later. These not only serve a bookmarks, but if you scribble a few words on them, they will remind you of why you saved the article.

It's amazing how much stuff you'll start collecting. You can start out with some folders piled on your desk. But it won't be long before you'll need a real file cabinet. I suggest you get one that will accommodate hanging folders (Pendaflex). These folders are available in different colors to color-code your files.

Every year, go through each folder and toss the stuff you no longer need. Sometimes you will toss entire folders. If you don't, you'll run out of room. You may not believe me now, but you'll see!

As for computer disks, all your articles, important letters, databases, and financial files should be backed up onto floppy disks and kept in a very safe place. Most people keep a copy off-site at a friend's house, or in their bank safe deposit box. Of course, always keep a hard copy of your articles just in case! Don't clutter your computer's hard disk with lots of needless stuff or you'll run out of room on the disk. Your computer runs slower when the disk is filled almost to capacity.

> *TIP*: There are several programs on the market to assist you in backing up your files. Look in the catalog, ask at the computer store, or check with user groups.

Try not to keep duplicates of information. It takes up space and makes your files difficult to manage. Try to follow the motto "if in doubt, throw it out." Information gets stale. There is so much information available to us that if you throw something out today, you can be assured that a similar piece of information will appear very soon! Don't collect information just to have it. Only keep something if you can identify a specific purpose for keeping it.

## What's Where?

Be sure to keep a separate file folder for each article and develop some form of keeping track of where you sent it. Some writers do this via their computer database. Others make notations on the inside cover of the manila folder in which they keep the hard copy of the article (along with any correspondence.)

If you're sending out two or three pieces a week, after a while you're going to forget what article went where, and when you sent it. Keep a calendar to remind you to follow up on an article for which you haven't received an acceptance or rejection.

Some people wait two weeks, some a month before they take follow up action. Some magazines report more quickly than others. My advice is to send a short fax after three weeks asking if they received your article and what the status is. Let them know when you sent it, the title, and a one- or two-sentence description. Give them some room to make notations and ask them to fax your letter (with their notations) back to you.

Don't phone unless your piece is on a breaking news story. Editors don't like being called by writers asking if the magazine received the article and if they're going to buy it. Also, you'll probably get a receptionist or assistant editor who doesn't know you from Adam (or Eve!) and could care less. A very short fax can accomplish more than a long (and expensive) phone call.

## It's the Time of Your Life

Everything about starting and managing a writing business is simple with one exception: time management. If you don't manage your time correctly, you will not produce articles and your business will fail. More people fail in this business, not because they write poorly or write on non-marketable topics, but because they never get anything done! They don't sell their work because they never have work to sell!

If you ran a store, you would have to be open a certain period of the day when you would expect customers. If you ran a service business (such as window washing), you would expect to reserve certain hours for doing the work. The writing business is no different. You must put aside time to create your product, sell your product, and manage your business.

Time and money are similar; you have a limited amount of each. If you don't manage your money correctly, you will not be able to pay the rent. If you don't manage your time correctly, you will neither finish nor sell anything.

No one can give you a magic formula to manage your time and make you a prolific writer of marketable material. You'll have to find what works for you. But other writers have discovered some tactics that might assist you.

> Some rise an hour earlier each day and get their daily chores out of the way (feeding the cat, doing laundry, going grocery shopping, etc.)

> Some do the opposite and stay up an hour later to do home-bound chores (pay bills, vacuum the rugs, etc.)

> Many use public transportation as much as possible so they can work at their writing instead of fighting traffic.

> Some tell people not to call or come by during the time they set aside for business. They turn on the answering machine and let it do its job.

Most writers try to combine outside activities so they make fewer trips. They set aside one day for research, calls, library work, and outside errands so they can get uninterrupted writing time most days.

Many writers use a small tape recorder while driving to dictate a few pages of some article that they will transcribe when they get home.

Many bring work along if they know they're going to spend time in a waiting room (doctor, accountant, dentist).

Productive writers use their time wisely, even if it's in fragments. They don't take an attitude that "I only have an hour before I have to _____, so why start writing?"

The best thing you can do for yourself is to create a schedule and stick to it. Get out a calendar and decide what hours you're going to write, go to the library, and do other chores. Be flexible and realistic. If you have a bridge game on Tuesdays at 10 AM, fine, put it on your calendar. Then schedule your business time around such outside commitments. Think of yourself as a company executive who has many areas to oversee. You can only do so much each day; schedule your time so that you get the most done.

You will have to make some choices. Many PEs fill their day with activities to pass the time. But if you want to be a productive writer, you may have to drop a pottery class or a golf game to reserve time to work on your business. Don't fool yourself into thinking that you'll find the time if your schedule is already filled to capacity. It won't work. If you want to do this business, you'll have to create time for it. You must devote 10 to 20 hours a week to your writing effort if you wish to be successful.

# 9

. . . . . . . . . . . . . . . . . . . . . . . . . . .

# COMMERCIAL WRITING

## Not for Everyone, but Maybe for You

I'm going to discuss a segment of the writing industry that may or may not be for you. All I ask is that you approach it with an open mind before you decide. Before I define commercial writing, I want to whet your appetite.

Commercial writing has several advantages. It's fairly easy to break into. You'll have a chance to build a regular clientele and you can expand your business as much as you like. After you get established, instead of you chasing the work, the work will chase you. In fact, it's possible that too much work will come your way and you could be in danger of having to work full-time just to keep up. Finally, commercial writing pays well.

If commercial writing is so great, why didn't I introduce it earlier? Because getting started in the commercial writing field is usually not a passive activity. It takes time, energy, and sales ability to get going. Plus, you have to write well and know what type of writing you can sell. I usually suggest that PEs start out as freelancers in the magazine world before they market themselves in the commercial world. But if you already have an aptitude for writing, you may want to start in the commercial writing arena.

Some types of commercial writing require face-to-face selling. You'll often have to, in Hollywood terms, "take a meeting" with those who hire you. PEs are often uncomfortable sitting across the table from a 28-year-old advertising agency junior executive, trying to land a writing assignment.

> **COMMENT**: Don't panic. I'll show you how you can minimize some of this face-to-face contact. As a magazine freelancer, you'll probably never meet the person who buys your product. In commercial writing, many times you will.

Another reason I recommend freelance feature writing first is that it's easier to find commercial writing clients after you've been published a few times. To most clients, it won't matter if you've been published in the East Tennis Shoe Fish Wrap News of Hee Haw, Florida. To clients, being published is one of the credentials used to decide if you can do the job. It's not the deciding factor, but it's surely a selling point.

This is not to say that you can't break into commercial writing without being published as a freelancer. Thousands have. But it's easier if you have a clip file of work to show potential clients.

## Wanted: Writer for Hire

Commercial writing is defined as work that is done on behalf of a client who will use your product for a commercial purpose (that it, to make money). It might be used to sell, motivate, educate, persuade, or describe. Most often it's used to help sell a product or service on behalf of someone in business. The usual goal of commercial writing is to help someone make a buck.

---

**COMMENT:** There are many avenues of commercial writing that you can do on behalf of nonprofit colleges, hospitals, trade associations, community groups, churches, etc. But most work will come from the business sector.

---

Commercial writing includes just about every type of printed presentation you have seen - advertisements, articles, booklets, brochures, case histories, catalogs, circulars, data sheets, direct mail packages, fliers, instruction manuals, sales letters, speeches, technical papers, and so on.

There is one common denominator. You get the money, but not the recognition. There is no byline. There is no evidence that you actually did the work. This is work for hire (as discussed earlier) and all rights are owned by the client.

Still, there are advantages to being a commercial writer:

**Money**: You can make far more money as a commercial writer than as a freelance worker. A 1,500-word piece that you might sell to a magazine for $200 might sell to an ad agency for $800.

**Regular Work**: Freelancing is uncertain. In commercial writing you can build up a small clientele that will give you a steady stream of assignments.

**Demand**: There is always a demand for commercial writers who can get work done by deadline. There is less competition than in the freelance world of magazines.

**Work Is Assigned**: You don't have to dream up topics once you get established. Clients will come to you with projects. You won't be writing articles in the hope (prayer) that they will sell, as a freelancer does.

There are also disadvantages:

**No Recognition**: As I said above, there is no by-line. Your copy will be used under a corporate logo or somebody's name. The client is credited as the author, not you. You don't exist.

**Lack of Variety**: Much commercial work is the same. If you write press releases, after a while you'll be able to do them in your sleep, since are all very much alike in style.

**Client Dictates**: The client may come to you with ideas of what she wants promoted, the key sales points, or themes that should be emphasized. There may not be much input from you. The client gives you the plans and the lumber. You're just the carpenter who builds the house.

**Work Flow**: While you might have steady customers, the work may come in spurts. Many commercial writers either have too much work or none at all. One week you might have to get three pieces done for one client when another client calls and wants revisions on work you turned in last week. Other weeks can be slow. There are often tight deadlines, meaning you'll have to burn some midnight oil. Commercial writing can be stressful if not managed properly, and it's hard to manage

this business properly! If you refuse to take work,
it may not come again. If you take too much, you
become swamped!

By now you should have a pretty good idea of what commercial writing is all about. Later, I will talk about the different genres (that word again!) of commercial writing. But first, you must understand who the customers are and what they're usually looking for. I'll cover the three main commercial markets in which PEs are most successful.

## The Corporate Market

Corporations (for profit as well as nonprofit) and businesses large and small are, by far, the largest buyers of commercial writing. Banks, insurance firms, utilities, distributors, manufacturers, high-tech firms, small service companies, medical organizations, professional organizations and one-person offices all need written material that you can provide. From advertisements to press releases to technical writing to sales literature, the business sector will probably be your best customer.

Large corporate entities have different needs. For example, the advertising and sales departments need you to turn out copy for brochures and product announcements. The personnel department may need you to provide an article on health benefits for the company newsletter. The public relations people might need you to provide press releases and feature articles. The manufacturing division may need you to work on a new manual, proposal, or other documentation. Executive administration may call on you to write a speech or quarterly report.

There are two basic ways of approaching the corporate market. Some PEs target their efforts to a particular division, such as sales. They will write material for corporations in many industries. This works well for PEs who have a broad business background.

I think a better way is to specialize in one industry. This is similar to choosing a genre, as I presented earlier. If you came out of the retail industry, you should be able to write for the retail industry. If you spent the past ten years as an engineer for a computer chip manufacturing company, you could concentrate on commercial writing for any chip company in the country.

## The Ad Agencies

Agencies are the second largest market for commercial writing services. However, you probably won't write ads or TV commercials, since this is usually done by in-house staff.

Agencies bring in freelance talent to help with direct mail, catalog, and one-time promotions. An agency may get a contract with a company whose business they don't know much about. For example, say a manufacturer of hydraulic pumps comes out with a new product to be used at salt water sites. They might want to do a mailing to construction firms, or create a press kit to be sent to engineering or heavy equipment trade magazines. How many ad agencies are knowledgeable about the hydraulic pump business? The agency that gets (wins) the contract finds a freelancer who specializes in the heavy equipment or industrial media and hires him or her (you) to do the work.

Agencies, especially larger ones, keep lists of freelancers who have various specialities. Also, some agencies specialize in one or two industries. (Several San Francisco agencies handle only high-tech clients from Silicon Valley).

To find out what agency has what clientele, go to the library and look in the *Standard Directory of Advertising Agencies* (a.k.a. the "Red Book"). Published by National Register Publishing Company, it lists some 5,000 agencies along with their specialties and major accounts.

---

*TIP*: The Red Book is updated several times a year but still is always out of date. Companies change ad agencies as often as we sharpen pencils.

---

## Public Relations People

PR firms come in two flavors: small one- or two-person outfits, or small divisions of large advertising agencies. The job of the PR staff is to get free advertising (a.k.a. publicity) for the products or service of their clients. Most often this is done by writing press releases, feature articles, speeches, and newsletters about their clients' products or services.

Like their advertising counterparts, they also bring in freelance help for certain projects or special industries.

There are many very small PR agencies. You should be able to get some overload work from the established ones that have a regular client base.

For more information on PR agencies, look in *O'Dwyer's Directory of Public Relations Firms*, (published by J. R. O'Dwyer). A larger library will have this directory of some 2,000 PR firms and their areas of specialization. O'Dwyer also publishes the *Directory of Corporate Communications*, which lists corporate in-house PR people at some 4,000 companies. (Of course, it's also always out of date!)

## Why They Come

Remember the line from the movie *Field of Dreams*, "if you build it, they will come"? Corporations, advertising agencies, and PR firms will come to you for three basic reasons:

> **Overworked and Understaffed**: The client's staff writers are busy with other projects, can't finish a certain project by deadline, or someone just quit. Often, clients run lean, meaning they only keep enough full-time staff to cover their ongoing work and farm everything else out. Some have no writers on staff and farm everything out!

> **Quality and Speciality**: Some agencies only need super-quality work done occasionally; regular staff (of lower paid people) handles the day-to-day stuff. But when an agency needs a top-notch writer or one with a specialized knowledge, they go outside for help.

> **Money**: Advertising agencies and PR firms don't want the small one-shot client. Often they have a requirement that a client commit to a large advertising budget. (Agencies make money from commissions on ads they place with magazines.) Corporations with small budgets must use freelance commercial writers because they can't get an agency to take them on. Also, corporations don't want to hire full-time writers for one-time or quarterly projects. Freelance commercial writers are much more cost effective.

As you can see, there are strong motivating factors for clients to seek you out to write for them. However, before they seek you out, you have to seek them out. And before any of this seeking takes place, you have to have a product to sell. So, let's look how other commercial writers do the business as well as map out a strategy that works well for PEs.

## Your Market Segment

Commercial writers are of two types: the specialist and the generalist. There are good arguments for being one or the other; your decision will usually depend on geographic location as well as what type of commercial writing you want to do. However, most of you will decide to be specialists, not only in subject matter, but in specific market segments as well.

To succeed as a specialist in commercial writing, you must know what you're going to sell: you must be an expert in your genre. I beat this into the ground earlier. In commercial writing it's even more important that you know your area of expertise because you won't have much time to climb the learning ladder. Businesses will contract with you to immediately step in, take over, and get the job done, quickly and correctly. Most often they look for writers whose career backgrounds match the writing subject they are assigning.

This should work for you. You should be an expert in your field. (That's why it *is* your field!) You're not selling creativity or personality; you're selling the ability to put words on paper that will fit the needs of someone who will use them to make a buck. It makes sense for an insurance company looking for a freelancer to hire someone with a background in the insurance business, rather than in agriculture.

When I talk about specialization, I mean the same genre concept discussed earlier. However, in some areas of the country it's necessary to broaden the perspective. Say you write on banking topics. If you live in a small city with no bank headquarters, you will have difficulty getting assignments. However, if you broaden your writing perspective to finance or service businesses, your chances increase.

> **COMMENT**: *There are limits. If your genre is home and small office construction, don't try to pass yourself off as an expert on building nuclear reactors, skyscrapers, or suspension bridges!*

In commercial writing, you'll have to choose one or two market segments. What are market segments? These are just the different types of writing people will hire you to do. The list below includes most of the ways you can make money in commercial writing.

| List of Commercial Writing Catagories | | |
| --- | --- | --- |
| Advertising | Manuals | TV spots |
| Booklets | Ghost articles | Trade materials |
| Brochures | Press releases | Training books |
| Business plans | Newsletters | Video scripts |
| Case histories | Radio spots | Annual reports |
| Catalogs | Sales letters | Fliers |
| Circulars | Seminars | Direct mail |
| Data sheets | Slide shows | Speeches |

As you can see, there are many areas in which you can work. But you can't do them all. Some, such as TV commercials, require a level of expertise gained from working in either the public relations business or the broadcast industry. My suggestion is do what you know best. If you've had experience writing new employee handbooks, then you could market yourself to companies that constantly hire (and fire) people. If you've had experience putting together sales catalogs, you could sell yourself as a catalog copywriter.

If you don't have a lot of specific industry experience you can be a generalist. Instead of writing for one industry, you market yourself as an expert in getting press for all types of small businesses and professionals. Both general PR work and ghostwriting are easy to get started in, especially if you've had any experience doing freelance article writing described earlier. Doing publicity work for a law firm is not all the different from doing it for a retail store.

Much PR work and ghostwriting does not require specialized writing knowledge. Even if you've never written a press release in your life, you can learn the basics quickly. The next chapters discuss PR writing and ghosting at length.

## It's the Money, Stupid!

You probably won't find commercial writing as interesting and fulfilling as freelance work because you don't usually get to pick your topic. If your client makes garbage disposal units, you'll write about clogged drains. If your client is a roach exterminator, you'll write about bugs. Because most commercial pieces are written to motivate a customer to buy something, the creative and educational content of most articles is low. Facts, features, and benefits! Repeat them enough times in print and someone is bound to buy. That's the purpose of your endeavor.

But you'll be paid for it, and paid well. Many variables determine what you'll earn.

Experience is always a factor. If you're a newcomer, obviously you won't earn as much as an established pro. But it doesn't take long to become an established pro! One solid piece that a client loves can catapult you into great demand. A man from Ohio was hired by an insurance agency to write a brochure on a new type of variable annuity the firm was selling. The client loved the work. The PE sent copies to other insurance agencies and soon the word got around on who to call for insurance promotional material. In six months he went from rank beginner to pro status.

Another factor is the client's perceived price of your service. Perceived prices are almost always wrong. Clients will say "Well, Mary, I believe the going rate for a two-page press release is $75." Why? Because that is what she paid the last writer. It means nothing. You can charge $100 or $1,000 if you like. The going rate is whatever the market (in this case, your client) will pay! You'll hear figures bandied about, but none are carved in stone. Prices vary all over the board. You'll find that some clients expect to pay $500 for a brochure and some expect to pay $1,000. But none will pay $5,000, nor do they expect to get it for $150.

---

*TIP*: When the client quotes a going rate, professional writers will ask where that figure came from. The pro then raises it by 50% to see what the reaction is. Sometimes, however, the client's going rate is more than what the writer would have charged! There are no rules!

---

Competition is another factor to consider, but don't put too much stock in it. If you see an ad in a trade journal or newspaper for a writer, or you hear of someone through the writers' grapevine (join a writers' group!), call and ask them what they charge for a press release, brochure, article, etc. It's not necessary to be anonymous; tell them you're just starting out. Most will cooperate with you. Many PR writers will tell you a range of prices they charge.

If you call posing as a potential client (you can say you're a consultant to XYZ), remember that some writers may give a low-ball figure to avoid scaring a client away. When they meet face to face, the rate goes up! (Don't do this yourself. It's bad business!)

---

**TIP**: Ask established commercial writers to send you their literature (brochures, rate-sheets, sample work) so you can see what others are using to market themselves.

---

You can charge by the hour or by the project. While you might expect most writers to work by the hour, this is not the case. Most work on a project basis, and some list their prices on a price sheet, often giving a range. Hourly fees can scare away many customers, especially small businesses. (They are terrified of having that meter running with no maximum.) You'll be more marketable if you tell a prospect over the phone that you charge, say, $280 for a two-page press release, $800-$1,500 for a feature article. If you go after longer projects such as a large proposal or heavy-duty technical documentation, you'll have to quote an hourly fee since you won't have a good idea how long the project will take. Hourly fees seem to range from $30-$100 an hour.

Here are some prices I've seen PEs charge when this book went to press.

| Prices For Commercial Writing Projects | | | |
|---|---|---|---|
| Brochure 8.5x11 | $750 | Sales letter | $250 |
| Newsletter | $425/page | Business plan | $1400 |
| Manual | $40/hour | Tech writing | $50/hour |
| Article 1500 wds | $800 | Speech | $900 |

Most of these rates and fees are conservative. You'll find commercial writing pays well when you have both the specific knowledge and the writing skills that are in demand in your area.

While there are many categories of commercial writing, I'm going to outline two: ghostwriting and PR writing. While not the highest paying, these are the best for most PEs starting out.

As I said in the beginning of the chapter, commercial writing is not for everyone. But if you think you might like it, give commercial writing a try. There is no penalty for failing, only for not trying.

# 10

## GHOSTWRITING

### Being a Ghost

You can be a ghostwriter. No, I'm not talking about writing the autobiography of some celebrity or famous business person. I'm saying that you can earn good dollars writing about your area of expertise and signing someone else's name to it. That's all ghosting is.

Believe it or not, there are a lot of ghostwriters out there. Obviously, they try to be inconspicuous. However, they have to walk a thin line between anonymity and marketability. And you will too, if you work as a ghost.

Many people have a strong desire to see their names in print as the author of an article. Most reasons are professional, not personal. Let's say you're a young lawyer who specializes in tax law. Wouldn't it be nice to see your name as the author of an article printed in the Sunday paper about local businesses using a little known tax strategy? Not only would this article bring you some business, but reprints of it could be effectively used as the promotional material you send to clients. The same case can be made for dentists, doctors, veterinarians, CPA's, financial planners, insurance agents, consultants, and proprietors of just about any service-oriented business.

Although work which does not carry your byline is considered ghosted, I like to make a distinction between ghosted and PR material (see next chapter). Ghosted material carries a name, but not yours. PR material, on the other hand, is unsigned.

While advertising is viewed with skepticism, information appearing in an article or news story has credibility. This is what business people and professionals are after: an article that not only promotes their services, but also provides enough information to pass as news. For example, a young surgeon who has done a number of operations using lasers could not take an ad proclaiming his competence. However, an article about laser surgery, the risks, advantages, costs, etc. along with a picture, could go a long way in building this surgeon's practice. An article with a byline can promote a person or product, educate people about a service, gain visibility for a company, and enhance the "author's" reputation within his or her industry or community.

While just about any writing can be ghosted, most ghosts write articles, speeches, and sales letters. I suggest you ghost feature articles since you should have some experience and knowledge from the previous chapters of this book. As I said earlier, once you've been published under your own byline, you've established yourself as a professional writer. You can use these clips to promote your ghost activities.

---

**COMMENT**: *Freelance feature writing under your own name and ghost feature writing under the client's name are not exclusive of each other. Many people do both.*

---

You can be a specialist and market only to a narrow range of customers, such as plumbers, eye doctors, or divorce lawyers. Or you can be a generalist and market to a broad category, such as small business, healthcare, law, etc.

## Ghost Prospecting

The best way to market your ghost service is by direct mail. You could cold call all day, but unless you hit the right person at the right time, cold calling will be a waste of time.

Your first step is to create a list of potential clients. Visit a library that has a business section (most city libraries have one). Tell the reference librarian that you want to find people or companies in your city, state, nation, or world (I suggest you start with your immediate locale!) to market ghostwritten feature articles. The librarian should be able to give you some local directories from which you can copy names.

Don't overlook the Yellow Pages, as well as the newspapers. Depending on your genre, there will either be too many prospects or too few. If you find few, rethink and broaden your genre. If there are too many, you may want to narrow it. For example, if you write on computer programming, not that many people in your area will need or want a ghost writer. But if you enlarge your scope to computers or technology, many people and firms will be interested in finding someone to write feature articles that might be published.

> *TIP*: Again, think of derivatives. If you write about computers, I'll bet some law firm would hire you to write an article about the use of high-tech research methodology in their practice.

Finding names and places to send a sales letter is not much different from finding magazines to send articles. It just takes a bit longer because there is probably no single compendium of prospects for your subject area. But with a little thought and some research, you should easily come up with a list of two or three hundred possibilities. I know that sounds like a lot, but it's realistic. Hundreds of outfits out there need your services; they just don't know it.

An excellent marketing activity you can do is sit down (with friends or family) and brainstorm a prospect list of possible business groups (medical, law, insurance, retail). Write down actual company names *and* the types of articles that might appeal to them. Two or three days cogitating on this (and nothing else!) should yield a terrific list of ideas and prospects.

> *TIP*: Enter commercial prospects, along with addresses and fax numbers into your computer database. You can then generate form letters offering your services.

Don't just get names of companies. Get names of people! A guaranteed turnoff is to send a "Dear Sir or Madam" letter. So, part of your effort will be to call and ask for the name and correct spelling of the owner or CEO. If someone asks why, tell them that your company is updating its vendor list. (Everyone wants to be a vendor!)

I said above that most cold calling is a poor use of time. However, when you're out and about doing errands and happen to be near potential clients, stop by and leave your flyer and "generic" sales letter (see below) *sealed in an envelope* with the owner, receptionist, or clerk. If you know the name of the person you want to contact, put it on the envelope. Otherwise just put "Confidential To Owner" (manager, senior partner, chief of medical staff, etc.) Don't ask to see anybody and don't make a sales pitch.

Even if you meet face to face with your intended client (victim? . . . just a little humor), simply ask her to read the contents of the envelope and contact you if she is interested. Then get out. Unless you're experienced in cold-call selling, you'll probably cause more harm than good if you try to explain what you do. It's better to let them digest the information and contact you.

## Ghost Letters

Most how-to books on ghosting instruct the writer to put together a high-powered sales letter full of hyperbole. I disagree. All you need is a simple dignified letter telling the prospective client what you do and how she will benefit. A letter usually includes four parts, but remember that nothing is carved in stone. You'll have to tailor the letter to the prospect. Obviously, a letter to a doctor would be different from one sent to the owner of a hardware store.

**The Grabber**: You want an opening statement that gets the attention of the reader. Unfortunately, most people go way overboard on the hype. I prefer a simple statement of fact, or a statistic, or an "assertion."

> *I am a ghost. But I'm not the kind you see at Halloween.*

***

> *There is an alternative to advertising and the results are better.*

***

> *You can be an author without writing a word.*

Do you get the idea? Come up with a good first sentence or two that will lead your reader into the rest of your letter. Remember, if you can't write an interesting letter, no one's going to have any confidence that you can write an interesting article.

**The Benefit**: The next section of your letter should inform your prospect why your service is *a solution*. You're not selling your service or the features of it. You're selling benefits. You can mention two or three article titles that, if published, could help the client's business.

> *Advertising is good, but business and professional people should include publicity as part of their marketing. If an article such as "The Best 10 Ways To Find a Lawyer" or "What Not To Put In Your Will" were published in a community paper under your name, do you think your practice would increase? Of course it would.*

***

> *Studies by the Dry Cleaning Institute have shown that a well-coordinated print publicity campaign has a greater and longer lasting effect than advertising and at lower cost. What if you authored an article titled "The 5 Best Ways to Remove Spots" and it was published in the local paper in which you already advertise? Think about it. You say you're not a writer? I am, and I become you on paper!*

You don't have to go into a long dog-and-pony show to make your point. If you can get your prospect thinking about your service, you've done your job.

**The Billboard**: In this section, say why you're the person to do the job. Talk about your experience in the particular industry, your writing credits, your contacts with the media, or, if possible, mention other clients via testimonial.

> *I don't draw attention to myself; after all, I'm a ghost! But I've spent many years working in and around the medical profession as a nurse, claims examiner, and administrator. I've written practice-building material for other pediatricians. In addition, I've been published under my own name in Docs and Kids magazine (see enclosed). I can help you, and you can afford me.*

***

> *After ten years of working as a buyer for Macy's, I decided to step away and enter the editorial business in helping small retailers get the most for their limited promotion dollars. Because I know your industry, I can write the kind of material the local press is looking for and will publish. I'm also affordable.*

In this section you try to show the prospect that you're probably the best qualified person he can find to be his ghost. Be sure to mention that you're not going to cost them their firstborn!

**The Action:** The final section is where you ask the reader to take one or several actions. Since you should always include a short flyer about ghostwriting (see below), direct your prospect to read it. Then tell him to call or fax you with his requirements. If you plan to call him, state it in the letter.

> *Give me a call, or fax me a fax. I can be your ghost by wire! We need never meet. I have several ideas for possible assignments and would be pleased to hear yours.*

\*\*\*

*Can we get together? I think you'll find the time quite worthwhile. I'll call you next week to ask for an appointment.*

\*\*\*

*Keep my card. There are not that many ghosts around with the knowledge of the computer industry. Do call me if you want some solid publicity ideas.*

The above is only a guideline. There is no one right way to sell ghost services. Most people who do ghostwriting have several different "generic" sales letters on their computer. They choose one and customize it for each prospect or group of potential clients.

## Ghost Flyers

Because many of your prospects will not know what a ghostwriter is, you must impart some education. Part of this is via your introductory letter. The rest can be through a nicely composed, tastefully done flyer. While some ghosts have a tri-fold brochure, I suggest that you go with a short one-sided, one-page flyer that you can clip (don't staple) to your letter.

The purpose of the flyer is not to sell *you*, but to sell the service of ghostwriting. Some PEs title their flyer "The 5 Questions Most Asked About Ghosts" and do the flyer in a question-answer format. Another tried-and-true method is to compose the flyer in three-column format and title it so that it looks like it was a magazine article on ghostwriting. Another is to use ghost testimonials by making them up and just using initials of the supposed client. (I don't like this format, but people say it works.)

You need to follow three rules:

(1) Sell the benefits. Yes, you need some verbiage about what ghosting is (what you read above) and the process (next section). However, you must hammer home that, by hiring you as a ghost, your client should be able to get an article she "authored" published (no guarantee). She will reap all the benefits (actual and perceived) of being published. This will be a good thing for her business life, her social life, her chances for advancement, her ego, her company, and her sense of accomplishment.

---

*TIP*: A main reason people hire ghosts is ego. They want to see their names in print in a newspaper or magazine. Even if it's in the *Maybury Shopping Mall News*, they want to trot it out and show friends, clients, associates, bosses, and family. Most people think they have something to say (debatable) and want it said.

---

(2) Write a *short* solid paragraph on your background, qualifications, publishing credits, education, etc. No hype is necessary. It should read like a mini-resume. If you have particular industry experience, make sure you mention it. End the paragraph with something like: "I've got the qualifications, expertise, and experience to do the job."

(3) Get professional help with your flyer layout. Obviously, you should write the text. After all, if you can't write a convincing argument for using ghosts, you shouldn't be one! But take the text to a someone who does desktop publishing and get some ideas on the graphic layout. You don't need a fancy layout, just something appealing to the eye and not cluttered. Leave lots of white space. Go for the dignified look. It shouldn't look like a flyer for a used car lot or furniture store.

---

*TIP: You might be able to trade a graphic person's time for your writing time. She does your flyer; you do an article on her business. It's worth a try! Make sure you get your artwork back from the graphics person. Don't let her keep it since you may want to use it again.*

---

Other than those rules, the rest is up to you. Hopefully, you were able to get the literature that other ghosts use. If you can find a writers' organization (ask at the library), you'll meet several ghostwriters. Ask for a copy of their stuff (if necessary, tell them you plan to pass it on to an associate who is a potential client). Study their flyers. If you find that your new ghost friends are successful, then adapt their flyers to yours. But don't spend a lot of money on the flyer. A nice black-and-white piece on good bond paper will work fine. Don't have it quick-printed, just have a few hundred copied from the laser printer output.

## Should You Publish Your Price?

This is a perennial question among commercial writers. Some have elaborate price sheets with figures for every possible type of ghost writing (even if they only do one or two types). Others never print or mention a price in their letters, flyers, or sales materials.

I don't like the price sheet idea. However, I know that prospects always have the question in their mind: "Can I afford this?" After all, people have an idea what a lawyer, plumber, or doctor visit is going to cost. But who knows what it costs to have a ghostwriter perform a service? It's not exactly a service your client considers every day!

I suggest that in your flyer or in your letter you add some verbiage to the effect that your services are affordable. Mention that you don't work by the hour, but instead, by fixed price. Also mention that most articles run between X and Y dollars. By giving a range, you don't lock yourself into a specific price. More importantly, you don't get some client who assumes you will do a 2,000 word project for $150.

> *Quality costs, but probably not as much as you think. Articles in the area of 2,000 words cost in the range of $800 to $1,500, depending on the complexity and amount of research needed. All work is done on a fixed-price basis. Of course, there is no charge for any consultation. Actually most meetings are held by phone and fax! (I'm a ghost, remember?)*

A paragraph like the above should work for you. You want to put your client's mind at ease that he can afford you and that you won't be working on the clock. Of course, if the assignment is very difficult, you might decide that a time-and-materials bid is the best for you. But for most work, charge a fixed price.

---

*TIP*: When talking about prices for commercial ghostwriting, you might compare the cost of hiring you to the cost of an advertisement. Your services will often be cheaper and more effective than paid advertising.

---

## The Ghost Kit

Some ghosts like to create elaborate packages of sample articles, copies of clips from published works, copies of articles from the media about the benefits of ghostwritten material, testimonials, resumes etc.

My feeling is that the bigger your market, the smaller your package should be. A letter and flyer should suffice. If you have the material and the money, go ahead and assemble and mail a nice package. But for most of you, it's probably not necessary.

However, if you write for a very specialized market, like nuclear medicine, you'll need a well thought out and comprehensive ghost kit to present to prospects. You'll have to convince them that you have the necessary skills and knowledge about the discipline to do the job. I don't think you can effectively convey this with just a flyer.

If you have a some clips from freelance activities, you can include them in your kit. If you don't, consider submitting one or two possible articles to your prospects. This is not much different than freelancing with editors. Write two 1,500 word pieces and submit them to clients as you would submit to editors. If the pieces are any good, *and* you can convince the prospect that they have a good chance of being published, *and* you can convince them that a competitor will grab it if they don't, you should be able to make a sale.

---

**COMMENT**: *You're asking: "Will they steal the piece?" Put a copyright notice in bold print (not uppercase) at the top or bottom of each page and it won't get stolen.*

---

## Ghost Advertising

This sounds like a contradiction in terms, but many people who do ghost articles have found that a small ad in the right place is helpful in getting clients. The first key is to find the right place(s). The second is to create the right ad.

Obviously, you want to advertise in publications that are read by prospective clients. A large circulation is not necessary. Often a small ad in an organization newsletter can be very success-

> *TIP*: *If they offer to give you a reader service number, decline. Make readers respond by mail, fax, or phone. If someone takes the time to call or clip the ad and send you a note, they are interested. Those who just circle a number on a postcard are tire-kickers.*

small ad does not have room for lots of sales chatter. Just
o business. In a clear and concise fashion, tell who you are,
services you offer, what clients you serve, and how they
d contact you.

**I Ghost**. *Freelance writer specializing in computers, technology, and automation writes articles for you to publish under your name. Confidentiality guaranteed. Contact J.J. Tel/Fax 123-456-7890.*

\*\*\*

**Be Published**. *Your career and advancement opportunities can be enhanced by being published. Freelance writer specializing in medical and clinical topics will write for you. The celebrities do it, why not you? Contact Sue in confidence. Tel/Fax 123-456-7890*

Jse a two- or three-word hook to get the reader interested.
times, the hook is all that people read when they are scan-
classified ads. I also suggest that you not print your address;
es up too much space. If you have a fax number, use it. You
t want to only use your initials or first name.

epetition helps create an awareness of your service, so be
red to run the ad three or four times. (Sometimes you'll get
uency discount.)

Classified ads are easy to place. You usually pay by the word.
ype out your copy, enclose it with a letter saying what clas-

ful if the right people read it. So don't
circulation alone. As you read, make note
commercial writers. Give the advertiser
has worked for them. Most will be honest
highly competitive area.

> **COMMENT**: There is an old saying, "In
> lawyer starves, but two make a fortune
> lieve that several ads in a magazine fo
> than if you're the only one. When read
> than one person does ghosting, it legitin
> in their minds. The think: "If there are a lo
> must be a lot of clients. Maybe I should l

There is no need to limit yourself to l
though they will probably be the cheapest)
ily done by phone and fax.

You can run either display or classified
usually cheaper). Sometimes you can run a
sified section. Whatever you do, follow two

(1) If using the classified ads, make su
your ad in the section for *editorial services* o
special section for your ad if they don't alre
will be glad to). Don't let them throw you
other services or products.

(2) Keep the ad small. You don't want t
into advertising until you know if it will wor
mum is one inch. Don't let ad salespeople ta
bigger than three inches. However, if over ti
zine that pulls (ad lingo for "gets prospects'
ing the size of the ad.

sification you want it placed in, enclose your check, and mail it to the classified advertising department.

If you plan to run a two- or three-inch display ad, find someone to lay out the graphics for you. Some magazines have standards (called "mechanicals" in the trade) that you have to follow. Larger publications will gladly send you a media kit with a rate card. Most media kits will contain facts (and fiction) on the demographics of the magazine, their editorial schedule (magazines are planned up to a year in advance), and a mechanical sheet with their specifications. Just give this to the graphics person. They've seen these before and will know how to knock out a small ad for you.

As for the rate card, almost nobody buys display advertising from the rate card. It's like the sticker on the new car. You can almost always get a discount by just asking. Most magazines give a 15% commission to advertising agencies. Most will pass this along to you also *if you ask for it* (believe me, they won't volunteer).

Some magazines may be able to offer you what is called remnant space. This is space that, at closing time (usually two months before publication) hasn't been sold. Like Macy's, they have a half-price sale. Again, you must ask for it. Also, you must be able to get them artwork (that is, camera-ready copy) in a day or two. This should be no big deal if your graphics person has the copy on her computer.

---

**COMMENT**: *I'm not a strong proponent for advertising ghost services. Depending on your subject area, it might be worth a try, but don't spend much money or get your hopes up. However, if you see an ad time and time again for another commercial writer, it must be working for them, so go for it.*

---

## Ghost Terms

Before you speak with a client, decide on what terms you're going to do business. Many ghosts work only when paid in full up front. Some ghosts work entirely on spec and are only paid when the client accepts the work. I don't like either method. Instead, I suggest you ask for 50% of your fee up front and the other 50% on client acceptance. If you explain to your client (if she asks) why this is fair, most will have no objection. It's fair because if the client declines the work, at least you get paid a bare minimum for your time. If they don't like the work, they are not stuck for the entire bill. The risk is spread evenly between both parties.

> *TIP:* If a client has a difficult time paying half the fee up front, I would walk away. You could be dealing with someone who will cheat you with a bad check or by stealing the piece.

What happens if the piece is never published? Some ghosts give back 20% of the fee, but most don't. If you spell out to your client during the sales process (see below) that there's no guarantee the piece will get any ink, you should be all right. You and the client are going to work closely to hone an article that both of you think will be publishable. You both take a risk. It's not unlike a lawyer taking a client's case to trial. Neither client nor lawyer knows who will win, but the lawyer gets his or her costs covered either way. The same is true when a stockbroker sells a client a mutual fund or when a surgeon operates. The service is paid for regardless of the result.

## Ghost Sales - Five Easy Pieces

Making a ghost sale is not hard because most clients will already be sold on the concept, if your flyer and letter are good. Simply rehearse (with a friend or family member) what you'll say in person or when the phone rings. It should take about 10 minutes to cover all the bases. You usually won't close over the first phone call or visit. Most often it will take a second call to make the sale.

The first thing you should get across to the client is that most of the process can be done by phone and fax as opposed to meetings. This saves everybody time. If you tell clients that "this is how it's done," and say it convincingly, most will be glad to comply. You don't want to waste time driving, especially if the client is in a different city. *The fax machine is the best medium for handling this business.* Stress confidentiality (no one at the client's office will see you).

However, some local clients will want an initial meeting. There is not much you can do but put on your nice clothes and see the prospect.

---

**COMMENT**: *You might run into age discrimination when you meet clients face to face. Don't say I didn't warn you. I advise PEs to avoid client meetings, if possible, until the project is done.*

---

The second item you must get across is that, while you will do your best to produce publishable material, there is *no guarantee*. Make sure you repeat this enough so it sinks in.

The third part of the sale should be a nice three-minute speech on what you do, how you do it, and what the benefits to the client will be. Most of this information should be in your brochure. Rehearse this so you know it cold, but keep it short.

The fourth part is to get some information about them and their business. Ask them to fax you a resume and information on their firm.

The fifth part of the sale is to discuss the article. Most clients will have titles in mind. If they don't, propose one or two on the fly (after all, you're an expert in their field, right?). If there is no agreement on a title (there seldom is), tell them you will propose several titles when you fax them your contract letter or letter of understanding.

That's about it. No hype, no pressure, no urgency. In fact, it will often work to your advantage to mention (only if *they* call you) how you're quite busy and are not certain you can take an assignment this month. Anyway, don't beat anyone over the head. Just explain what you do and what the benefits will be. Emphasize that there are no guarantees. Tell them that you're a good writer who can create a publishable piece. Do all of the above in a matter-of-fact voice without hype or urgency. Practice your pitch. It's not a hard sell.

## Who Should Submit?

Some ghosts deliver their work and walk away. However, most assume the task of submitting the article to a specified number of publications. Remember, you will send the article off under the client's name and address. Some clients will give you copies of their letterhead for this purpose, but you can always make up your own on your word processor.

Is your job done after the last submission goes out? Possibly. Sometimes an editor will want changes or additions. She will contact the client, not you (she doesn't know about you). The client will call and let you know about the editor's request, so be prepared to work a little more on the piece. Even if it's a lot of work, you can't make an additional charge to the client. The client took the risk that it would not be published. Your risk was that you would not have to work more hours than your were fairly paid for in doing the piece. Anyway, most changes are minor.

---

*COMMENT: Many times submission is not an issue because your client will already have reserved space in a company newsletter or association mailing.*

---

## The Deal

After you've talked with your prospect, send a letter of understanding (known in government lingo as an LOU) along with a cover letter explaining the process you will follow.

The LOU should be short and sweet, and should cover only the terms of the deal: the scope of the work, the payment and terms, the risk, and the expected completion date. Don't make it overly complicated by using legal terms or by covering more than necessary.

Below is an LOU that covers the bases: You can adapt it to fit your circumstances. Some ghosts do not take on the job of submitting the work for publication. If so, your LOU should state this. Always, always, always make sure your client understands that there is no guarantee the work will ever be published. You can also put in verbiage about giving back a part of the fee (say 20%) if the article isn't published within a year.

---

*TIP: Sometimes putting in a 20% refund if the piece is not published will help close a sale because it gives the client confidence that her financial risk is limited.*

---

I use this simple letter of understanding as our agreement. Please sign and enter the date below.

I will write one article containing approximately 1,500 words and two photos. My fee for this work will be $800. The first half of my fee ($400) will be paid upon agreement of a title. The second half is payable upon delivery and your acceptance.

While the work is in development, I will retain all rights. Upon acceptance and payment, I will sign all rights to the work to you.

I will submit the work, under your name, to the publications we agree upon when we determine the title. Any fees received for publication belong to you.

You understand that, while I will do my best to create a publishable work, there is no guarantee that it will be published and that my fee is not contingent upon publication.

Should editorial changes be requested by the publication receiving first rights, I will be happy to make them at no charge.

## The Ghost Process

Agreement on titles and submissions may occur before or after the signing of the LOU. Nothing is carved in stone. Often the ghost will write up a mini-proposal and send it off to a prospective client. This proposal will include title suggestions, names of magazines and papers to submit to, a short synopsis of the article, and why it's likely to get some ink.

Many times the client will have an exact title in mind for you to work on. In that case, you can flesh out the contents of the article from your own knowledge and research, or from talking with the client.

If you don't put the details of the agreed-upon title and publications for submission in the LOU, make sure you do it in a separate letter. You don't want to end up in a situation where the client tells you that she "thinks she understood what she thought you said!"

Either way, you must reach agreement with the client on what you're going to write about as well as the main points the piece will cover. Once the two of you decide on the title, collect either half or all of your fee, depending on your terms.

If you're going to write an article that will profile the author, the company, or a product, make sure the client sends you *all* of the background material you will need.

> *TIP*: If possible, get a resume of the "author" you are ghosting for as it will help you write in his style. If your client only has a high school education, it's unlikely he will write like a college professor!

When you write the ghost piece, you must understand one very important fact: The article must not be a blatant sales piece. It's important that it extols the virtues of your client's product or service in a *subtle* way. The article must present news and information that's important to the readership, and it must be fair and objective. You're not writing an advertisement. The PR piece must meet the same journalistic standards that a regular freelance piece would, even though both you and the editor will know it's a publicity piece.

When you read the publications you plan to submit to, you will probably not be able to pick out the freelance material from the ghosted material. This is how it should be. However, you should pay particular attention to how other authors present material that is really advertising but done in a journalistic format.

On the other hand, sometimes an entire article will be on a particular product or person. This is what the editor wants. For example, if a local company comes out with a new product or service, publications want to profile it. When a new franchise moves to your area, editors want to run pieces on the business, especially if the service or product is popular in other parts of the country. For example, when the first company that produced "quick" signs for businesses opened in my area, the local print media ran all types of articles on the service. After all, it was new and different.

This is the key: new and different. You can always get ink for a publicity piece if it tells a unique story. Whenever you do a ghost job, ask the client what is new and different about her business or service. If nothing is new, make something new! Editors don't want old and boring!

---

**COMMENT**: *A skill you bring to the client is your ability to see her business or service from the media standpoint and to create work that will get media attention. This is part of why she is paying you. You're not just putting words on paper.*

---

Some articles are not designed to directly pitch a particular business or service, but are written to give the "author" visibility and prestige. Professionals often hire ghosts to do articles about a segment of their service, but the piece never mentions them or their firm directly. For example, a doctor might hire you to write an article on "How To Choose a Physician" or "Deciding Where To Have Your Baby." Often, they want these articles written in the first person as advice columns. But many editors will not run such pieces because they smack of self promotion. An experienced ghost will suggest to the client that the piece be in the traditional journalistic style of the reporter's (third person) voice. This way, the article has a better chance of being published.

You should understand that the entire ghost process is client-driven. When you do freelance work, you decide what does and doesn't go into the work. When you write as a ghost, your client has the final word on what's written and how it's styled. After all, the client is paying for this privilege. The client has the right to be wrong.

> **COMMENT**: *However, the client should only be wrong over your objections. Make sure you tell her your feelings and concerns. But if she stands firm, then you have to accept it.*

When you or your client come up with a title or concept, you should decide what type of article it will be (consult the article types presented earlier). One type you should always suggest to the client is the case history or testimonial. Trade journals love the reader take-away of case histories. Clients like them because case histories can easily be turned into advertising and promotional pieces. Editors as well as readers tend to believe case histories, especially when they primarily contain quotes and experiences of real customers. For case histories, contact the client's customers and get information on:

- What the problem was and why it was an important one.
- Solutions that were considered.
- How the customer determined that your client's product was best.
- What was done to solve the problem.
- How the solution made improvements in the customer's company.

The process of developing a ghost article is an iterative one. You do your research, write the piece, and fax it to the client. The client will make corrections or suggestions and fax it back. You rewrite the piece and send it to the client. It may end here, or you and the client may ride the merry-go-round several more turns.

## Does the Ghost Materialize?

In a word, no. Confidentiality is the key. You never, never, never reveal a client without the permission of that client. You also don't show the work you did for one client (even with the name crossed out) without permission. Remember, the client wants the community to think he or she wrote the article. Even if everyone knows that the client couldn't spell CAT without help, and even if everyone knows that he or she probably hired a ghost, never admit to the fact without the client's permission.

An interesting turn of events is that clients often leak the fact that they hired a ghost. It's become sort of fashionable to have someone else write for you while you take the credit. Actually, having a ghost is a subtle sign of power and prestige. People think, "Well, she's too busy and important to sit down and write so she sketches it out and hires a ghost."

---

*TIP*: Many ghosts use this concept in their marketing materials. When they pitch to a high ranking executive or public official, they play to the person's ego.

---

If you want to use a client as a reference, call him and say that you would like to show "his" work to another prospect without mentioning names. Make sure you alert your client to the possibility that the prospect might remember seeing the piece, remember who "did" it and thus, know your client's secret.

## A Few Miscellaneous Notes on Ghosting

I've spent much of this book pontificating on the thesis that you can make an income writing about what you know from your life's work, vocation, or hobby. Ghosting can broaden your range.

If you have an aptitude for writing and for research, you can ghost almost anything. If you have expertise in a client's area, so much the better, but not all clients require it, nor could they all find ghosts if they did.

If you have the "gift of ghost," someone else's expertise will flow on to your screen. If you can extract the necessary information from a person then synthesize it into coherent paragraphs, you can write on just about any topic. It's not uncommon for ghosts to write on heavy duty scientific projects as well as ordinary run-of-the-mill business assignments.

Clients may come to you with an article already written and want you to "punch it up" in an acceptable style. You may add a few topics and subtract a few paragraphs to come up with a publishable piece. Is this ghosting or editing? I don't know, but either way, you should be well paid.

The best qualification you can have is to be sensitive to the egos of your clients and be able to show them at their best. You have to be flexible with the client in order to produce an article that not only meets your standards, but those of the client.

If you can work well with people, understand their egos, and be willing to give up the credit, you can do well as a ghost. And the word will get around.

You will be surprised at the types of people who approach you for ghost jobs. Most will be intelligent people who simply can't write. Some will be too busy, and a few will just not want to do the work involved in writing an article.

There will be some clients you'll want to steer clear of. These are the people who want you to collaborate with them on a book that's sure to make a zillion dollars, and of course, you will share half the profits. Dream on! If you do ghost work on spec, sooner or later you will get burned by a non-payer.

Ghosting can be a good business for the PE. It's easy to get into, does not require a long list of references (confidentiality discourages references), and the pay can be pretty good.

But another area of commercial writing is also a possibility for the PE: public relations copywriting. Like ghosting, it's not for everybody, but it might be right for you.

# 11

· · · · · · · · · · · · · · ·

## P R   W R I T I N G

### Flacks, Hacks, and the Media Staffer

The first cousin to ghost work is public relations work. They are similar in that both are well paid. I classify the difference between the two by noting that ghostwritten items are usually done with the intent of getting a byline for the client. PR writing, on the other hand, is always unsigned.

If you decide to investigate the avenue of PR writing you'll soon learn that both freelancers and the paid writing staff of newspapers and magazines will consider you a class below themselves. Every PR person knows the reason and almost every reporter and editor also knows the reason. But, the media people won't express it. In a word, it's jealousy. PR people are paid far better than most reporters and editors, and this is considered immoral! Not surprisingly, PR people are labeled hacks and flacks.

> *COMMENT: It's a good piece of rationalization which works to the mental advantage of media staffers. It's always nice to believe that someone is lower on the totem pole than you. All prejudice is based on such an assumption.*

Yet, what happens when reporters and editors either quit their jobs or are laid off? They go to ad agencies and PR firms, become media consultants, or join the PR department of some company or government agency. They become what they previously disdained.

> *COMMENT: The whole "attitude" that media staffers have about PR writers is nothing more than a cover-up of their envy for what PR people often earn.*

So, if you ever hear garbage about someone not being a "real" writer because she creates print PR, you know to look to the source. It's probably some lower paid reporter or overworked editor.

> *COMMENT: I believe that the arrogance and snobbery of many print media people is "compensation" for the low pay and long hours. If you think they don't like PR people, you ought to hear what they think about TV and radio anchor people!*

## Your Contribution is Valuable

Most newspapers and magazines would find it very difficult to cover their markets without the constant flow of information provided by PR writers. In most papers today, editors and reporters hardly leave their desks. They don't get the news; they distill it! From the mountain of press releases that come in, they choose those that seem promising, make a few calls to verify a fact or two or get a different quote, and send the release to a copy editor for tomorrow's edition.

What would happen if no more releases from public officials and government agencies were sent? What if no business news releases were sent to the business editor? What would happen if the scene/lifestyle editors received no information from clothing manufacturers, no announcement of new products from home improvement firms, no reports about new food products from processors, no interior decorating ideas from furniture makers? What if the flow of photos, bios, and news releases from college and professional sports promoters suddenly ceased? What if industry associations stopped sending background stories on technical subjects and new products to the editor in charge of computers and technology? How would the travel section look if tour companies stopped sending articles and pictures about exotic locations?

The media needs a constant flow of information from the PR community. There is no way any paper, even one as well staffed as the *New York Times*, can fill all its pages solely from information gathered by their staff reporters. If you look at the number of stories a paper has each day contrasted with the number of editors and reporters, you'll understand why the media desperately needs the services of PR writers.

---

**COMMENT:** *A large part of most papers are wire service features. Many of these are contributed by public relations people either directly to the service or through a paper that subscribes to the service.*

---

Attitudes toward PR people are changing due to the downsizing and reduced readership of many papers. Newspapers are not in the business of reporting news; they are in the business of selling ads and subscriptions. The news-content is just the vehicle. In many cities, a PR writer who can consistently supply a paper or magazine (for free) with the type of news that helps sell papers is more highly regarded than your average paid reporter. The city editor won't admit this, but the managing editor or publisher will!

It's a fact of business life that most media (print and electronic) entities could not stay in business without hundreds of PR people supplying information.

## Is It PR or Advertising?

PR and advertising are terms that confuse most people, and rightly so, because if you look at the intent of each, it's often hard to tell one from the other. The purpose of PR and advertising is to get a message to the public through the media. Whether the message is about an upcoming charity event, a new dry cleaning process, the opening of a new law office, or whatever, the intent is the same.

However, advertising is a paid-for commodity. Someone buys space or time in the media and presents the message. Most often the message is to inform the customer about something he should buy.

PR is free. The message is deemed by the editor to have some kind of news or information value to her readership.

The job of the advertising copywriter is to see that the ad gets noticed by the reader or listener. The job of the PR writer is to create news and information out of what is usually an advertising message.

I'll go into more detail later, but here is a simple example. A dry cleaner gets a new machine that will remove any stain known to mankind. He could take an ad out telling people to bring in their stained clothes. He would pay for this ad.

Or he could write up a ten-line press release announcing the availability of the new process. Would an editor print it? Probably not. Where is the news value? Where is the reader interest?

Or, he could hire you to create a PR piece on the new cleaning technology now available. You would write about how this will revolutionize the cleaning industry, allow people to keep their clothes longer and save money by not having to replace badly soiled articles. And, in passing, you would mention the name and location of the cleaning store. Would this get printed? It sure has a better chance than the above. Why? Because there is news and information value.

You've heard the job description of "spin doctor"? Your job is to put a "spin" on something that is rather mundane, so that it will appeal to an editor's sense of news and information.

## I Don't Preach Advertising

I don't recommend that PEs use whatever writing talents they have for advertising, although I have nothing against advertising work. I believe that public relations work is not only easier to grasp, but is more suited to PEs. For one thing, you don't have to be a Ph.D. to create good PR.

Advertising, however, is another matter. You may think you could write a good ad for some product or service. More than likely you can't. Go ahead and try. Pick some product you know a lot about and compose an ad that would fit in a 3x5 space.

Unless you have a background in buying psychology, media graphics, marketing demographics, and can blend the message of the product with the content of the media (an ad for beer is different in *Sports Illustrated* than in *The New Yorker*), you're not going to make it in the advertising world. Advertising requires a specific set of skills that you have to develop over a long period of time. Such skills are not picked up in a few weeks.

Doing PR work is not as difficult. Far fewer variables are involved, and once you learn the basics, you can apply them over and over for different clients. PR is not that different from freelance writing. You take something common and make it uncommon. You create something interesting from something boring. It's really a lot easier than creating good advertising.

---

**COMMENT**: *A main reason I discourage PEs from advertising work is that they would have to learn all about the wonderful world of graphics. Advertising is visual; PR is not. Outside of knowing how to take a picture, you don't have to know much about the graphic arts for PR.*

---

## The PR Menu

There are three main menu choices when it comes to doing PR work. The first is called house work. This is the creation of internal publications such as brochures, newsletters, annual reports, catalog copy, as well as the occasional direct mail piece. I urge PEs to stay away from most house work because it will often be more involved and take more hours than the average PE will want. If you desire full-time work, fine, go after house work; but make sure you have a solid background in graphics. For most of you, there are better choices on the menu. I won't discuss house work in detail, as I believe trying to give you a background in graphics is beyond the scope of this book

**COMMENT**: *Many, many freelance people specialize in brochures for companies or industries they know. This can make you a lot of money if you want to devote the time. You're probably looking at a lot more than a 20-hour week to turn out good house copy.*

The second alternative, and the one I recommend, is media work. Writing press material is not just confined to the print media; TV and radio also need information; and you'll find clients who will want you to compose items for the electronic media. The creation of most promotional press releases is not difficult to master. The real learning curve for most PEs is finding out how to "work" the media. Clients hire you not only for your writing skills, but also for your knowledge of what the media is looking for, and your ability to get ink.

A final avenue that appeals to PEs is grant writing. The general public probably has little knowledge of the grant process, yet grants are the lifeblood of many government, charitable, and educational institutions. I cover this in the next chapter.

The theme of this book has been to show you how you can make some money writing about what you already know, mostly from your previous career. PR work is not as limiting. If you learn and understand the basics of creating good media or proposals, you can apply the knowledge to many different areas in which you may not be expert. Say you were a science teacher before you retired. You could certainly create press material for a company involved in bio-tech or write a grant proposal for a hospital looking for funds for special equipment. But, with the same skills, you could also write press releases for a computer store or shoe manufacturer. You could write a grant proposal for a nonprofit council seeking funds to retrain laid-off defense workers.

Remember that press is press, and grants are grants. Once

you learn the style and develop a feel for how to create news from non-news, you can create press for almost anyone. And most grants follow a certain structure and seek to answer the same questions. Learn the process and you can write proposals for many different organizations. It's a skill, not a talent; a craft, not a gift.

## The Media

Media people have assumed an exalted status in our society. When you find out that someone at a party is an editor or reporter for some media organization, does your behavior change? You bet! Who would you rather talk to at the party: the editor of the woman's page or a life insurance salesman? Take a quick look at some of the most successful TV shows. They're about media people (*Mary Tyler Moore, Lou Grant, Murphy Brown, Home Improvement, Bob Newhart, WKRP*). We see media jobs as glamour professions and the people in them as larger than life.

It's just not true.

However, one absolute fact of life applies to all people who work in the media: they are busy. They have important deadlines to meet and they don't have time for idle chatter. People who work in the media have a reputation for being rude and brusque. This is a perception of non-media people who don't understand the pressures of getting out a paper or putting together a news show. What looks effortless is, in reality, a process with a million details and ten million things that can go wrong (and sometimes do!).

In dealing with the media, always understand that time is their most important currency. Their deadlines are real. If they can't meet them, the publisher or station owner will find other people who can. Media people are not interested in you, where you've been, what you do, what you've done, what you can do, or how you do it. All they want is your story and they want it quickly.

Another concept you should know is this: there are many types of media out there! Most of you, if asked about available news media, would name the largest regional paper, the three network TV stations, one or two talk-radio stations, and perhaps a local magazine. There are many more than that. Look in the Yellow Pages under newspapers, radio stations, television stations, and publishers. No matter where you live, more outlets for information are out there than you're aware of. It will be your job to know who covers what.

> **COMMENT**: Don't always go by circulation. Many special newspapers and radio stations target certain demographic groups (blacks, Hispanics, seniors, etc.). None of them have huge audiences, but taken together, the numbers are sizable.

In the larger city newsprint media, you should know three important editors. The first is the city editor. This person usually oversees a staff of general assignment reporters who may cover your area of expertise. Most often these areas are defined along the lines of subject matter and geography. For example, there might be a reporter who covers city hall, one who handles issues on health and welfare, and another who might cover the courthouse. But on smaller papers, reporters wear more than one hat.

The business editor will also have a staff of reporters whose assignments usually are made by industry groups. One might cover computer and technical stories, another the retail area, and another finance.

It used to be called the women's page, but this part of the paper has expanded in scope. Now the editor is usually called the lifestyle, scene, or features editor. Reporters here cover subjects like sewing and cooking, health, entertainment, advice, new books, travel, and anything else that's not business, sports, or news-event related.

Large TV and radio stations are often organized like papers; however, most have smaller staffs. At smaller stations (as well as newspapers), reporters may not be assigned special subject areas; they cover whatever assignments the news director hands them.

> **COMMENT**: *How can they do this? It's simple. They rely on PR material being sent to them. Most of their work is done for them by writers like you!*

## Making Contact with the Media Elite

There are two schools of thought on making contact with the media. But first understand that these people *are* approachable - maybe not directly, but if your story is good, you will get through. Of course, there are limits. It's unlikely you will speak with Dan Rather or the business editor of the *New York Times*.

> **COMMENT**: *And you don't want to. Most TV and radio anchor people just read the news, they don't write it. The Times editor is probably more interested in space allocations (against the sports section!) and staffing problems than in content. These people can kill your release, but not promote it. That's left for junior staff.*

You must also know who to contact and how to find them. This is no big trick. Get on the phone and ask. You can call the largest or smallest paper in the world and ask who covers what topic. Just remember that media turnover is rapid and "hats" change so often that many staffers are not sure who does what!

Now to the two schools of thought concerning media contact. The first school says that PR writers (often called publicists) should make the rounds either in person or by phone to the movers and shakers of the local media. If you live in a small population area or you're dealing with a small publication or station, by all means, call the names on your list and just introduce yourself and ask if they're looking for any stories in particular.

The second school says to wait until you have a piece you want to submit and then call around, introduce yourself, and tell them a piece is on the way (but don't pitch it).

Both schools of thought are founded on the concept that by making contact with the media, you can forge a friendship that will help get your pieces printed. Media people are human; they like to associate a voice or face to a name. There's no problem with you doing either of the above; no damage will be done. However, I don't think it's a good use of your time.

The Canton school of thought is this: Wait until you have an item, then pitch it to the right person via a quick phone call.

If I had just written a press release for a client company that developed a new software-only voice mail system that runs on a PC, here is what I would do: Call the paper and find out who is reporting on business technology (this week!). When I find the person, I'd say "Susan, this is Al Canton speaking. I'm a PR writer. Can I have 30 seconds to make a pitch? [yes] I have a release on an important new product from one of our local technical firms. It's a real innovation in voice mail technology. Would you have any interest?" If she says no, I thank her for her time and end by saying, "OK, no problem, Susan. I just wanted to give your paper first crack at it before I sent it off to KXYZ. When I get another item, I'll call you. Thanks." Ninety percent of the time she will then say, "Well, why don't you send it to me." I tell her I'll send it and follow up with, "Hey, I know you're on deadline [they're always on deadline], but are you looking for any other stories . . . I have several clients in the technology area"? Sometimes they will tell you what they are looking for, sometimes not. Finally, I ask if I should fax it, mail it, or both?

Remember, these people are busy. They talk and think in sound bites. If you tell them you only want to do a 30-second pitch, you'll sound like a pro and you'll be treated as one. If they want to know more, try to resist them. I say something like "Susan, it's pretty involved and the release has all the facts. It's really going to be a hot product. The company is New Voice Technology. You'll find the piece interesting. Would you like me to fax it?" Note that I gave her some information, but I left her in suspense. I was also quick and to the point.

When I send the piece, I'll send a short cover letter thanking her for her time and telling her to call if she needs more information. I end it by saying something like "If you find yourself looking for material on computers, technology, or software, give me call. I might be a good source for you. Being an expert in the area, I know where some of the bodies are buried!"

When and if you decide to contact a media person use common sense. There are a lot of pieces that the media will publish that don't need personal contact and where contact would probably be a waste of time. For example, if a financial industry association hired you to write a press release on a public seminar they're giving on "Investment Trends of the 90s," there's little reason to call a paper and inform them of the event. Most papers will publish an inch or two about upcoming business events. If you called a reporter, he or she would ask, "Why are you calling me on this?" Media people expect you to use some professional judgment on whether or not to bug them. They expect you to know what their paper routinely publishes, and they expect you to only call them on special items.

---

**COMMENT**: *There is some ego involved here. Many reporters like to be queried; it gives them a sense of power and self-esteem. But they want to be queried on important pieces, not run-of-the-mill, mundane stuff.*

---

When it comes to the electronic media, you can forget about contacting the on-air people. With some notable exceptions, most local news anchors are hired for their looks and voice, not their journalistic abilities. Most stations have an assignment editor. Non-talk radio usually has a person who wears the "news director" hat in addition to other hats. You can always call the station manager or his/her assistant and ask to whom you should send your releases.

Remember: professionalism is the key. Act like a professional and you'll be treated like one. A professional publicist is quick and to the point. Being able to make good conversation is not considered a professional ability and too much of it is unwise. It's this simple:

> *Mr. Jones, this is Al Canton speaking. I'm a PR writer. Can I have 30 seconds? Are you the person I should send a story about an innovative real estate service offered by a local firm? I think the firm is one of your advertisers, so I thought your paper (station) would want first crack at this. Fine. By the way, to what other areas are you assigned? OK, I'll note that in my database. Thanks. I'll get this to you ASAP. Is it OK to fax it? What's the number?*

The next time you call Mr. Jones, build on the previous contact by reminding him that you sent in that real estate story he did. However, always ask permission to speak and always be brief. And when Mr. Jones inks your piece, send a brief thank-you note.

---

*TIP*: Buy a box of plain white fold-over cards that just say "Thank You" on them. These are the kind new brides use for wedding gift thank-you notes. Write a sentence such as "John, Thanks for running the real estate story in Monday's edition." Sign your name. Don't gush, and don't pander. A quick note like this will go a long way in getting your next piece printed.

---

## Targeting Your Markets

With any business or service, you have to determine just who your market is. A public relations writer can have a very broad market or a very targeted one, depending on the scope you want to pursue. If real estate is your background, you can definitely market agents, lawyers, escrow companies and others affiliated with the real estate industry. But if you wanted to, you could also market your services to the building trades, the insurance industry, and certain retail outlets (such as furniture and hardware stores - places people spend money after buying a house).

I keep coming back to this point over and over again: Think in derivatives. What do you know that you can apply outside your immediate field? For example, I'm a computer expert. I know these machines inside and out, as well as the software that runs them. But most people aren't interested in computers; they're interested in what they can do with them. Thus, I try to write on how business can profit from the use of technology. This is what people want to read about and what editors want to publish.

A woman in Nevada worked in the gaming industry as an accountant. Most large casinos have in-house PR people and don't use freelancers. However, from her years in the casino business she learned a lot about customer service. She seeks out small businesses and sells them on having her do press pieces on the innovative ways they serve their customers. She writes pieces about doctors who make home visits, insurance agents who go to the scene of a client's house fire, stores that deliver on holidays, repair people who guarantee their arrival time, etc. The news media likes these kinds of pieces, and she does very well.

A Houston man who was a contracts administrator for an oil company sells his PR service to small subcontractors and helps them announce new services or accounts through the oil trade press. He also does PR pieces for equipment manufacturers and start-ups.

A retired nurse in Detroit writes news releases for several small substance abuse centers and convalescent hospitals. In addition, she writes press material for medical rental companies and gets these published in hospital in-house newsletters.

I don't care what you did in your former job. If you can write, you can make money doing PR. If you were a homemaker all your life, you have areas of knowledge that can be translated into a PR writing service for some sector of the economy. It might relate to children, decorating, food preparation, education, gardening, or nutrition.

The magic method to finding your market is to follow the money trail. Ask yourself "who makes money in my area of interest and expertise?" Ask yourself "who is selling product and service to my area of expertise?" There will be more people than you think. This is how you can define your market. Let's take an example.

You sold furniture for the past ten years and are now retired. Obviously you could sell your services to furniture stores and manufacturers. Let's assume that there are no independent stores in your locale, and that the large chains won't hire you since they have their own PR people. So, who sells to the furniture industry or makes a living from it? Here are a few: decorators, paint stores, cabinet makers, carpet stores, office purchasing managers (who buy chairs and desks), hardware stores, home insurance agents, delivery companies, upholsterers, fabric stores, and even orthopedic doctors.

---

*COMMENT*: In the film It's A Wonderful Life, the character Jimmy Stewart plays discovers how many lives he touches. This theme carries through in the business world where one item affects many other sectors of the economy.

---

Another PR market is the netherworld of advertising agencies. While it may take a while to crack this market, if you're persistent, it can be done.

Agencies make commissions by selling advertising. While some larger firms have a PR department, most don't. However, they have clients who often need PR services and they will refer clients to freelance PR writers. Obviously, they want to refer clients to people they either have used in the past or are sure can do the job. Therefore, it may take you a while to get the trust of advertising people.

A final market you should consider, not only to sell to, but for referrals, are the organizations and associations in your area of interest. Also consider the associations related to your expertise. Think derivatives!

A Boston woman has a client that is an association of purchasing managers who specialize in buying computer parts and accessories. She also does PR for small firms that these purchasing managers buy from and often gets referrals from the association itself. It happens time and again where a buyer finds a product from a small company and suggests that the company get the word out so they can sell more (and lower the price). The company asks to whom they should turn and the buyer suggests that the company call the buyer's association for some referrals. This is how the woman picks up several projects a year and is a classic case of how PR people find clients.

## Stocking Your Sample case

What are clients buying? They want your writing skills and your knowledge of the media. As you can see, this is not much different from marketing ghostwriting services.

While the term portfolio is sometimes used to describe samples of one's writing, most often it refers to graphic samples. I prefer to call a collection of sample articles the "writing sample case." You have to stock your sample case with specific examples of your writing so that a client can browse through them and see how good you are.

Obviously, once you get some clients and have real samples along with the resulting news clips, your sample case will be complete. However, to get started without any clips, you need to demonstrate that you know what you're doing. The best way to do this is to create five sample press releases for mythical clients. For example, if you write on business technology, you could create a press release on how state-of-the-art answering equipment has given rise to services which allow businesses to have an e-mail drop point (especially from the Answer-Right company!) You might also have a press release on how law firms are able to do on-line research from databases around the world and how the firm of Monkfish, Flounder & Carp won an important case because of it. You could have a press piece on how portable computers have made the insurance reps (especially agents of the Town and County Insurance agency) more productive.

---

*TIP*: Keep sample press releases on your computer and use the merge feature to put in a prospect's company name if you decide to do a mailing to prospective clients.

---

Many PEs have found the addition of a flyer useful. Again, it's important to sell benefits, not features. This does not have to be fancy, but it should cover all the points on how a client will benefit from a public relations effort.

Finally, you should have a cover letter prepared. This is probably the first thing (maybe only thing) a prospect will read, so it should be a grabber. It should also be short, with a great opening sentence. You don't want hype, but you do want something beyond "I would like to introduce XYZ company to my services."

---

**COMMENT**: One of the best opening lines I ever saw simply read, "You need me." The second paragraph was also one sentence saying, If, after reading this letter, you don't think you need me, than you REALLY need me!" The letter went on talking about the benefits of public relations via press releases.

---

One other item might be included in your sample case. This is information of value that the prospect might keep and refer to later. Lots of PR writers include a sheet that has the names, addresses, and phone numbers of different editors (news, sports, business, etc.) of three or four local papers. You can put this on your letterhead or your flyer and headline it with something like: "Whether or not you use my services, these are some of the people in our area who you should be aware of, and who should be aware of you!"

Finally, you should have business cards printed up. They can be fancy or simple. You can get simple ones from most quick printers or large office supply stores like Office Depot for less than $20. Give yourself a title, such as Media Writer, Public Relations Specialist, or Contract Journalist. Don't forget to put your fax number on it. If you use one number, just list it as "Tel/Fax (123) 456-8765". Also, many people are putting their e-mail address on their cards and letterhead. If you have one via CompuServe, America Online, etc., it's probably a good idea.

---

*TIP*: *Stay away from the title "Freelance Writer." Unfortunately, the word "freelance" is often taken to mean anyone who can't get a job!*

---

That should about do it for your writing sample case. Some PR writers put this material on disk, some include very short cassette tapes, and some prepare expensive four-color brochures. My advice is to save the glitz and glitter. Unless you're going after some very high profile company, the good old time-honored folder with some writing samples, a flyer, and a letter should be all you need.

## Marketing Your Targets

Several strategies have been successful for PEs who write PR. I don't think any one is better than the others, and it's a good idea to try several.

Direct mail to clients is the most traditional and probably most effective way to get the word out. However, instead of sending out all of your sample case items, just send one mock-up press release along with a letter and a flyer. On cold-call mailings, you don't want to spend a lot of money on postage. In a first class postage business envelope, you can get 4 or 5 sheets of paper, depending on the thickness.

It's a good idea to follow up your letter with a phone call. Thus, it's not a good idea to send out a hundred letters on one day because it will be impossible to follow up with calls in a timely manner. I suggest you send only five letters a day so that you'll have time to follow up three or four days later.

A follow up phone call is not a big deal and no reason to get nervous. Accept the fact that you will not speak with most people you call; they will be traveling, in a meeting, on another line, etc. Also, the purpose is not so much to sell them as to demonstrate that you're a person who takes the writing business serious enough to follow up on your mailings.

If you can't reach a person, go with voice mail when available. If they don't have voice mail, leave your name and number with the secretary. If she asks what it regards, tell her your call pertains to the letter you sent Mr./Ms. So-and-so last week. Don't explain. Just say "Would you kindly let Mr. Jones know I called?" When the secretary says "yes," thank her and hang up.

If you get voice mail, leave a short message that goes something like this:

> Mary? This is Al Canton speaking. I'm the PR writer who sent you the material you should have received a few days ago. I hope you got it. I think I can really help your business in an affordable way. Please call me back at 555-1234. Mornings are best for me. Again, Al Canton, the writer, 555-1234.

If you reach the person to whom you sent the material, ask him if you were able to pique his interest. No matter what he says, tell him you would be glad to meet with him in person or to work with him via the phone and fax:

*Hi, Mary, Al Canton speaking. I sent you material about my PR writing services. Was I able to pique your interest? Can you see the value of favorable PR? [yes]. I would be glad to meet with you in person or we can do everything by phone and fax. The choice is yours. [phone, fax] Fine. What ideas do you have that the media might be interested in? [not sure.] OK, tell me about your business (practice, store, etc.) and let's see if we can develop some.*

---

**TIP**: Practice your phone call out loud over and over. The best method is to have a friend play the client, hook your tape recorder to the phone (or use your answering machine), and practice, practice, practice.

---

One of the most effective marketing techniques is the simplest. I call it the retail drop-off. Prepare a bunch of envelopes with your sample case information and keep them in the car. Whenever you go into a store that's either locally owned or franchised, ask if the owner is in. Tell the clerk you just want to drop off the envelope and you'd like to do it in person. If you go to a store on a weekday morning, many times the owner will be behind the counter. Let me give you an example of what happened when, out of curiosity, I went into a store that sells wild bird seed and other birding stuff (I'm a city kid, afraid of bees, bats, birds, snakes, and most forms of wildlife!):

*Hi, I'm Al Canton. This is an interesting store. My wife will love this place. I never knew it was here. I was visiting the store next door. You know, I'm a PR writer and I know the media will love reporting on your store. It's really unique. Why don't you look some of this stuff over when you get a moment and see if it interests you?*

It's that simple. No pressure. No hype. You can vary the message for almost any store. Even something as mundane as a dry cleaners or pet store. OK, it's a bit harder to come up with something unique about a dry cleaner, but with a little imagination, it can be done:

> *You know, I'll bet there is a story in here somewhere that would capture the attention of the papers. Maybe it's you! Anyway, why don't you take a look at some of this stuff and I'll give it some thought also. We can get together later.*

I can virtually guarantee that the average shop owner has never been approached by a PR person before. They will be receptive to your ideas as long as you're affordable. And who is more cost-effective than you? Certainly not a newspaper advertisement!

---

*TIP*: Don't waste time with large grocery or department stores. However, small stores, restaurants, service businesses, and professionals are good targets. If you write for the professions and are in a medical or legal building, just drop off a few envelopes with the receptionist asking him or her to give it to the office manager or managing partner. (Maybe get the name and scribble it on the envelope.) You have nothing to lose.

---

Another marketing tactic is to obtain referrals from local advertising agencies. You'll have to do some research to find out what agencies represent what types of businesses; for example, some just handle large law offices. Often, the reference librarian at any library with a business department can lead you in the correct direction. If there is a local advertising agency association, they may publish a list of members and their largest clients.

You will have to write an in-depth letter telling the agency what you do, why you're good at it, and the type of assignment you want. This letter must be good. Remember, you're selling to the masters of sales: ad people. Ask them to please start a file on you (some PR people enclose a manila folder with a pre-written tab) and to keep you in mind for possible PR projects that are too small for their own staff to handle. Emphasize that you specialize in short deadlines and try to make them feel comfortable with your level of knowledge in your area of expertise. Also emphasize that you're not looking for long-term commitments, but are only interested in one-shot projects. Send them all the stuff from your writing sample case and also mention that you will occasionally send them copies of future releases for their files.

The key to dealing with agencies is repetition. Agencies get one-time letters from wannabes all the time. But they never get that second or third letter. Make it a point to send some material (make up some hypothetical releases on *their* clients) every five or six weeks. If you do this with a dozen agencies, you'll eventually get referrals or subcontracted projects.

---

*TIP*: Never mention anything about finder fees or fee splitting. It's unprofessional.

---

Another target for marketing letters is associations and industry trade groups. Again, the librarian can help you get a list together. There are several strategies you can follow. You can seek the associations as clients, or ask for referrals. In the letter, start by asking for a copy of any printed media they publish so that you can add it to your files. Then explain your service and your availability. Ask if they keep a list of people like yourself that they make available to the membership, if you can attend a meeting, and if there's a mailing list available. Don't ask for free materials or a press pass; offer to pay meeting and mailing list fees, if any.

You should use the same strategy with associations that you use with advertising agencies. Choose the most important ones in your area of expertise and send them some material every 5 or 6 weeks.

---

*TIP*: *If you do any speaking tell them that you're available to speak and willing to fill in if there is a cancellation. Program chairpeople keep a list of potential last minute substitute speakers.*

---

Networking is another marketing method; however it has been a bit overdone in the past three or four years. There are a number of networking or "leads" clubs that you can join. The sole purpose of these organizations is to talk about being in business and to exchange referrals. Everybody comes to the meeting with the name of one client and these names are made available to the entire meeting. Many clubs only allow one member from each type of each business. Thus, there might only be one insurance broker and one real estate agent. You can bet that there won't be any PR writers!

Do these groups work? They can work if done correctly. Unfortunately, a name pops up at one of these meetings and the person gets called by 10 people offering some kind of service. By the time the 11th person calls, the businessperson is not a happy camper. Some clubs prohibit phone calls and only allow mailing.

Many networking clubs meet in the very early morning and have a $10 or $15 per meeting fee which pays for the breakfast. If you can find the right leads group, it might work for you. It depends on what you write about and where you live. I think it's worth a try, but not to the exclusion of other marketing methods.

And while I'm talking about networking, it's obvious that you have to spread the word within your own network; your banker, your tailor (your candlestick maker!). You do PR, right? Well, if you can't spread the word to everybody about your own business, how do you expect them to have confidence that you can spread news of theirs? So, make sure that you tell everyone you meet about your service. There is a simple way to do this. Whenever you meet someone new (like at a party), always ask them what they do (or did). When they tell you, reply "how interesting." Pause. They will almost always ask you about yourself. Simply say, "I'm a professional writer." Pause. They *will always ask* what you write. "I specialize in writing media releases and PR materials for doctors (or small business, or furniture stores, etc.). Here's my card. You say you were with XYZ company? What do they do?" The concept is to make your statement and back off. No one wants a dog-and-pony show about your writing business. If they ask, that's one thing, but don't give them a sales pitch.

Tell everyone about what you do. For example, when I'm at the pet store buying cat food, even if the clerk is only 16, I tell her while she rings up the sale:

> *You like working here? [yes] It sure beats my job. [what do you do?] I'm a writer. I do media releases, you know, public relations, for dentists and doctors. Oh, here's my card. Give it to your dentist. I'm sure you can't wait to see her!*

No matter what market you write for, tell everybody about it and try to give them a card. Sure, most of them will get tossed. But if one out of a hundred gets you a client, the other 99 served their purpose!

---

*TIP: When talking with people, follow two simple rules: Be brief, and be matter-of-fact. Use plain conversation, not a canned sales pitch.*

---

A final avenue for marketing is the writing group. Almost every community has some sort of writers' organization. Most meet monthly. Some areas have separate groups for fiction and nonfiction writers.

There are two types of people in writers groups. The majority will be people who write as a hobby and are not trying to make a business out of the craft. If they sell something, fine, but they have outside income (or day jobs) and their writing is a sideline. The minority will be people who are serious and knowledgeable about the business side of writing. They may not be doing it full time, but they make enough from it to be considered a second income. Obviously you should try to meet and get referrals from both groups. However, you'll have better results from those who take a serious business interest in the craft.

At the start of most meetings, everyone introduces themselves and mentions what type of writing they do, what they just sold, or if they need help researching a topic. This is a perfect time for you to say that you're available for referrals from anybody who can help you.

When you meet other writers during the breaks or after the meeting, don't try to sell them. During the course of the conversation, simply let them know that if they come across someone looking for a PR writer, they should keep you in mind. "Jack, if you get backed up, or hear of some work you don't want, keep me in mind. I'd really appreciate the help." Or "Joan, since you do features, if you come across someone needing PR stuff during your research, let me know, OK?"

To sum up marketing, I'll leave you with the two golden rules:

**Persistence**: Why do you think companies run the same ad over and over? One-shot marketing doesn't work. A single letter to a client or agency will probably not work. But if you send stuff out each month, a legitimizing effect takes place. After three or four letters (all somewhat different) an agency, association, or potential client will believe that you're not just a wannabe but that you're a real business entity. They get letters all the time from people they never hear from again. When a piece of work comes up, who will come to mind? The guy who sent them a letter three months ago or the gal who has been sending marketing material every six weeks? You don't have to send out a hundred letters on the first of each month. Just make a list of 30 to 60 possible letter targets and send out one or two each day. At the end of the list, start over.

**The Casual Word**: You've heard the old saying that 80% of the business comes from 20% of the customers; or 80% of the sales are made by 20% of the sales force? Well the majority of your business will actually come from word-of-mouth and casual contact. Most of your assignments will result from someone who knows someone (who knows someone!) who mentions you to them. Here is an example of the process. You write for the insurance business and send a marketing letter each month to a large insurance agency. Does the agency ever call you? No. But the office manager attends an insurance association luncheon where she meets a colleague who is getting ready to do a marketing campaign and needs help. The office manager tells the colleague that when she gets back to the office she'll fax your name to her friend. Another scenario is where you casually mention your writing business to someone *you feel* couldn't possibly use your services. Yet, they have been looking for someone like you for a long time. You get the job.

---

**COMMENT**: As someone once said "I'd rather have luck than talent."

---

A simple statement such as "This is a great store. You should get the word out. I know how to do it" can work wonders. They will always ask how and they will usually be pretty interested in what you do and the results you can get for them. You don't have to beat people over the head to sell your services. You're not selling aluminium siding or vacuum cleaners. You have an interesting service that has probably never really been explained to your prospect. Not everyone is going to be interested. Maybe not even most. But, enough professionals, associations, agencies, businesses, manufacturers, and institutions are looking for someone just like you. If you get the word out, you can make it as a PR writer.

## The Art of Making News

You must master two skills to make money as a PR writer. The first, and more valuable, skill is in distilling from a client what is newsworthy. The second is in knowing how to structure that information into a piece the media will use.

I believe that what your client is really paying you for is your ability to create news. An 8th grader can learn to write a "proper" press release. However, it takes creativity, imagination, and media-moxie to develop a rather mundane item into something the paper wants to print as news. So, let's look at a few ways that experienced PR people make news.

**Find Something Special**: Look for the attributes of a client's business, product, or activity that distinguish it from the competition. Remember, to be newsworthy a subject must have some distinct quality to the subject. Editors are experts in determining if the subject of your piece is news or puff. Thus, you have to *make* it news. This is done by showing how your client's business or service is special, unusual, and different from others in the community. Say your client is a veterinarian. Nothing special about that. But, if she works out of a van and does home visits, there is news value here. It's different. Wrap this around a theme of how home pet health care is less stressful for owners (and pets!), and you have news!

**Investigate the Customer**: Why do customers use the products or services of your client? Any successful business has something that keeps the clients coming back. It may not be anything distinctive, it may simply be something they do just a little better than others. If your client owns a beauty shop, there is not much news value in that. But if her clients keep returning because all of the staff have also taken courses in psychology so they can listen and understand the problems of the clients then give "arm chair" advice, you have a news item.

**Tie-in to Other News**: If there is a local angle to any national news story that you can relate your client to, you have a newsworthy piece. This is the single easiest way for you to get ink for your client. The possibilities are endless. There is almost always a way to tie your client's business or profession to either a national news event or information. It may take some creativity, but it can be done. Look for ways any event or news story relates to your client. For example, whenever the government comes out with a provocative study, editors look for a local opinion or commentary. When the government came out with the information that Mexican food was high in fat, a savvy PR writer in Portland faxed a mock-up of a press release to several local restaurants. The piece talked about how Mexican cuisine can be prepared without high concentrations of fat. In an hour, she secured a client, rewrote the release and shot it off to the paper, where it was used as a side-bar to the paper's main story. She made a quick $100. Whenever government studies are released, new surveys come out, or new products are announced, there is almost always a way for you to tie in to the big story.

**Become the Story**: What can you and your client come up with to create some news? I'm not talking about elaborate stunts such as bungee jumping off the Goodyear blimp! How about doing a telephone survey on some topic related to your client? Say your client is a dentist. How about a quick survey on the top 10 fears of seeing a dentist, or how much money the tooth fairy is now paying kids for a tooth under the pillow? Sure it's frivolous. But, it's interesting *and that's what matters*.

You're not marketing your ability to put words on paper in an organized fashion so much as you're selling a client on your ability to see the newsworthyness of his or her situation. And it all comes down to what I preached earlier: Think in terms of derivatives; open your mind to the realm of the remotely possible instead of the narrow cause-and-effect corridor.

> **COMMENT:** There are many ways an editor CAN BE fired, but creating a boring publication is the one sure way he or she WILL BE fired.

## Press Release Mechanics

Before you learn how to craft a good press release, let me go over the basics on spacing, paper, etc. While there is no absolute single standard, most PR writers follow several conventions.

First of all, don't even think about a handwritten press release, and don't consider anything but 8.5 x 11 white paper. Use only one side of the page and try to leave wide margins. Never single-space your press releases.

*COMMENT: Some people like to use brightly colored paper, such as electric pink, for their releases. Don't do this. It's hard to read, and most editors already have tired eyes by the time they open your release.*

If you have a letterhead, use it. Somewhere at the top put the words FOR IMMEDIATE RELEASE; or if you prefer to have your release held, write FOR RELEASE DECEMBER 1. Make sure you enter the date your release was written or sent. The date can go either at the top or bottom of the page.

Always include a contact name and daytime phone number at the top of the release, as well as an address. The contact person is not necessarily the person who wrote the release; most often it will be your client unless he/she wants you to handle all media contacts.

*TIP: When you put your phone number, also include your fax as well as a nighttime number. If they are all one number, write: (123) 345-4565 Tel/Fax (24 hrs.) Remember, large papers are staffed around the clock, and the person on the night desk may call you.*

There's endless debate over how long a release should be. I go with the conventional wisdom that one page is best. However, many writers feel that two pages and even three are OK. Never send more than three pages. If the story is long and complex, you should make it into an article, not a press release.

Never staple the pages together. Editors hate staples.

Write in simple short paragraphs using only three or four sentences. Make every word count. Try to start each paragraph with action-oriented words. If you're going to send the release to a TV or radio stations, make sure you phonetically spell out difficult names or foreign words.

---

*TIP*: *The Zen school of PR people believe that the visual appearance of the release is important. A page having large blocks of text tends to intimidate the reader so that he/she skims over it. Short paragraphs leave lots of white space and tend to entice the reader into the piece.*

---

Make sure you put your releases through your spell checker. Also proof your release carefully. You're writing to people who make a living with words. While one misspelled or incorrect word will not kill your release, a piece with lots of errors will be sent to File 13 (the trash).

At the end of your release, skip two lines and put three pound signs (###) or -end- to signify that there is no more material. Don't put the old teletype notation of 30. The editor will think you're trying to be cute. Editors hate cute.

The following sample should give you an idea of a format that you can follow.

## Press Release Style

Contrary to what many news editors will tell you, writing press material is simple. And that's part of the problem. Because it's so simple, people don't think their releases will be effective unless they make them complex. While the purpose of your release is to entice as well as convey news, there must be a balance here. Too many writers try to make their releases cute and neglect the news value. Or, they err on the other side of the scale and pay no attention to the interest factor of the reader and simply load the piece with too many facts and figures. The key to effective releases is in achieving a balance between the interest content and the news content.

*The Wonderful Life Media Company*
FOR IMMEDIATE RELEASE                    *123 Maple Street*
Contact: George Bailey                        *Bedford Falls, NY 11111*
1-1-95                                              *TEL/FAX (222) 333-4444(24hrs.)*

## 2000 AD: THE BIG COMPUTER CRASH

It won't make a sound, but it will be the largest explosion ever to occur in US industry. It is the year 2000. No, not what will happen in the turn of the century, but the year itself. Every program on every computer in every company will be affected. It may sound trivial but entire companies may shut down because some vital computer program cannot process the change of the century!

Some programs use logic that fail to recognize the fact that the year 2000 is greater than the year 1999. Such computer applications only recognize the last two digits, thus 00 is less than 99. Bam! What happens to a health insurance program that, in order to prevent fraud, compares a date-of-birth to the current date and decides to only write a check if the birthday is less than today?

A lot of hand-wringing is going on in computer centers throughout the country.

One popular solution is New Date from Wonderful Life Software. This suite of programs will search existing programs and change them so that dates greater than 1999 won't crash the computer.

Donna Reed, the president of New Century says, "we can't stop the calendar, but every company can and should prepare for the future."

Wonderful Life can be reached at 555-444-3333, 3008, Market St., Bedford Falls, NY, 99999

### ###

The best way to learn press style, besides reading lots of newspapers and magazines, is to put yourself in the persona of the editor. What does she want? She wants readers. How does she get readers? By providing them with information they want in a format they find fun or interesting to read. So, if you think like an editor as you compose your release, you have a good chance of producing a piece that any editor will publish. Again, balance is the key.

The first paragraph is important, but in my opinion over-rated. Traditional journalism classes teach that the first paragraph should have the five W's: who, what, when, where, and why. This is how releases were written up to about twenty years ago. Today, the first paragraph is more likely to be a hook, something to grab the interest of the reader and draw him into the story. The five W's, of course, must be covered in the release, but to say that they must be in the first paragraph is wrong, judging by today's standards. However, until you develop a "effective"style of your own (one that gets ink!), I suggest that you put the five W's as close to the top as you can.

> **COMMENT**: *Many people credit (?) the electronic media for the change in how print journalism is presented. Many also point to USA Today as a leading factor in how style has preempted content. Take a journalism class and see what I mean!*

The second traditional rule is that press material is structured in descending order of importance. The most important information is at the top with the lesser points flowing toward the bottom. Again, this rule is a good one to follow, but you'll see it broken time and time again.

Keep your sentence structure simple and use strong action-oriented language. You're not trying to write a Pulitzer winning piece. You just want to impart information to an editor so that she will be both interested and informed enough to want to print it or seek more information. Many writers err by trying to be cute in making their press material read like a mystery novel instead of a factual account. Now, I'll be the first to say that a small amount of cute is OK for human interest value, but there is a limit to how far you can go; and it's not far! As I said earlier, editors hate cute!

Use the common tongue. In other words, don't overestimate the knowledge and intelligence of your average reader. Use simple words and make sure your message is understandable to anyone at any education level. This is especially true when your release is on a technical topic or about an industry for which the average reader does not have a basic understanding. For example, if you have a client in the plastic injection molding business and you're doing a piece on how the company recycles their waste products into new plastic items, make sure you don't lose the editor with a lot of technical jargon. Instead of saying "the thermal sensor diode on the new vacuum extrusion device is sensitive to the molten epoxy in such a way as to not accept any mixture that might become resistant to re-manufacturability" just write "the new process employs a special sensing device that prevents hot plastic from becoming contaminated to an extent that it could not be remelted and reused." Remember: Editors don't print what they don't understand.

Avoid hype. Don't fill your releases with claims that can't be positively proven. If your client is an ice cream store, don't say her ice cream sodas are the best in the city. No editor will print that as news because it's an advertisement. However, if you can get Mrs. Harrold's 6th grade class to sample several ice cream parlors and if they vote 3 to 1 that your client's ice cream is the best in the city, you have an item editors will be interested in printing. An important concept to understand is that press re-leases mimic actual newspaper stories. Thus you must put forward a good degree of objectivity if you want to get an editor to print your piece.

PR writers spend far more time developing headlines than they should. Most editors will read past the headline. It's your copy that interests them. While many editors may not know much about your subject, they all know how to write headlines that will grab their readers. So, come up with a headline that you think summarizes the gist of your message and let them rework it. Don't spend hours and hours trying to come up with just the right phrase. A simple rule in headlines is to show action or create a visual image. Instead of "Big Bucks Bank Creates Easy to Qualify Mortgage," try "Been Foreclosed? New Bank Program Has 2nd Chance Program." Instead of "Insurance Agents Increase Customer Service in Emergencies," write "Cash, Compassion, and Concern: How Agents Help Tornado Victims." Both of these headlines evoke visual images and are active, not passive.

Try to use a quote in every release. Editors like to print stories that have the words of experts, witnesses, opinion makers, as well as the man or woman in the street. Quotes give your release a sense of now and they help to humanize the topic. In the above example of the plastic mix, you could hammer home the point by a quote such as: Chief engineer Jim Smith says, "What this technology really means is that we won't slop hot plastic on the floor anymore!" Quotes should be used to illustrate a point, not make it. Quotes should be short. This is not the time to recite someone's version of *War and Peace*.

> *TIP*: Need a quote? Get on the phone and call an "expert."
> Tell them you need a quote for a press release you're do-
> ing on such and such; give them a 25-word synopsis and
> ask their reaction. Sometimes it's a good idea to get a quote
> from a competitor of your client. It gives your piece objec-
> tivity and veracity.

## Picture Perfect

I'm not a fan of sending pictures along with your releases
unless you are positive they add to the piece. While pictures can
tell a story, most will only illustrate. The famous picture of a
fireman kneeling on the sidewalk outside a burning house giving
CPR to a cat told an entire story (by the way, he saved the cat).
However, pictures like that are rare.

> *COMMENT*: Editors complain that most pictures they get
> are either hazy, fuzzy, out of focus, or color Polaroid prints
> that can't be used. If you send photos, send good ones.

You should follow two basic rules in deciding whether or not
to send a photo. The first is to send one if there is a central
"photo op" in your story. Is the piece about a building, an invention, a new product, or anything that will make an interesting
picture? For example, a piece done for a builder who just completed a new office building would be well served by a photo of
the building. However, if the piece is on a company that does
telemarketing, would the editor print a picture of a telephone?

The second rule is to send a photo if the piece is on an individual person, such as a new doctor joining a medical group. If
the piece concerns someone famous, then a picture should be
sent. For example, if a sports personality has made an appearance at your client's store, by all means send the photo.

*TIP: My rule of thumb is that if you're in doubt whether to send a picture, don't send it. Save your money. You can always write "Picture available" at the top or bottom of your release and let the editor call and ask for it.*

If you do send a picture, follow a few rules. First, don't ask for it back. Second, avoid the standard head and shoulder mug shot as well as the group shot. Take an action shot of your client doing something (besides talking on the phone!). Finally, attach a caption by printing it on a separate piece of paper, cutting it, then taping it to the back of the shot. Here is an example:

For Immediate Release

Surgery Without A Cut
Photo Caption

Doctor Smith is pictured with a patient who has just had a new surgical procedure that removes kidney stones using lasers.

Your picture should be in black & white, even though many publications are running color. Most papers only use color on the front page, and it will probably be a cold day in you know where before your piece ends up on the front page! While some papers do encourage color, B&W is a safer bet.

*TIP: Some PR people take a picture in B&W as well as color. They have two inexpensive 35mm cameras.*

Papers love 8x10 photos, but 3x5 are acceptable and will save you a bundle of money. When it comes to developing, make sure the picture is not too dark. When printed, pictures become darker and if yours is dark to begin with, the paper won't run it. Mention to the lab that does your work that you expect the print to be reproduced.

*TIP*: Why not forget pictures and suggest that the paper send their own photographer. This often works, so try it.

## Creating the Client's Press Kit

Here is another marketing possibility for you. By now you know that today's media is lazy. In the old days, reporters spent as much time out of the office as they did in front of the type-writer. Today, they expect the news to come to them. And it does! The media expects those who want coverage to do much of the work. Thus the press kit was born.

The press kit is several pieces of information, all relating to a product, a person, or a story. There is a great misconception that press kits have to be fancy as well as expensive. Not true. They only need two ingredients: They must tell the story about what they represent so that an 8th grader can understand it, and they should have some originality in their presentation. The reason so many press kits are expensive is that they actually lack a good story so the writers try to make up for it by lots of glitz. It doesn't work.

Also, there is no standard list of what items a press kit should contain. You can include or leave out any items you like de-pending on the situation. You also don't have to spend a fortune on fancy covers. A nice pocket folder from an office supply store will do fine. Be sure to label the front of it.

---

*TIP*: *Media people get so many glitzy press kits that they are numbed by them. Simple is best. You want them impressed with the story, not the fancy paper or embossed covers.*

---

Here are the items commonly found in press kits:

**Bio**: Writing a bio is easy, if you follow the formula. Keep it to no more than two double-spaced pages and don't begin with "Ms. Smith was born in. . . ." The lead paragraph should relate directly to the story. For example, the lead on a bio on a female lawyer who practices labor law might read *"When Ann Smith attended law school, dealing with gruff teamsters was not what she imagined she would be doing for a living ten years later."* You want the lead to be catchy, but not cute.

The next paragraphs should remain current and highlight items about the subject's relation to the story that the media will find interesting. Toward the end, work in a paragraph with a transition that will lead into the overview of the past. *"Although Dr. Jones loves New England, a small part of his heart is still in his native Austin, Texas, where he was born in 1948."*

Recap any interesting childhood experiences, education, and early career moves, leading up to how he entered his particular field. Don't tell every event or you'll lose your reader. Keep it short and snappy.

Finally, wrap it up with a paragraph that points to the future as it relates to the story. This might be: "Ann sees *labor law evolving beyond the workplace and into family law. . . . As one of the area's experts on labor law, she is in demand for speaking engagements as well as interviews. . . . Her views are widely quoted . . . ."* In the last paragraph, you want to make a statement of purpose, of why this person is special and should be taken seriously by the media. Avoid heavy hype, but a little bit of puff won't hurt.

*TIP: The best way to practice bio writing is to do your own. After you've written it, cut out about 20%. After you finish your personal bio, you'll find it far less difficult to write someone else's bio.*

**Photo:** A press kit must have a photo. The media expects it. It should also be an 8x10 black-and-white head shot. If the story is about a product, event, or place, a photo is even more important.

*TIP: Lots of photo studios specialize in doing publicity photos. Look in the Yellow Pages and have your client get a dozen or so pictures done. It's not expensive.*

**Clips:** If your client has past news clippings about himself, the product, or service, you want to include these with the press kit. However, if none relate directly, then do some research and find some news stories that have been written about the subject. For example, if Dr. Jones has no clips on himself, and you're doing a press kit on how he is performing a new type of eye surgery, find some information on the benefits of the surgery. Reprints from other publications tend to legitimize your press kit. Journalists are herd animals. If it was covered in Hippopotamus, Texas, then maybe it's worthy of coverage in Platypus Falls, Montana.

Don't overdo press clips. They're used to support your kit, not to tell your story. Photocopy them and use both sides of the paper so that no one clip is more than one page. These are only going to be glanced at by the media.

**Canned Feature:** This is a newspaper article you write yourself. I've spent most of this book showing you how to do this, so if you haven't read these previous chapters, you should! However, newspaper writing is just a little bit different from magazine writing. Newspapers are aware of the short attention span of readers so your piece must be brief and scannable. Also, load up on quotes. Reporters like to have subjects tell their own stories; it makes the reporter seem objective. Keep paragraphs short and the piece focused on the story. Think and write like you're the reporter.

**Vital Stat Sheet**: Because the media expects you to spoon-feed them information, inclusion of a fact sheet will endear you to them. They love this stuff. Find ten to twenty facts and statistics about your story. This is easy if you have an almanac or set of reference books. Otherwise, engage the help of a librarian.

You may have to think abstractly. For example, if you're doing a press kit on a lawyer who specializes in environmental law, you might find the number of environmental cases each year that are decided, along with the damage figures. You might find some figures on how many environmental lawyers practice in the region or how large a law firm must be to afford hiring such a person. If your client is a retail store, find statistics on how many similar stores are in the country, their revenues, as well as the failure rates. Give the media this kind of info and they're going to love you!

**Quote Sheet**: This is nothing more than quotes about the story from other people - the more famous, the better. Again, you'll have to think abstractly. If your press kit is on someone who sells health insurance, quotes from well-known people and politicians on healthcare issues could be included. If you're doing a kit for a company that makes computers, quotes by leading authorities about the computer industry will help. The media people will know how to work these quotes into their story. You simply supply them with the words, they'll do the rest. A little bit of library work should find you all the material you need.

**Backgrounder:** If the business or project is concerned with highly technical material or is associated with difficult-to-understand subjects (such as law, medicine, computers, etc.), you might want to suggest to the client that a background document be written. This is just a piece of any length that explains the history and the details of the main story. It's not going to be quoted, but media people do read them to help educate themselves on a subject that is not within their everyday domain.

These are easy to write. Make believe you're writing a section that will appear in an encyclopedia or textbook. If you sit down and read a technical piece from *The World Book*, you'll quickly learn how to put a backgrounder together. It's just facts, stats, and detail; no style, no quotes, no puff. It's the easiest writing you'll ever do.

> *TIP*: Many PR writers have their clients compile the background material and then charge a fee for editing and rewriting. If your client can't develop background material on his subject fairly easily, he shouldn't be in that business!

## PR Is Easy to Do and Easy to Find

PR work is just about tailor-made for the active PE. If you like getting out and meeting people, being a PR writer will put you in contact with people from all walks of life. If I were to pick a second career for most of the PEs I meet who seek something to do, I would suggest public relations. It's not hard work, there's a demand for it, and it can pay a pretty fair wage. There is no reason you can't charge $150 (which is on the low side) for a one-page press release that took you an hour to think up and an hour to write. Do two a week for fifty weeks, and you gross $15,000. It's done every year by people like you.

# 12

· · · · · · · · · · · · · · · · · · · ·

## GRANT WRITING

## A Little Known Writing Business

Have you ever wondered how the government and non-profits decide to whom to give money? If you haven't, you should, because there may be a bit of profit in it for you. The grant process is worth getting to know.

The competition for grant money is intense. Yet the vast majority of grant proposals are so poorly written that, even in a time of abundant funds, most organizations don't stand a chance of winning grants. Many organizations will pay you to help develop a grant proposal. The high stakes justify your fee. Who are these clients? They are most often community groups seeking funding for a specific project - a shelter for battered women, an after-school sports program, a plan to help the homeless. Without doubt, some organization related to your area of expertise is looking for public or private funding via a grant. And the money doesn't flow without a winning proposal.

Grants are the lifeblood of local and state government agencies, nonprofit charitable, and educational institutions. Grants keep these organizations going, yet obtaining them involves a good deal of time and effort. Many organizations spend up to an estimated 35% of their time, people, and resources preparing grant applications. This is important business because, without a constant flow of grant money, many organizations would disappear in a flash. No matter where you live, organizations and agencies right now are trying to land one grant or another.

The literature on the subject of grant writing points repeatedly to one fact. Most grants are rejected not because the cause or need isn't well substantiated, but because the *proposal* is badly conceived. Most grant applications are poorly written and dull, dull, dull.

If you know or can learn how to prepare a readable, persuasive proposal that might help an organization win a government or private grant, you have the basis for a very nice little writing business. A writer who can bring to a grant application both clarity and emotion without hype or tear-jerking will find many customers.

Who are these customers? Most are nonprofit organizations that do not have their own base of funding. It might be an organization requesting support for a new animal shelter. It might be an organization seeking funds for a program of art therapy for developmentally disabled people. It could be a rural hospital in a poverty area seeking a grant to build a new wing. It might be a local government agency hoping to win matching federal money for a new sewage plant.

Not all proposals are from nonprofit organizations. A business looking to win a contract from the county to haul garbage might seek the services of a grant writer.

Around 30,000 private foundations are funded by families or corporations or special interests who have money to give away. But they don't give it to just anybody. The grant process is the game that's played, and those with the best proposals win.

As a writer, you can contract out your services to help grant-seeking organizations create a winning proposal. Your first role is to present the aims and goals of the organization so that the grantor will be convinced initially that your client is a serious player. The second role is to present in your client's proposal the specifics of how the grant objectives will be fulfilled.

Grant writing is not much different from editorial writing I discussed in earlier chapters. You'll do research to determine what the best story should be.

Grant writing also involves the PR skills mentioned in the previous chapter. You'll package information into a cohesive, succinct proposal that will sell the foundation or funding agency on your client's ability to utilize the money properly. All in all, it's not much different from preparing a press kit. It's just more focused.

## The Parts of the Grant Package

Most grant proposals are not much longer than 20 pages, double spaced. While there are exceptions, your client doesn't have to publish *Gone With the Wind* to win a grant! Most grants have the following ingredients:

**Introduction:** Sometimes it's called the *executive summary*. It's never more than two pages, which sum up and sell the proposal by presenting an accurate and compelling synopsis of the material that will follow. It often conveys a subtle sense of urgency . . . "if we don't get the money, the world will come to an end!"

Many times the introduction is the only part of the application that's read. If it's poorly done, an evaluator (who might have 300 applications for a single grant) won't read the rest.

If you've learned anything about writing from this book, you should be able to write a sharp, well thought out introduction.

**Organization Summary**: This is a brief history of your client's past track record and summary of what the organization represents. This is a commercial for the organization. It flies the flag and tells the evaluation committee that the group is not only important to the constituency it serves, but to the community at large.

This is also an easy piece to write. It's basic PR stuff done in a who, what, why, when, where format.

**Statement of Need**: This presents the reasons why the grant is desired in the first place. It states the problems that the money will address. It mentions how widespread the problem is, why other means of support are not available, and why the organization's approach to the project is unique and best. However, this section does not go into great detail on the "how"; it only stresses the "why."

Again, anyone who knows how to write a simple magazine article can put this section together with little effort.

**How the Grant Will Be Spent**: This is the meat of the proposal. The granting agency wants an overview of how the money will be spent, what products or services will be delivered, and how the winner will take the project to the public to possibly raise more money.

While the foundation won't want specific details on how every dollar will be spent or every move that the organization will make, it does want enough detail to understand the organization's approach.

This is the hardest part to write because every word must count. If the section is too long, you'll lose the evaluator's attention. If it's too short, the screening committee may think the group doesn't understand the problem. This section is usually what makes or breaks the application.

If the client's ideas for spending the money are not really new or unique, the writer must work with that concept and talk about tried and true methods for addressing the problem and how the requesting organization can do it best. If, on the other hand, the group is requesting funds for a revolutionary new program, this section must explain why existing programs don't work.

The grant writer's skill in understanding the power of words, ability to paint word pictures, and talent to sell, are what organizations look for when they hire a writer. These are not difficult skills to attain, but they are necessary ones.

**The Evaluation:** Just about every funding organization wants to know how the project will be evaluated. Funding groups want to know that the organization is not going to take the money and run! They want detailed specifics on how the organization will evaluate and report the use of the funds.

Often, really good proposals lose because they don't pay enough attention to this section. A good grant writer must remember that the funding organization must answer to someone - a board, Congress, a company president, etc. An application that proposes elaborate evaluation processes is going to make the evaluation committee feel safe about granting the funds.

They'll have something to show their boss for their efforts!

> **COMMENT**: Sometimes the evaluation and reporting procedures are more important to the grant evaluators than anything else in the proposal. They may need this to look good so that they can get more money to give away!

**The Budget**: This will not be your responsibility, but you should be familiar with how to present one. Knowing how to use a spreadsheet will be invaluable in developing a format for the budget pages.

It's often helpful to guide your client in how to detail certain amounts via footnotes. If you've had experience reading or preparing quarterly or annual reports in your career, you'll know what I mean.

> **TIP**: Preparing budgets for nonprofit groups can be a profitable business of its own if you have the financial background. Many nonprofits lack this skill and hire consultants for the task.

## Grant Format and Style

The most often used format for grants is the traditional outline method using roman numerals for each section. The second format is the narrative. No matter what format you choose, keep it short. Length is not an improvement from the standpoint of most evaluators. Many, many grant proposals are only nine or ten pages.

Most people think that grants should be written in tight, boring, academic style. Wrong, wrong, wrong. Use the same straightforward, confidence-inspiring tone you would use in a magazine article. Hype will kill you, but so will indifference. The proposal must impart to the reader that your organization has all the abilities to make good use of the money as well as enhance the reputation of the funding organization. Instead of saying "The XYZ organization has done this, that, and the other thing . . .," say "The XYZ agency has won local admiration and national recognition from involvement in past projects involving this, that, and the other. . . ." Paint word pictures without exaggeration.

---

*TIP: If a grant proposal is done correctly, which is not all that hard, the funding agency will break down the door to give your client the money. Not because your client is so good, but because most proposals are so badly written that the funding agencies have no confidence their money will not be wasted. A little salesmanship can go a long way.*

---

## Place Your Bets, Place Your Bets

Finding associations and nonprofit agencies needing your services is easy, and selling them is even easier, *if you want to take a risk.*

In the first place, unless you live under a rock, tons of organizations in your community constantly seek money from either local funding sources, or regional, and federal sources.

The best way to find them is to decide where your interests lie. If you have a background in health care, you might want to seek out clients among hospitals or disease support groups. If your background is in science or engineering you might be interested in approaching educational institutions. If you have an interest in construction, you might look at groups seeking to build shelters. If your career was in food service, perhaps you are interested in meals-on-wheels type programs. They're all out there waiting for someone like you to come along and help them put a proposal together.

An almost sure-fire method of landing a client is to do some research and come up with a grant that the organization either doesn't know about or doesn't have the resources with which to respond. For example, if, in your reading, you learn that some state agency is seeking to fund programs for training workers displaced from defense cutbacks, contact the agency and get the facts. Condense it into a sharp three page sales letter and send it to various private and public educational institutions. If you can convince them that they have a chance to land this grant because of your skills, knowledge, and abilities, you might just win a contract.

Here is where it gets risky. Many grant writers start out by working on contingency. This means that if the organization doesn't win the grant, the writer doesn't get paid! True, you might end up doing a dozen or so grant proposals for free until your boat comes in. But, you hone your craft, and when you do win one, you have a track record that you can take to the next client.

Should you work on speculation? If grant writing interests you, then this is great way to start. If you propose to an organization that you won't charge them unless they win the grant, it's hard for them to refuse you. However, I suggest that PEs only use this method to get started. Once you have a track record, insist on your fee irrespective of the outcome of the proposal.

## Where Your Fee Comes From

Many times, the fee for the proposal is included (hidden) in the proposal under "publicity." Most proposals have a budget line item for publicity to not only reach the public whose needs the grant is intended to meet, but also to make sure the sponsor gets the credit it expects!

Another way the writer's fee is included in the proposal is under the heading of "outside administration." Many organizations don't have the staff to take on more work, especially for short-term projects so they propose to hire the skills they need to carry out the project until the money runs out. You are one of the skills they hire!

Finally, your fee can be hidden in a budget line item often called "Preparation of Final Report." Almost all granting organizations require a final report, which is a candid sorting out of how the project worked or is working. This is an important document as it can often lead to further grants! Funding groups know that it takes time to put this document together, and they want one that will help them look good; thus they don't mind if the grant winners spend a few extra dollars on this part of the project.

---

*TIP: If you write the proposal, you will almost certainly get a chance to write the final report. However, make sure that your agreement says you get paid separately and that the final report is not part of your fee for doing the up-front proposal.*

---

## What Will They Pay?

If you develop a track record of writing winning proposals, you can charge anything you want and still have clients begging for your services. After all, the few thousand dollars they're going to pay you is peanuts compared to the amount of money they're going to receive. If you write a proposal that nets an organization $200,000 and helps them keep five people on the payroll, your $5,000 fee is a small price to pay.

If you decide to start out by charging a fee, I suggest you give a client a fixed price amount instead of an hourly rate. You'll have to "guesstimate" how many hours it will take, apply an hourly figure, and come up with a number.

If you're going to work on speculation, since you're taking a risk, you should charge more; perhaps almost double. However, you have to be careful that you don't end up charging more than the client can pay.

If your client is going after a $50,000 grant that will take you 80 hours of work at $30/hour, your fee would be $2,400. However, on spec you could probably get away with $3,800 or $4,000.

Some grant writers charge a percentage of the overall grant; anywhere from 2.5% to 5%.

There is little useful information I can give you on how to set your rates. You'll have to snoop around, ask others, and try some negotiation with potential clients.

---

*TIP*: Everyone has a friend of a friend who knows someone at some organization or agency. Ask them to find out what these potential clients pay outside (contract) grant writers.

---

## Doing Good Works

PEs often donate their writing services to pet causes. It makes them feel good and keeps them active. It's also a good form of marketing. It allows them to meet many people in the community who will have need for their services. Doing volunteer work for your favorite cause can help you get started and provide you with a good reference for that first paying assignment.

Many PEs belong to a charity, religious group, or educational institution in which they have a great interest. If this is the case, you might propose to the organization that they contract with you to provide public relations materials, ghostwritten articles for the officers, as well as any grant writing that might be necessary. You could ask for a small monthly retainer and do the work as it comes up. Once you have some experience, it's very possible that a retainer will be offered to you by either a paying client or wherever you do volunteer work.

Grant writing can give you opportunities to work in a wide spectrum of areas. You'll find that most grants are structured the same, only the numbers and the causes are different.

But there are a few other areas available to the PE who has developed what personnel people call "good communication" skills. Indeed, knowing how to work with the media can open many doors of opportunity.

# 13

· · · · · · · · · · · · · · · · · · · · · · · · · ·

## OPPORTUNITY KNOCKS

## Other Possibilities

There are lots of other writing business possibilities for PEs with special talents and backgrounds. However, I don't cover them in detail because they require a level of experience the average PE does not have. Here are a few:

**Speech Writing**: Many business and professional people are called upon to give speeches; usually at some industry or association dinner meeting. These are busy people who don't have the time to research or prepare a 30-page double-spaced document which would be about a 40-minute speech.

To be an effective speech writer, you must have excellent interview skills. You must be able to get into the mind of your client so you can think the way he or she thinks and write the way he or she speaks. You must totally understand the client's position on a topic as well as the points he or she wants to get across to the audience.

If you've had experience writing speeches for yourself during your career, or if you have a background in teaching or sales, you may have the skills to be a speech writer.

It's an easy service to market, but hard to sell. Get a list of executives or professional people and send them letters telling them about what you do. As for fees, it's typical for clients to pay from $1,500 to $3,000 for a 30-minute speech.

---

*TIP*: Sometimes the client's company will pay the fee for speechwriting if the client is a top executive. Also, get your fee before the speech is given. You can't repossess a speech!.

---

**Business plans**: If you have financial management or executive experience, there is always a good market in helping new companies write business plans.

Most business plans are not really designed to be followed like a blueprint in order to build the business. They are most often used to impress financial investors to lend money to a budding venture.

Writing business plans can be an especially good opportunity for those who have expertise in businesses that are formed over and over again, such as restaurants, retail stores, and even medical practices.

If you have the skills, you can charge from $2,000 to $5,000 to create a business plan.

*TIP*: You can buy "boiler plate" software packages that you can adapt to most any businesses. They not only have the verbiage, but they come with a spreadsheet to create the budgets and cash-flow projections. Ask your computer user group members for suggestions.

**Annual reports**: If you think that companies publish annual reports to enlighten their stockholders on the results of the company, think again. These pieces are actually designed to impress financial analysts and lenders. While the Securities and Exchange Commission requires that publicly held companies disclose certain information, it doesn't require them to put out long, detailed, glossy presentations.

However, companies spend an enormous amount of their funds for these puff pieces, and they often hire writers (or their advertising firm hires the writers) to do them. Many times, money is no object so a 50-page report can gross the writer from $5,000 to $10,000.

Do understand that these can be long projects that drag on for several months. In addition you'll have to deal with many levels of management. Some projects may require your full-time attention (in which case you must charge much more).

The best way to find these clients is to network with advertising and graphic design firms.

**Institutional Advertising**: This type of advertising is not designed to sell a product or service but to gain a favorable image for the advertiser. Many government agencies, associations, and nonprofits hire writers to create brochures and handouts, as well as print media text and graphic pieces.

---

**COMMENT**: *Of course you've seen print ads for anti-smok-ing, say-no-on-drugs, a mind is a terrible thing to waste, buckle up for safety. . . .*

---

You'll also find large hospitals and law firms creating promotional pieces that are upscale and highbrow. They want to get their names out to the public and in the process create a favorable image without sounding crassly commercial.

If you have a marketing, sales, advertising, or copy writing background, you might find opportunity doing such projects in your own town or city. The key ingredient is imagination. If you can come up with a concept to market the services of a law firm or a medical practice, accounting firm or a government agency that needs image advertising, you can make a nice profit for little actual work. It's the idea they're buying, not the effort.

A good way to market this is to come up with an idea for an ad for a professional firm, put the text down on paper with a description of the graphics. Put a copyright notice on it and send it to the managing partner or CEO with a letter saying this is the type of work you do. Tell them that if they are interested in this piece or perhaps another, they should call you before you approach a similar firm.

There is no end to the possibilities that PEs can come up when they have specialized talent from their previous work life.

## The Most Important Section in This Book

Forget about fear. Forget about rejection. Take some positive steps to enhance your life and the lives of people who could benefit from your experience. You have a lot to offer the world.

Don't be influenced by others; remember what I said about conventional wisdom. There are a lot of know-it-alls out there and they all seem to find it easier to say "can't" than "can."

As I said earlier, I'm not into the rah-rah hype presented by many positive-mental-attitude speakers, so I won't close with a rousing pep-talk. My thesis is simply that you can find happiness and modest financial reward from your own small writing business. It will help keep your mind active and enhance your retirement years. If this appeals to you, I urge you to give it try.

Whatever endeavor you decide upon, the important thing is to do what makes you happy. You've earned it. You deserve it.

---

**COMMENT**: Please write me, care of the publisher, and let me know your questions, thoughts, comments, criticisms, and (I hope) about your success. I will reply to as many of you as I can.

---

# Appendix

# 1

# WRITING SAMPLES

## A Good General Interest Piece

Following is a sample article that most PEs could write from their own experience or with a little research.

I picked it because it's a simple topic with almost universal appeal. Articles like this can be be sold over and over. This one has appeared in print nine times and still in circulation It normally goes for $200 to the larger markets.

Editors love to run this kind of piece in the life-style section of newspapers, or in the child-care section of women's magazines. They know that people with kids want to read it.

Notice also that the author included a couple of sidebars (separate mini-articles) that can be used to augment the main piece. Sometimes, just the sidebars are sold for $50-$75 each.

Marilyn Pribus                           One-time Rights

1234 Maple Street                     Approx. 1,300 words

City, XX 12345                  (in three parts)


NOTE TO THE EDITOR: This piece has a factual article on pp. 1-3, a single page sidebar on p. 4, and a humorous first-person picky eater story on pp. 5&6. Any combination of the three sections could be used.


## PICKY, PICKY, PICKY


by

Marilyn Pribus

Nathan, two, used to eat everything in sight including food. Now he'll eat only grapes and graham crackers. Five-year-old Sara and her father kept a vigil over her uneaten spaghetti dinner until he surrendered at midnight. Again.

THE TRAP.

It's worrisome and frustrating when your child refuses to eat. Parenting is nurturing, and when a child starts eating without help and says, "Dis good, Mommy," we mentally give ourselves gold stars. Parents of fussy eaters, however, often feel they are failures or inadequate.

*Just Say No. That's what kids do at two and it isn't necessarily about food. While they may have developed certain dislikes, they also relish this new power of choice, and rejecting food is one way to express it.

*Appetites Slow Down. Children generally triple their birth weight in the first year. Around eighteen months, however, growth slows and appetites lag. A child of three or four gains only 4-5 pounds a year. Children grow in spurts, ravenous one week and nibbling the next, but they actually have a very accurate hunger level. In fact, in that respect their bodies are more accurate than adults who eat for pleasure rather than survival, and are inclined to finish everything on their plates, especially the expensive fare.

*Attention getting. Persistent or exaggerated pickiness may be a way of acting out at an age when a child can't say "I'm scared. Something's wrong." Things to consider: changes in the family, at school or with friends. Pickiness can also be an attention-getting device. If it seems possible that this is true, try addressing the need for attention in a more positive way.

THE SOLUTION.

If you could toss the TV set, it would help, because when cereals are named for cartoon characters and candy is touted as a "snack food," it's hard to compete. And when kids hit the "real world" they may ignore the whole wheat habits you've tried to instill. Nevertheless you can take action to sidestep or correct problems centered around food.

*<u>Trust Your Child</u>. Children are capable eaters and know how much they need. Don't let food become a focus of conflict.

*<u>Tender Taste Buds</u>. Youngsters generally prefer foods that are mild in flavor, neither very hot nor very cold and brightly colored rather than beige or mauve. They also like one-thing-at-a-time kind of foods they can readily identify rather than those camouflaged in a casserole.

*<u>Kids are 'Neophobes.</u>" If it's new, they don't like it, especially food. It may take many exposures to a new menu item before they are willing to accept it into their diet.

*<u>Offer Control</u>. An important step in avoiding or overcoming problems is to let children feel in control of their eating. It's important for them to know they can taste a food and not finish if they don't like it. This way they'll be more likely to try something new later.

*<u>Division of Responsibility</u>. There are food responsibilities for both adults and children. Parents should provide appealing, wholesome food and a pleasant atmosphere. They should teach good table manners, respect for the feelings of others (including the cook by simply saying, "No, thank you," instead of "Gross!"), and discretion about removing something from their mouths when they don't want to swallow it. Parents must <u>not</u> impose their ideas of how much a child should eat, not even with a too-fat or too-skinny youngster.

The children's responsibilities entail having good table manners and choosing how much -- or whether -- they eat. Making them responsible for preparing themselves an alternative meal reduces the payoff if the pickiness is an attention-getting ploy. Having children help with cooking can also be a good strategy.

The entire question of food and feeding usually reflects the relationship between a parent and child. When children are forced to eat, or are treated overbearingly at mealtime, it is clear their feelings don't matter. Youngsters who are fed attentively and courteously, however, get a clear message from the time they are very young that they are loved and respected.

-##-

SIDEBAR: AVOIDING PICKY EATER PROBLEMS

1. Make mealtimes pleasant. This isn't the time to discuss broken toys or broken hearts. Talk about the funniest thing you saw today, about accomplishments or books or a movie.

2. Whenever possible, put control of the diet in your child's hands. Let your youngster dish up his or her own plate at home, for example. At a pot luck or cafeteria, don't even look! If your little one wants red Jell-O for salad, dinner and dessert, it won't hurt once in a while.

3. Encourage sampling new foods, but don't require children to finish something they don't like. Make servings small enough that you won't be upset by wasted food.

4. Keep healthy food available. Little tummies may do better on six small meals than on three big ones. Have snacks in the pantry and fridge for any time but one hour before meals.

5. Let the children plan the menu now and then with the help of a four basic food groups chart.

6. Don't invest yourself in your child's eating habits. Don't pay cash money and never force a child to stay at the table over a cold dish of something.

7. Never use food as a reward.

8. If you find your child is eating less than previously, carefully squirrel away the money you're saving. Invested judiciously, it may help you during the voracious teenage years.


SIDEBAR: THE PRINCE OF PICKY EATERS

I planned to be the perfect mother. My sons would never whine, squabble or pick at their food. Actually, they didn't whine or squabble much, but when it came to eating -- brother!

The older boy was the problem. This is the son who now must go to the local gourmet grocery when he visits to get exactly the right ingredients for the gourmet meals <u>he</u> cooks. But when he was three he'd eat a carrot stick here, five or six Froot Loops there and occasionally a bit of exactly-the-right-kind of white bread toasted with exactly-the-right-kind of yellow cheese.

Childrearing books suggested broccoli florets with a peanut butter dip, dainty sandwiches made with cookie cutters, and wheat germ smuggled into cookies. They also said eating problems stemmed from power struggles between mother and child. Please!

I served oatmeal cookies baked minus raisins (vile contaminants), perfectly peeled apple slices without a trace of revolting red skin, pancakes griddled with smiling faces. He sat with nose wrinkled and mouth shut tight.

And then a miracle. My husband and I had a chance to take a week's vacation and a friend kept our kids along with her own. I warned her about my picky eater. "Don't worry," she told me blithely, "he won't starve."

How right she was! I came home to discover he'd been eating fried chicken, baked beans, even the dreaded raisins. I may have been losing the power struggle, but I wasn't dumb. I copied her menu item for item, including the paper towel "panties" on the "drumbones" to keep the fingers clean. The next night I served fried chicken.

With panties.

"Don't like chicken," came the automatic response.

"Oh?" I said blandly. "Mrs H. said you ate two pieces. She said you liked the panties."

He frowned.

Then I managed to abdicate control of his diet. I feigned rapt interest in my own chicken's panties and with Oscar-worthy nonchalance I said, "It doesn't matter to me if you eat or not."

He watched me from the corner of his eye, but I didn't blink. And that was the beginning of the end of the power struggle I'd been so long in recognizing.

- M.P.

Marilyn Pribus lives in _____,_____. Her former picky eater now passes the fridge like a vacuum cleaner.

About The Author

Marilyn Pribus is an author, a mother (and grandmother), a teacher, and a para-professional in the field of mental health. While serving as a Listener and Trainer of Volunteers for the Alexandria, Virginia, suicide prevention hotline, she met a writer who encouraged her to submit her work.

Since the 1978 publication of "The Love Bucket" (which has since sold more than 20 times as a reprint), she lists over 400 sales of fiction and non-fiction. She is a member of the Mystery Writers of America; International Food, Wine, and Travel Writers Association; and Sisters in Crime.

Ms. Pribus also works as a freelance editor. She has conducted writing workshops and taught yoga, swimming, folk guitar, and banjo. With her Air Force husband, Glenn, she has lived in many states and overseas. Since the completion of his military career, he has also turned to freelance journalism. They often collaborate on assignments.

(This bio runs about 150 words.)

## An Experience Piece for a Magazine

The second writing sample is an article I wrote that appeared in the Spring 1994 edition of Information Systems Management, a rather highbrow (and expensive) quarterly for data processing executives (and those who want to be).

"Reengineering IS" (IS stands for Information Systems) is about double the length of the articles that I suggest you start out with. However, most feature writers find that it's often easier to write longer articles than the short ones. They also find that it doesn't take much more time or effort. When you get paid by the word, long is good (ask Dickens!).

I did not enclose a bio because I had written for the magazine previously and I knew they would not print one. I also left off my social security number because they already had it on file.

I was paid $500 for the piece. It took me four or five hours to write and four or five months to receive a check!

While this piece is about 3,500 words, it can easily be reworked it into pieces about half that length and submitted to other magazines.

This is a perfect example of a piece based upon experience. There was absolutely no research done for this article. I made an outline of the points I wanted to cover and just let the words flow. After two or three rewrites, it started to make sense! After the fourth, I sent it off.

You should be able to do this same type of experience article in whatever genre you choose.

Alan N. Canton
1234 Elm Street
Platypuss Falls, NY, 12345
(123) 123-3456 Tex/Fax

One-time Rights
Approx.3,500words

### REENGINEERING IS: The Arguments Every CIO Will Hear?

by

**Alan N. Canton**

Reengineering is all the rage. It is all you hear today by the pundits, vendors, soothsayers, as well as anyone who either wants to separate your wallet from its contents or who may have a covert hidden agenda. Everyone wants you to trade in your Schwinn for a Lincoln.

As a consultant to IS executives, I've seen the snake-oil vendors, the great pretenders, the fantasy makers, and fast-buck takers spin webs of cotton candy around a tough-minded CIO such that he or she joins the CIO's clarion call to re-invent the corporation, reengineer the business, and to unload what everyone is made to think is an unwieldy information substructure, for a new, better, different, improved, up-to-date, state-of-the-art, with-it, slick, whiz-bang computer configuration. (You can take a breath now!)

If reengineering means taking a total look at the *raison d'être* of an IS division, I am the first person to sing its praises. If you are going to assemble your best team of insiders and hire a good group of consultants to take a hard look at how you produce, serve, manufacture, create, inform, educate, market, and/or sell information services to your user population so that the entire business entity has a chance of being in business by the change in the millennia, then I am on your side.

But that is not what is going on out there. Reengineering is becoming not only a marketing mission, but also a political effort to get you, the CIO, to believe that if you just bring in some new hardware and some full-color, object-oriented software, all the company's problems will be history.

But hey, it is a wonderful tune the choir sings, and nobody can blame you for humming along. However, you really ought to ask yourself one basic question, like, who is really conducting the orchestra? There are a lot of people with hidden agendas out there trying to convince you to engage in an effort to reengineer your data center operations. Before you can determine the basic prime directive of reengineering for your company, you would be well advised to do some analysis on just who in the company is yelling for this effort, and why.

I am reminded of the film *The Godfather* where the old don tells Michael how to recognize a traitor. He says that the "family" member who first approaches Michael to have a summit with the other clans is the culprit.

OK, you are not the Mafia, but your organization may not be all that different structurally. There are always people who are not happy with the status-quo. This can be good. It gets people thinking and keeps the moss from growing. You want executives and staff who are not afraid of change. But you also have to understand that some people see change as a way to mask their own failures - as a cover-up, if you will, of their own inability to perform. Also, some people see change as just a fun-and-games thing. Change means chaos, intrigue, politics, and sometimes excitement. After all, how scintillating is working in a claims adjustment department with technology that has been around since pre-Cambrian times?

So I ask you, who in the entire business entity wants reengineering? From people within your own IS division to your colleagues in senior management, you must ask yourself if they have another agenda? Let's take a look at the usual suspects who propose the panacea of reengineering and what they might have to gain, lose, or fear.

**Your Own Systems and IS Operations People**

Do you want to hear what true panic sounds like? Use the word "downsizing" in or around the keepers of your Pondasaurous 5000 mainframe. Maybe it is no longer panic (as it was 10 years ago) but just simply apprehension. At any rate, the systems group does not want to lose its power base within the business entity and there are many good reasons why they shouldn't. If central control of the information function is necessary (and in some firms such as banking, it is) these folks will propose a reengineered (i.e. less costly) centralized configuration as merely a method to keep up with the times. This is all well and good.

However, in many businesses, the concept of a central, monolithic IS is no longer necessary. With the availability of cheap hardware, simple networks, and reliable software, information can be distributed to where it is used and needed most: the department.

Many within your IS department will propose reengineering to install a complex client-server network configuration that only they can set up, and only they can understand. They will still be masters of the information universe and answerable to no one. With client-server, since no one really knows what it is, they will be even more omnipotent, more priestly, more powerful. By controlling downsizing and the proliferation of ad-hoc departmental data centers, your IS gurus protect their own turf and can reestablish their own powerbase within your division as well as the entire business entity.

The operations area is also suspect. In the past, they have opposed reengineering and seek to "protect" the company from the danger of users having access to too much computing (i.e. informational) power. However, by now these folks have learned that they can't turn back the clock. The desktop workstation is now the information source of choice for most users. So, by proposing a complex reengineering scheme, such as client server, the operations people hope to prevent the disintegration of their function: from being the hardware technology gurus to mere caretakers of repository information (i.e. they make the back-ups!).

**The Dot-People**

Every good-sized company has a group of people who, while reporting to specialized areas on the organization chart, also have a dotted line running to the CEO. Sometimes these people serve as special assistants to senior management. Other times they are staff or executives "on loan" from one of your "friendly" sister departments for a special project. There are probably dot-people assigned to you. Some CIOs are plagued by a plethora of these gnats hovering all over their divisions, trying to make sense (and report to senior management) of things they will never understand in a million years since most of them can't spell CAT unless one of the junior programmers spots them the C and the T. (A little editorial, true, but honestly, these folks can drive you crazy!)

Most of these people are called upon to fight fires or perform some specialized "project" and then move on to something else. They are sort of in-house consultants. Like many people who have no prime directive, they often lack enough work to fill their day. The concept of reengineering has become the vision of a full-employment act for the dot-people. They have no idea about the "truth or consequences" of the process but will make all sorts of wonderful predictions to senior management because any change in the business entity can and will mean more special projects and fire fighting.

When the "special assistants to the president" come to your IS department and start talking about the wonderful benefits about reengineering all of your operations, you should understand that most likely they not only don't know what they are talking about, but they also don't care to find out.

Change is their prime directive. Any change is good change. An organization that is stable, healthy, and has effective and efficient IS operations is an organization that probably does not need the services of too many "special assistants." These folks hate stability.

The dot-people are great readers and researchers. They often know what everybody else is doing in the industry, but often have little idea how their own company "works." But that is not an issue to them. When they read that a competitor or a colleague in a related business is going through a mystical process called "reengineering," they will clamor mightily for you to jump on the bandwagon. They truly believe in what Steve Jobs at Apple told his people who were working 20 hour days in development of the Macintosh . . . . "The journey is the reward."

Bringing in new machines, new software paradigms, embracing client server configurations, and instituting new IS procedures is the "journey" to the dotted line people. Please, do understand that the work and energy of these people is not always wasted. Sometimes clear-thinking dot-people are necessary healers for a company or IS division that is sick. But so many times I have seen them "cure" a basically healthy patient to death. Dotted line people are concerned with form over substance. They are often "herd" type animals. If Amalgamated Consolidated increased profits by 18% after reengineering their information services, then it stands to reason to these people that your company will follow the same form. It makes no difference to them that Amalgamated is in the iron ore business and your company sells insurance. To them, substance is not substantive! Process and form are all they understand and they believe that a form or process that is successful in one company will be the same with all. These folks love to go from one cure-all to another. They came at you with "structured methodology."

Then came CASE. Next was object technology. Now they speak about TQM, client server, and, of course, reengineering.

The dotted line people make great critics. But every IS director should remember what George Bernard Shaw said about critics. While driving around London and seeing all the statues of famous writers, Shaw remarked "Never pay attention to what the critics say. In all of London there is not one statue erected in honor of a critic!"

**The Users**

The pundits who look for the rhyme and reason of business decisions usually credit the user community with spearheading the reengineering effort. The adage is that they are sick and tired of waiting months (years) for their information needs to be delivered. Thus, over the past ten years, they have installed zillions of PC's to do what IS has never been able to install: simple productivity tools. When it comes to spreadsheets and word-processing and simple data capture, the users are right. These tools are more efficient than anything IS has ever proposed, much less delivered.

So, the pundits conclude that the users are the real protagonists behind the reengineering boomlet. But this is just not the case at most firms. Users don't want to run their own departmental data centers. Users don't want to learn, nor are they all that interested in technology. For instance, the engineering department responsible for the development of new widgets does not want the responsibility of maintaining a groupware set of software programs. Yes, the department may want groupware, but surely not the baggage of running its own computer and network center.

Thus, when the users come to you, the CIO, and extol the virtues of reengineering, they think they will be getting something for nothing. I am reminded of what a past CIO at Pacific Gas & Electric said to me several years ago: "It is not so much what users believe that is troubling; it is what they believe that is just plain wrong that scares hell out of me!"

The agenda of the user is simple. If reengineering will help them do what they are paid to do and what they like to do, then yes, let's get on with it. When they call for massive decentralization into low level departmental data centers or clusters, it will be your responsibility as CIO to give them a "reality check" and explain how radically their roles and responsibilities would change if they get what they think they want. Let them know that services they take for granted, such as support, analysis, and good old creative thinking, may no longer be available in any one centralized location. Make sure they understand that senior user management may have to play a more "political" role to attain the resources they will need in order to run their own little information centers. Some of their time and energy will be diffused talking (fighting?) with several layers of management instead of just the IS department.

It has been my experience that when users make the argument for reengineering, the CIO must realize that they probably have not thought the concept through. He or she should understand that the users are not calling for the end of civilization as we know it; they just want their backlog of requests trimmed down. And they think they will be able to do it themselves. After all, anyone who can program a spreadsheet can surely master the simple concepts of UNIX or parallel processing! No, they are not stupid, they just don't understand. But a good CIO should.

**The Big Guns**

CIOs live a perilous existence. They get their butt kicked for everything that goes wrong (or has ever gone wrong) in the business entity, and they are the first group signaled out to either cut costs or improve on the bottom line. Whatever it is, you can blame it on the IS group. Profits down . . . must be IS's fault. The new product didn't sell, must be IS's fault. Lost a big client, must be IS's fault. Hey, let's cut their budget and reorganize them and perhaps business will pick up!

What is really needed is a shakeup of either senior management, or at least their thought processes. What is probably required is for senior management to take some risks in the marketplace, be more creative, more customer responsive, and generally more aggressive. But today, we have many large companies with very complacent management that instead of looking deep down for the answer to a falling bottom line, look for a quick fix. And reengineering the IS area is being sold as the best quick fix of all time!

In many companies, senior management embraces the IS reengineering bandwagon as a replacement for creative thinking. It is a turn inward. If we are failing, it must be because of something we are doing internally. Maybe our information flow needs to be fixed. Maybe new reporting systems will improve our profits. Maybe, maybe, maybe.

Instead of doing some serious research into what the marketplace might want, and then taking a risk on delivering that product or service, so many senior executives believe in the quick fix of technical reengineering. If we just change our computer system, all will be well. Sometimes reengineering is an indication that a company is idea-bankrupt. Instead of serious risk taking, a company in trouble will embark on a total reengineering of its central data processing plant, in the hope that out of the smoke and ashes will come a new revitalized, streamlined, responsive business entity.

CIOs around the country must fight the flattery of their colleagues. Any CIO of any mettle knows that his department cannot carry a company that produces poor or unneeded products or services. However the CIO is told by the highest executives how important IS is to the business and that so called reengineering, say installing a client server configuration companywide, will position the firm for the next century. It often sounds good, but it is not often the truth.

The agenda here is two-fold. I say it again. Many senior executives honestly believe in the silver bullet. It is so much easier to tinker with the IS area than to sit down and work on new business products and services and take the risk they will fail. If a company is not making much of a profit, it seems so much easier and safer for management to sit on its butt and do some internal tinkering, than to come up with the master plan for the next five years.

The second agenda is the so called herd instinct. Everybody is doing it, so it must be a good idea. Downsizing, rightsizing, reengineering, client server, array processing, OOP, and the other buzz words all find their way into the in-flight magazines that senior management digest between Peoria and Boise. Some reporter writes about how some company in East Tennis Shoe, Nebraska, has installed an enterprise-wide client-server network, and profits have zoomed. If it worked there, maybe it can work here. Do we want to be the only company with a centralized IS function? Hell no, we have to keep up with the times.

**So, What's a Manager to Do?**

I know I sound like a traditionalist. It is not true. I have just seen too many companies attempt change just for the sake of change. I have seen many CIOs bombarded with what seem to be good arguments to form a reengineering task-force for their departments. And I've seen CIOs simply cave into the pressure to change what is a perfectly efficient department into one with GUIs, and servers, and networks, and objects, and paradigms, and open systems, and chaos.

As I said earlier, reengineering must be a companywide project, not just some senior manager's scatterbrained idea to tinker with the IS department. This is the concept that the competent CIO must communicate when the subject of reengineering is brought up. If you don't know where you are going, any road will get you there. And that is what is happening at so many firms. Reengineering mania takes hold because it fulfills so many needs and desires for so many people in the organization. It seems that everybody might benefit for change, except the entity as a whole.

The CIO is perfectly positioned to counsel senior management because he or she is witness to the entire organization's entities, since IS must service all of these diverse users. By knowing and understanding the hidden agenda of the players in the reengineering game, a CIO can help prevent senior management from inventing a company where each department does its job with perfection, but where none of the entities are able work together as a functioning business organization. In short, the CIO can prevent an Edsel.

Reengineering is often a great idea. Sometimes it even works. But when it used as a tool for furthering the political or promotional aspirations of the players, or when it is employed as a reactive internal process instead of a proactive response to the marketplace, reengineering becomes just another well-argued silver bullet that never reaches the target.

###

# Appendix

# 2

. . . . . . . . . . . . . .

## R E S O U R C E S

## A Word On Resources

One good thing about starting a professional writing business is that you don't have to "know" too much to get started. If you've finished this book, there is not much more you need learn (beyond that from actual experience . . . which is the best teacher!) for you to be successful.

Most books like this one try to overload the book buyer with a ton of references so as to either make the book longer, or make the author imply that he or she is knowledgeable because of all the references he or she listed and presumably read!

I'm only going to list reference material that I know will be of some use to you. There is no need to run right out and get everything at once. However, as your business interests develop, these are some of the items you will want to take a look at. I list the ones that I have *actually* used or read and which I recommend.

## On-Line Information Systems

Note: Many on-line services offer free trial subscriptions. Check user groups, computer stores, as well as magazines and newspapers for a chance to sign on the system for 10 or 15 free hours. Most also have special software (low cost or free) for either PCs or Macs.

> *America Online* - 8619 Westwood Center Drive, Vienna, VA 22182, 800-827-6364. This runs neck and neck with Compuserve. However, most beginners feel more at ease with AOL. There is a writer's forum as well as a forum for seniors, called Senior Net (see below).

> *CompuServe Information Service* - 5000 Arlington Centre Blvd., Columbus, OH 43220, 800-848-8199. This is the oldest major information system available for general use. It has more "stuff" on it than AOL and is probably a little better for research. It's the favorite with tech-heads.

> *Senior Net Online* - 399 Arguello Blvd., San Francisco, CA 94118, 415-750-5030. This is an organization, more aptly stated an "electronic community" of senior citizens who share an interest in computers and what computers can do. Senior Net is actually carried by America Online as one of the special interest groups. Besides just being an on-line discussion group, Senior Net offers discounts on high-tech products to its members, as well as good prices on a number of books and publications. In addition, the organization has many learning centers throughout the country where

they teach computer classes. Senior Net is well worth checking out.

## Government Publications

Note on government publications: Most of the material found in government documents is not copyrighted and is in the public domain, which means you can include it word for word in your articles. Government documents can serve as idea generators for articles . . . or can be the articles themselves (along with a few words of your own!).

. IRS publications are not bad references, however they are often out of date. You can pick some of them up at the larger IRS offices.

*IRS* 800-829-9676, Publication 334: Tax Guide for Small Business, Publication 583: Taxpayers Starting a Business, Publication 587: Business Us of Your Home, Publication 937: Business Reporting

*Small Business Administration* - 1141 L Street NW, Washington, DC 20416, 800-827-5722. SBA has all sorts of publications at low cost that relate to starting a business. They also have seminars in various parts of the country on subjects relating to home businesses.

## Software

A ton of software is out there for writers, and most is very good. In addition to wordprocessing software (a must-have) is graphic software, page formatting programs, dictionaries, etc.

Below are the programs that have versions for both the Mac and the PC.

*Microsoft Word* - Microsoft Corp. Many consider this as the best wordprocessing program out there. It's the program I use.

*WordPerfect* - WordPerfect Co. (Novell) This is the close runner-up to Word. Millions swear by it. I hate it. But you might find it a bit easier to use than Word.

*FileMaker Pro* - Claris Corp. Hands-down the easiest database program to learn and use. Most people will never need anything more. It's also great for doing labels and envelopes.

*FoxPro* - Microsoft Corp. This is a powerful database which uses the so-called relational model. It's overkill for most people, but if you want the best, this is it.

*Quicken* - Intuit Corp. This is the finance program of choice for most small businesses. It's really an automated checkbook program that will also print a zillion different reports. Unless you hire employees, you probably won't need any other program to keep your financial records. Intuit also makes the best tax software (MacInTax for the Mac and Turbo Tax for the PC).

*PageMaker* - Adobe Inc. Professionals use PageMaker to compose documents that contain graphics. Contrary to popular belief, PageMaker is not that hard to learn. However, the new version of Word contains many of the features of

PageMaker. If you plan to write a book, use PageMaker. It will make your life very easy when it comes to page numbering, indexing, graphics, etc.

*American Heritage Dictionary* - Wordstar Corp. This is a terrific dictionary program that interfaces with most word processor programs.

*PhoneDisc* - Digital Directory Assistance, Inc. This is reason enough to get a computer with a CD-ROM. This CD has 9 million (that's right, 9 million) business names, addresses, and phone numbers. It's actually a listing of the nation's yellow pages. It's a snap to use and is available through most mail-order software houses.

## Business Books

There are many how-to-run (start, succeed etc.) business books out there. They all pretty much say the same thing. Most of them cover marketing, sales, and finances in a generic manner.

*Small Time Operator* - Bernard Kamaroff (Bell Springs Press, 1987). If you're only going to read a general book on how to run a business, I think this is the best.

*Easy Financials For Your Home-based Business* - Norman Ray (Rayve Productions, 1993). All you ever need to know about keeping your books and dealing with taxes.

*Homemade Money* - Barbara Brabec (Betterway Books, 1994). Barbara covers every conceivable way someone can make money by working from home, including writing. She has good info on starting a newsletter.

## Writing/Business Books

Like business books, there are a ton on books on writing. I think a few of them are really terrible, but even the worst book can teach you something. I don't endorse any writing-method books, but I do recommend some writing-business books you could use, especially *Writer's Market*.

*Writer's Market* - Writers Digest Books. This is a must-have. I talked about it at length earlier. Don't write from home without it!

*Tools of the Writers Trade* - Dodi Schultz (ed.) (American Society Of Journalists and Authors, Harper Perennial). This is another must book for writers. It's a collections of tips and secrets from writers on practical matters such as equipment, marketing, travel, supplies, motivation, etc. Some of it is out of date, but most of it is terrific. Buy it, you'll like it.

*The Address Book* - Michael Levine (Perigee Books). This simple book has the names, addresses, and phone numbers of over 3,500 celebrities, corporate execs, experts, etc. When you need a quote, you have someone to call!

*Write To $1,000,000* - Carol O'Hara (Cat*Tale Press, P.O. Box 10, Orangevale, CA, 95662-0010,

(916) 726-3548). This is a one-of-a-kind anthology of astounding success stories, tips, secrets, and inside information, written by twenty-four talented, determined men and women from all walks of life who "made it" in the writing business. This is my favorite book on writing and motivation. Buy it and read it. You won't be sorry.

*Using Public Relations* - Patricia Bario (Capitol Marketing Solutions, 1993, 800-452-4351). This is a good, short, little book that will give you a quick background on the wild world of public and press relations. (Written by former President Carter's deputy press secretary.)

## Magazines/Papers

You can go broke subscribing to all the writing and business magazines available. However, it will probably help you get started if you pick up a few of them.

*Writers Digest* - The grandpa of writing magazines, this monthly publication has articles on everything concerning writing, both fiction and nonfiction. I disagree with many of the articles concerning multiple submissions, but I find a lot of the stuff in WD worthwhile. Note: WD also has its own correspondence school as well as an entire line of writing books through their own book club. If you're going to be a writer, you should read this. I do.

*Home Office Computing* - This monthly magazine has a huge circulation and contains lots of good articles about getting more out of your home computer. It's not very technical so most of you should understand it. Give it a look-see.

*PC Magazine, MacUser* - Both of these are published by Ziff-Davis and are the leading magazines for PCs and Macs. They tend to be more technically oriented than others, but their software reviews can't be beat.

*PC World, MacWorld* - These two, published by PCW Communications, are the main competitors to the Ziff magazines. I like these better because they are a bit less technical and are concerned more with using the machines as opposed to how they work.

*Wall Street Journal* - I talked about this wonderful publication earlier. If you've never read it, you have a surprise. Most of it is on human interest topics having a business slant, not hard-core business or investment features. If you want to learn to write, read the WSJ. It's expensive, but worth it.

*USA Today* - Hated by many, this paper is, in my opinion, the most influential paper in the country today. Its articles are short and to the point; critics call it McPaper or McNews (after McDonalds, not Macintosh!). If you want to find out what the public at large is interested in, pick up a copy.

# Reference

Ideally, every writer should have an encyclopedia, either hard copy or on CD ROM. However, a full set of books take up a lot of space and the CD ROM versions of encyclopedias are not all that easy to use or timesaving (until you get over the learning curve, which can be difficult if you don't use it often). Here are three reasonable substitutes.

> *The New York Public Library Desk Reference* (Prentice Hall). This is the first place I turn when I need to know something about a particular subject. It's easy to use and the print is large enough for my old eyes to focus! If you are going to have only one reference book, make it this one.

> *The Dictionary of Cultural Literacy* (Houghton Mifflin). This is the second place I turn to find a fact. If you studied "it" in school, something about "it" is in this book. Because the subjects are in alphabetical order, the book is simple to use.

> *The 19xx Information Please Almanac* (Houghton Mifflin). When you need to know who won the 1937 World Series, or the population of Chad, the Almanac can't be beat.

# Index

# dering Information

## Please Print

_____

_____

_____

_____ Zip _____

one _____

Please send me _____ copies of **The Silver Pen**.

Price is $22.95 plus $3.00 for shipping. California residents please add 7.75% ($1.78) sales tax. Express delivery available for an additional fee to credit card customers.

Method of payment:

❏     Check

❏     VISA          VISA   MASTERCARD

❏     Mastercard

Card Number _____

Expiration Date _____

Name on Card _____

Signature_____

Adams-Blake Publishing
8041 Sierra Street
Fair Oaks, CA 95628
**Tel/Fax (916) 962-9296**

Unconditional 1 year guarantee:  Books purchased directly from the publisher may be returned for any reason for up to one year from date of purchase for a full refund. No questions asked.